Understanding Intellec the Public Sphere and the Arts

At the Interface

Series Editors
Dr Robert Fisher
Dr Daniel Riha

Advisory Board

Dr Alejandro Cervantes-Carson
Professor Margaret Chatterjee
Dr Wayne Cristaudo
Dr Mira Crouch
Dr Phil Fitzsimmons
Professor Asa Kasher
Owen Kelly
Dr Peter Mario Kreuter

Dr Martin McGoldrick
Revd Stephen Morris
Professor John Parry
Dr Paul Reynolds
Professor Peter L. Twohig
Professor S Ram Vemuri
Revd Dr Kenneth Wilson, O.B.E

Volume 78
A volume in the *Critical Issues* series
'Intellectuals, Knowledge, Power'

Probing the Boundaries

Understanding Knowledge Creation
Intellectuals in Academia, the Public Sphere and the Arts

Edited by
Nikita Basov and Oleksandra Nenko

Amsterdam - New York, NY 2012

Cover illustration: The Three. Nikita Basov and Oleksandra Nenko (2011)

Cover design: Inge Baeten

The paper on which this book is printed meets the requirements of "ISO 9706:1994, Information and documentation - Paper for documents - Requirements for permanence".

ISBN: 978-90-420-3462-4
E-Book ISBN: 978-94-012-0744-7
©Editions Rodopi B.V., Amsterdam - New York, NY 2012
Printed in the Netherlands

Table of Contents

Introduction	Intellectuals and the Transformation of Knowledge Creation *Nikita Basov and Oleksandra Nenko*	vii
Part I	**Intellectuals in Academia: Institutionalized Knowledge Creation**	
	The Rationalization of Academia: From *Bildung* to Production *Jeroen van Andel*	3
	The Democratic Intellect Reconsidered *James Moir*	17
Part II	**Intellectuals in the Public Sphere: 'Organic' Knowledge Creation**	
	Post-Apartheid Organic Intellectual and Knowledge Creation *Sechaba Mahlomaholo and Vhonani Netshandama*	35
	Walter A. Rodney and the Instrumentalist Construction and Utilization of Knowledge *Tunde Adeleke*	55
	Possibilities and Risks of Influencing Public Knowledge: The Case of Hrant Dink *Georg F. Simet*	83
	Not a Sin, but a Side Effect: Collaboration and Knowledge Creation by the Organic Intellectuals *Olga Procevska*	109
Part III	**Intellectuals in the Arts: Emotional Knowledge Creation**	
	Art and the Passion of Intellect *Carlos David García Mancilla*	129

	Emotional Intelligence: Literature, Ethics and Affective Cognition in J.M. Coetzee's *Disgrace* Claire Heaney	141
	Aesthetic Emotional Experience: From Eye Irritation to Knowledge Oleksandra Nenko	163
Conclusion	Knowledge Creation in the Intellectual Networks Nikita Basov	183
	Notes on Contributors	207

Intellectuals and the Transformation of Knowledge Creation

Nikita Basov and Oleksandra Nenko

*****

Today, with the emergence of the knowledge society, the ways of how knowledge is socially created change dramatically. It brings changes to the role and practices of *intellectuals* who are the knowledge creators and evokes new interest to the corresponding field of research.

There are specific trends taking place which mark fundamental transformation of knowledge creation mechanisms and practices of intellectuals. Some of them have been developing for centuries, some are the product of recent decades. However, all of them are reaching a point of intersection after which new logics of knowledge creation may emerge.

The first of these trends is that *social mechanisms are considered primary in knowledge creation* (1) increasingly frequently. This is particularly clear when we look at the transformation of scientific practice. Traditionally, scientific knowledge creation was presented in the literature as a process of individual work, which involved establishing facts and identifying patterns in their interdependence, followed by their further conceptualization into a form of rule or law. In the 1960s T. Kuhn addressed the social mechanisms of knowledge creation in the 'Postscript 1969,' after the wave of critics that followed the first edition of *The Structure of Scientific Revolutions*. He indicated that scientific communities form the basis of any normal science or scientific revolution; they are, in fact, 'elementary structures of creating scientific knowledge.'[1] He also pointed out that it is through explaining the changes in the structure of communities in science that we reveal and study the development of the science itself.[2] But Kuhn's remarks on the social nature of science were still of an esoteric kind for the science studies of that period.

The beginning of the 1970s evidenced dramatic change, as the Sociology of scientific knowledge emerged. It was presented in the chapters by D. Bloor, S. Fuller, A. Goldman and others.[3] According to the 'strong program' of the Sociology of scientific knowledge both the content and form of knowledge are entirely social in nature, and it is necessary to consider not only social factors influencing scientific knowledge creation, but social mechanisms of knowledge creation as well.

Almost simultaneously B. Griffith and N. Mullins stepped in with the idea of the 'invisible college,' an elitist scientific subgroup, whose distinctive features are: connectivity based around innovation, geographical dispersion of the members (alocality), and intensive interaction of formal and informal character (supported by D. Price, D. Crane and others).[4] This was followed by a wave of cross-reference studies lead by D. Price and E. Garfield.[5] They have shown the essential role of communication among researchers - through their links to each other in scientific journals - in increasing the speed of scientific knowledge growth.[6]

Later, in the works by G. Böhm, R. Crohn, B. Latour, R. Collins, N. Stehr and others the connection between knowledge creation and social interaction has been analyzed in detail.[7] It was clearly demonstrated that knowledge creation is socially determined.

Another important contemporary trend is the *interconnection and intersection of fields of knowledge combined with narrowing specialization* (2). This trend is composed of two macro-processes. On the one hand, in response to the social demand for deeper knowledge, specialization becomes narrow and intellectuals become experts in increasingly refined areas.[8] On the other hand, the need to create breakthrough innovative ideas demands that sufficiently different areas of highly specialized knowledge are connected. One of the most advanced approaches to innovations - open innovations methodology - is based on these connections of narrow fields of specialization.[9] The combination of diverse knowledge is demonstrated across most spheres of human activity. This is not just interdisciplinary collaboration within science, but cooperation between completely different types of knowledge (scientific and common, rational and emotional, technical and spiritual, etc.), as well as between various areas of activity, such as science, education, business, politics, etc.

Under such circumstances the image of an intellectual as a lone-wolf scholar is becoming obsolete. Such a *cognizer* - an actor performing cognitive activity - appears uncompetitive compared to intellectual teams that create fundamentally new ideas on the basis of heterogeneous and profound knowledge unattainable by a single researcher. Traditional practices of organizing collaborative cognitive activity, such as small research group or a scientific school specializing in a separate area of knowledge, also appear inefficient. The experts belonging to various spheres say that the dynamic development of contemporary society depends on the ability to overcome knowledge boundaries by uniting efforts of separate individuals and organizations to solve complex problems.[10] Thus, *creation of novel knowledge in contemporary society relies more and more on communication between actors in extensive networks which provide continuous and dynamical communicative interaction of individuals possessing competencies in various areas* (3).

In the search for new competences, experience and ideas to synthesize innovations, knowledge creation gradually ceases to be the privilege of a narrow circle of scientists; the number of knowledge workers and creative class representatives grows; and *the process of democratization of knowledge creation* (4) becomes evident.[11] What we see here is not just knowledge creation in P. Berger's and T. Lukmann's sense (as forming individual representations of the world through daily activity).[12] Nor it is what Schütz coined as a 'well informed citizen,' who doesn't agree to use the ready recipes offered by experts, and aspires to form his/her own understanding, to predict consequences and make an independent choice.[13] We face a much more groundbreaking process: democratization of the ability to purposefully create new socially significant knowledge, and thus the ability to be an intellectual. This ability becomes associated not only with scientists, but with all people, whose practices involve intensive cognitive activity, whether they are managers, teachers, business trainers, advisers, politicians, experts, researchers, journalists, or other practitioners. The knowledge creation activity takes place both within organizations (from small innovative firms to transnational corporations and government structures) and within temporary teams focused on projects (such as conferences, symposiums, round tables, consulting procedures, political activities, etc.). The Internet plays a significant role in the democratization of knowledge creation as it allows actors of various types to express and discuss different opinions in blogs, forums, and through other services, without discrimination. Knowledge generated in such a way is not always deep, but often appears even more socially significant than scientific knowledge. Science looses hegemony on knowledge creation it held through separating legitimate knowledge from non-legitimate and awarding diplomas of 'legitimate knowledge creators.' The key function of science at the turn of the century is no longer searching for Truth with a capital 'T' and to then disseminate it throughout society. Instead, the contemporary organizing feature of science is the co-ordination of knowledge creation networks that penetrate throughout society, networks in which everyone is a potential knowledge creator - an intellectual.

To understand this perspective of how knowledge is socially created by intellectuals analysis of various social arenas of intellectual activity offers exciting potential. Actors can be defined as intellectuals as far as they create socially significant knowledge while performing certain cognitive, communicative and emotional practices in the realm of various social 'infrastructures,' such as institutions and networks. This approach involves examining cases of knowledge creation by intellectuals in various environments and considering mechanisms used to create various types of knowledge.

A focused multidimensional analysis of knowledge creation by intellectuals requires bringing together researchers from multiple disciplines and with various cultural, intellectual, and professional backgrounds. This book offers the collective work of authors from Germany, Latvia, Mexico, Netherlands, Russian Federation, South Africa, Ukraine, United Kingdom and United States with background in Philosophy, History, Literature, Cultural Studies and Sociology. Our discussion initiated in May 2010 at the 3rd Global Conference *Intellectuals: Knowledge, Power, Ideas* resulted in the development of the first book *The Intellectual: A Phenomenon in Multidimensional Perspectives*.[14] However, we desired to go much deeper into the processes and mechanisms of knowledge creation.

As soon as we understand *knowledge* as a network of correlations of meanings embedded in communication networks we decided to create a book that would be not a simple collection of disparate chapters, but a socio-cognitive network of communication between the authors where their positions expressed in chapters are involved into a dialogue forming a coherent whole.[15] Thus, the book reflects the structure of the knowledge field which started to emerge in our face-to-face discussions in May 2010 and then evolved through distant communication between the authors. We came to the conclusion that knowledge creation is one of the main functions of intellectuals in three main arenas of their activity: the 'institutionalized' arena - academia - and two adjacent arenas: the public sphere and the arts.

Academia has always been a locus of knowledge creation, a 'sacred environment' purposefully formed to give 'adepts' an immediate intellectual identity. The horizons of *public sphere* are much vaguer, but nevertheless eminent since it is the arena of action where ideas are introduced, clashed and selected. Observing the public sphere we can reveal the social embeddedness of knowledge and principles according to which it is achieved. The arena of *the arts* is the most debatable, but probably one of the most enriching areas to study intellectuals and knowledge creation for here we can observe how knowledge emerges, not through rational scientific procedures but through aesthetical and emotional insights, and still remains knowledge.

In *Part I - Intellectuals in Academia: Institutionalized Knowledge Creation,* Jeroen van Andel and James Moir approach contemporary problems of rationalization and mercantilization of academia, as well as the transfer of economic thinking to its activities. Authors discuss the loss of the democratic ideal of shared knowledge and try to provide guidance as to how ideals of the 'pure,' legitimate and socially accessible knowledge should be re-established. Van Andel describes the contemporary problems that knowledge witnesses as the world view and academia as a fairway to the blooming of the 'human cognizing.' With the help of analytic layouts by Marcuse - the classical intellectual critic of the economization and standardization taking place in society - Van Andel underlines the damage caused to the humanistic ideals of 'Bildung' by the reduction of the academic environment to the 'factory' producing grades and degrees. Van Andel considers the silent acceptance of managerial enforcement by academic intellectuals to be particularly disappointing, allowing them to be removed from the public dialogue and to be placed in an 'academic' sideline.

This is followed by Moir sharing van Andel's attitudes towards 'Bildung' and knowledge as a public good, who also takes a closer look at the unfortunate consequences of the economic rationalization of the academia and narrow specialization of intellectuals that led to loss of democratization in knowledge creation and sharing. Moir suggests that academia should reconsider the 'input-output' model applied to its students and position them (and the wider public) as stakeholders. Knowledge production would then be replaced by knowledge creation and the knowledge economy should evolve into the knowledge society. For Moir the knowledge society is based on the 'knowledge from below' gained through life experience. To achieve it the learning process has to be dialogic, critical and dwell upon personal aspects that turn knowledge into being, i.e., personal development planning (PDP) and graduate attributes (GAs). Thus Moir recognizes the possibility for changes not in the transformations of the higher education institutions' regulation system itself, which in his mind will remain 'audit-driven,' but changes in the learning community through shaping of attitudes and values.

Authors of *Part II - Intellectuals in the Public Sphere: Organic Knowledge Creation* comprise Sechaba Mahlomaholo, Vhonani Netshandama, Tunde Adeleke, Georg F. Simet and Olga Procevska. These contributors approach the shaky ground of the public sphere as the arena of intellectual practice where applied, problem-focused, socially critical, ideologically inclined and public-involving knowledge is generated. In a way they continue the argument of the authors of *Part I* that intellectual practices suffer when isolated within the ivory towers of academia, and they suggest possible alternatives out of this dilemma through engaging the public and socially grounding knowledge. This part presents a number of cases, which make up a tense debate on the possible strategies and aims of intellectuals in the public space: to be representatives of the subaltern who lack voice and power, to create socially acceptable knowledge, to fight obsolete norms as class guerillas, etc. The theoretical discussion is rather tough, as authors, strongly linking to Gramsci and Bourdieau, expand on different mechanisms and tactics of public intellectual practice accentuating its main dichotomies: 'individually sustained' - 'collectively grounded,' 'politically conscious and ambitious' - 'oriented ethically, denying political component,' etc.

The part begins with a contribution from Mahlomaholo and Netshandama, who outline a unique case representing a combination of their own theoretical knowledge and intellectual practice as Black academics in the post-apartheid South Africa. They show the discrepancies between their subaltern class origins and their teaching position in the bourgeois system of education that allows them to become organic intellectuals sharing and creating knowledge with the community but hindering them to be objective in their research work.

Then Adeleke analyzes a similar case where a West Indian activist-intellectual, Walter A. Rodney, is presented as a 'Guerrilla' intellectual, who was able to construct and utilize knowledge instrumentally to advance the cause of liberation for the subaltern while being a representative of a prosperous class. Rodney transformed knowledge into a veritable weapon of resistance against domination and exploitation and set the example by immersing himself in the working class struggles.

Another case provided by Simet illustrates the mechanisms and risks of an attempt to influence public knowledge drawing on the example of a journalist Hrant Dink, an ethnic Armenian who lived in Turkey, stood up for the rights of Armenians and was eventually murdered. Simet's case presents a contrary argument to that of Mahlomaholo and Netshandama and Adeleke: Dink as 'public intellectual' is not trying to awaken the majority and provoke a class struggle and political awareness; Simet claims that Dink was acting on his own as an individual professional trying to change the discriminative perception of Armenians in the Turkish society of today. Whether his practice in a wider perspective is really or not politically disengaged we can judge from the tragedy of his death and its consequences: gunned down in 2007, Dink is a hero to some and a lawfully punished criminal for others.

In the final chapter of *Part II*, Procevska concludes the discussion by underlining that the ideological involvement or relationship with power holders and power institutions is a necessary evil for intellectuals, especially for public ones, who want their knowledge to be socially useful as well as distributed and acknowledged. Moreover, she regards the nature of knowledge, public in particular, as ideological (power-related). Doubting the 'autonomy ideology' of intellectual being, Procevska argues that in a contemporary (post-modern) world where the meta-narrative of Truth has fallen and socially meaningful identities are fluid, the public intellectual is always passionate, whether patriotically, civically, nationally (all this equating to politically), in order to feel engaged with community and in acting accordingly, create public knowledge. This situation is evident in all of the three cases mentioned in *Part II*. Procevska also shows how the ideology of autonomy has vanished, replaced by strategies of opposition (Dink, Rodney) or collaboration (Mahlomaholo and Netshandama) with the government for the sake of the subaltern, depending on the harshness of the ideological context. Therefore Procevska reconsiders the concept of the organic intellectual as an intellectual interpreter, whose identity is based on his/her interconnectedness with a particular institution, community or society.

Authors of *Part III - Intellectuals in the Arts: Emotional Knowledge Creation* Carlos D.G. Mancilla, Claire Heaney and Oleksandra Nenko net the third dimension of the intellectual activity, approaching the most provoking arena of intellectuals' activity - the arts. By considering the role and essence of emotions in cognition these authors correlate with previous parts. They underline the importance of strong emotional engagement during unfolding of 'being,' what also applies to the learning and knowledge creation processes considered in *Part I*. They suggest that emotional aspects of intellectual practice are real and have an importance of their own. This once again demonstrates the considerable role of emotions in the public intellectual landscape as posited by the authors in *Part II* who write of emotional connection with the subaltern as well as complex intellectual feelings of honor and dignity, who passionately describe their own public intellectual practices and excite emotional responses in the reader through the description of Rodney and Dink's tragical deaths.

Part III shows the historical dimension of emotional studies in their interconnections with the arts as an arena of concentrated manifestation of emotions. Mancilla reveals the corner stones of passions and art in modernity discourse. He describes distinction between rationality and emotions which led to rationalization of different spheres of life and to the disrupt concept of 'being.' At the same time he shows that considering art and aesthetic emotional experience gave modern intellectuals access to the lost completeness of life. Another interesting argument raised is that modern philosophy linked passions to suffering and to the passive behavior of the cognizing subject.

This statement, though debatable, is taken up by Heaney, when she regards Romantic concepts of true life and experience as openness to darkness of passions in her fine literary analysis of J.M. Coetzee's novel *Disgrace*. Portraiting the novel's main character Prof. Lurie, Heaney demonstrates his affective intelligence, which originates in classical art, and its role in decision-taking and committing actions throughout his life. This story is a significant example of absorption of the vital currents of art by the academic intellectual and ripening of affective intelligence in him. Heaney shows that emotionally-driven knowledge maintains crucial personal views and ideals in the situation when 'rational' knowledge is absurd or bankrupt.

The problem of the emotionally-driven knowledge is put into a wider environment of complex aesthetic emotional experience by Nenko. She starts by considering basic sensations caused by the materiality of the work of art, then discusses the intentional evaluative emotions aroused by the perceived concept of the art-work and concludes with the notion of intersubjective experience received as a result of awareness in correlations between the author and the spectator. Nenko argues that emotionally-driven knowledge engulfs all these components of experience - from primary sensations in one's own body to complex inter-subjective emotional awareness of the transcendent truth of life.

Concluding the analysis done in the three chapters of the book we argue that knowledge creation processes become gradually distributed through all social levels and spheres of social life and at the same time stay inter-connected via complex intellectual communication networks. This may give birth to a new mode of knowledge creation: a total, continuous and co-ordinated sociocognitive process. The time when a general theory of scientific organization as a main unit of scientific production was necessary has passed.[16] Today it is timely to work out a general theory of intellectual networks, which connect intellectual actors with equal opportunities for co-creating knowledge. Such a theory requires new concepts, new criteria of effectiveness, new models of optimal structures and new approaches to organization of the intellectual interaction that would allow continuous interactive real-time cognitive activity to take place, similarly (but not equal) to the processes occurring in the human brain, when neurons interact. This requires analysis of what we have called the *'intellectual landscape'* - a dynamic, complex, non-linear network structure, which consists of thousands of actors and other network entities and generates knowledge.[17] If properly organized, intellectual landscapes may act as *knowledge-creating systems*, specific forms of intellectual network structures intensively generating knowledge.[18]

What we see is a call for a new paradigm that will re-consider knowledge creation by intellectuals in society under the new circumstances. This paradigm will analyze mechanisms of purposeful knowledge creation as sociocognitive and describe knowledge creation as a collective cognitive process, run by intellectuals. This task involves inter-disciplinary analysis of individual and collective processes, bringing together cognitive, communicative and emotional dimensions and the synthesis of micro and macro levels using theoretical and methodological tools of cognition studies, social studies of knowledge, science and technology, discourse studies, interactions studies and communication network studies.

To make a step towards such a paradigm, summarizing some of the book's insights in the concluding chapter Nikita Basov describes the basic principles of collective knowledge creation through communication and emotional entrainment. He suggests the concept of a knowledge creation ritual, which describes the process of structural coupling between individuals and explains social knowledge generation in its co-evolution with communication and emotional energy. He also analyzes the mechanisms of knowledge creation in large-scale network structures - intellectual landscapes - and introduces the concept of cultural-cognitive domain as a main unit for analysing knowledge creation in these structures. Some of the principles of emergence and evolution of the cultural-cognitive domains are outlined. Finally, using the proposed approach he completes the knowledge creation cycle and attempts to address some of the key issues discussed throughout the book using the proposed approach.

With this book we try to call for re-considering knowledge

generation, to go into the broad field of intellectual activity looking for new insights and even to make a step towards a new paradigm of understanding knowledge creation as a 'democratic,' 'organic,' 'public', 'emotionally driven' collective cognitive process run by intellectuals. We hope our search will encourage other researchers to explore the fundamental principles of knowledge creation - for the benefit of transition to the knowledge society.

Notes

[1] T. Kuhn, *The Structure of Scientific Revolutions*, University of Chicago Press, Chicago, 1962/1970 (2nd edition, with postscript), p. 232.

[2] Ibid., p. 234.

[3] D. Bloor, *Science and Social Imagery*, University Of Chicago Press, Chicago, 1976; S. Fuller, *Social Epistemology*, Indiana University Press, Bloomington, Indianapolis, 1988; A. Goldman, 'Foundations of Social Epistemics', *Synthese*, Vol. 73(1), 1987, pp. 109-144.

[4] D.J. Price and D. Beaver, 'Collaboration In an Invisible College', *American Psychologist*, Vol. 21(11), 1966, pp. 1011-1018; D. Crane, 'Social Structure in a Group of Scientists: A Test of the 'Invisible College' Hypothesis', *American Sociological Review*, Vol. 34(3), 1969, pp. 335-352; B.C. Griffith and N.C. Mullins, 'Coherent Social Groups in Scientific Change ('Invisible Colleges' May Be Consistent throughout Science)', *Science*, Vol. 177(4053), 1972, pp. 959-966.

[5] E. Garfield, *Citation Indexing: Its Theory and Application in Science, Technology and Humanities*, John Wiley & Sons, New York, 1979; D.J. Price, 'Network of Scientific Papers', *Science*, Vol. 149, 1965, pp. 510-515.

[6] A. Shirokanova, *Prehistory of Distributed Research Teams*, 2010 (paper manuscript, used with author's permission).

[7] G. Böhm, 'Cognitive Norms, Knowledge-Interests and the Construction of the Scientific Object', *The Social Production of Scientific Knowledge*, E. Mendelsohn, P. Weingart and R. Whitley (eds), D. Reidel Publishing Company, D. Dordrecht, 1977, pp. 129-141; B. Latour, *Science in Action: How to Follow Scientists and Engineers through Society*, Open University Press, Milton Keynes, 1987; R. Krohn, 'Introduction: Towards the Empirical Study of Scientific Practice', *The Social Process of Scientific Investigation*, K. Knorr, R. Krohn and R. Whitley (eds), D. Reidel Publishing Company, D. Dordrecht, 1980, pp. vii-xxv; R. Collins, *The Sociology of Philosophies: A Global Theory of Intellectual Change*, Harvard University Press, Cambridge, MA, 2002; N. Stehr, *Knowledge Societies*, Sage, London, 1994.

[8] K. Deutsch, *Nerves of Government: Models of Political Communication and Control*, Free Press of Glencoe, London, 1963.

[9] H. Chesbrough, *Open Innovation: The New Imperative for Creating and Profiting From New Technology*, Harvard Business School Press, Boston, 2003.

[10] K. Clark and T. Fujimoto, *Product Development Performance: Strategy, Organization, and Management in the World Auto Industry*, Harvard Business Press, Cambridge, MA, 1991; P. Kitcher, *Science, Truth, and Democracy*, Oxford University Press, Oxford, 2001.

[11] В.С. Степин, *Философская Антропология и Философия Науки*, Высшая Школа, Москва, 1992; R.L. Florida, *The Rise of the Creative Class: And How It's Transforming Work, Leisure, Community and Everyday Life*, Basic Books, New York, 2002; E. von Hippel, *Democratizing Innovation*, MIT Press, Cambridge, MA, 2005; A. Raza, R. Kausar & D. Paul, 'The Social Democratization of Knowledge: Some Critical Reflections on E-learning', *Multicultural Education & Technology Journal*, Vol. 1, 2007, pp. 64-74; L. Santerre, 'From Democratization of Knowledge to Bridge Building between Science, Technology and Society', *Communicating Science in Social Contexts*, C. Donghong, et al. (eds), Springer, New York, 2008.

[12] P. Berger and T. Luckmann, *The Social Construction of Reality: A Treatise in the Sociology of Knowledge*, Anchor, New York, 1966.

[13] А. Шютц, 'Хорошо Информированный Гражданин. Очерк о Социальном Распределении Знания' в *Смысловая Структура Повседневного Мира*, ФОМ, Москва, 2003, с. 225.

[14] N. Basov, G.F. Simet, J. van Andel, S. Mahlomaholo and V. Netshandama (eds), *The Intellectual: A Phenomenon in Multidimensional Perspectives*, Inter-Disciplinary Press, Oxford, 2010, pp. 57-71.

[15] For details see: N. Basov, 'Knowledge Creation in the Intellectual Landscape', 2011, this volume.

[16] S. Fuchs, *The Professional Quest for Truth: A Social Theory of Science and Knowledge*, State University of the New York Press, New York, 1992.

[17] В.В. Василькова и Н.В. Басов, *Интеллектуальный Ландшафт: Самоорганизация Знания в Сетевых Структурах* (неопубликованная рукопись, используется с разрешения авторов).

[18] N. Basov and A. Shirokanova, 'From Distributed Knowledge to Intelligent Knowledge-Creating Systems', *The Intellectual: A Phenomenon in Multidimensional Perspectives*, N. Basov, G.F. Simet, J. van Andel, S. Mahlomaholo and V. Netshandama (eds), Inter-Disciplinary Press, Oxford, 2010, pp. 57-71.

Bibliography

Basov, N. and Shirokanova, A., 'From Distributed Knowledge to Intelligent Knowledge-Creating Systems'. *The Intellectual: A Phenomenon in Multidimensional Perspectives*, Basov, N., Simet, G.F., van Andel, J., Mahlomaholo, S. and Netshandama, V. (eds), Inter-Disciplinary Press, Oxford, 2010.

Berger, P. and Luckmann, T., *The Social Construction of Reality: A Treatise in the Sociology of Knowledge*. Anchor, New York, 1967.

Bloor, D., *Science and Social Imagery*. University Of Chicago Press, Chicago, 1976.

Böhm, G., 'Cognitive Norms, Knowledge-Interests and the Construction of the Scientific Object'. *The Social Production of Scientific Knowledge*. Mendelsohn, E., Weingart, P. and Whitley, R. (eds), D. Reidel Publishing Company, Dordrecht, 1977.

Chesbrough, H., *Open Innovation: The New Imperative for Creating and Profiting From New Technology*. Harvard Business School Press, Boston, 2003.

Clark, K. & Fujimoto, T., *Product Development Performance: Strategy, Organization, and Management in the World Auto Industry*. Harvard Business Press, Cambridge, MA, 1991.

Collins, R., *The Sociology of Philosophies: A Global Theory of Intellectual Change*. Harvard University Press, Cambridge, MA, 2002.

Crane, D., 'Social Structure in a Group of Scientists: A Test of the Invisible College Hypothesis'. *American Sociological Review*. Vol. 34(3), 1969, pp. 335-352.

Deutsch, K., *Nerves of Government: Models of Political Communication and Control*. Free Press of Glencoe, London, 1963.

Florida, R.L., *The Rise of the Creative Class: And How it's Transforming Work, Leisure, Community and Everyday Life*. Basic Books, New York, 2002.

Fuchs, S., *The Professional Quest for Truth: A Social Theory of Science and Knowledge*. State University of the New York Press, New York, 1992.

Fuller, S., *Social Epistemology*. Indiana University Press, Bloomington, Indianapolis, 1988.

Garfield, E., *Citation Indexing: Its Theory and Application in Science, Technology and Humanities*. John Wiley & Sons, New York, 1979.

Goldman, A., 'Foundations of Social Epistemics'. *Synthese*. Vol. 73(1), 1987, pp. 109-144.

Griffith, B.C. & Mullins, N.C., 'Coherent Social Groups in Scientific Change ('Invisible Colleges' May Be Consistent throughout Science)'. *Science*. Vol. 177(4053), 1972, pp. 959-966.

Hippel, E. von., *Democratizing Innovation*. MIT Press, Cambridge, MA, 2005.

Kitcher, P., *Science, Truth, and Democracy*. Oxford University Press, Oxford, 2001.

Krohn, R., 'Introduction: Towards the Emperical Study of Scientific Practice'. *The Social Process of Scientific Investigation*. Knorr, K., Krohn, R. and Whitley, R. (eds), D. Reidel Publishing Company, Dordrecht, 1980.

Kuhn, T., *The Structure of Scientific Revolutions*. University of Chicago Press, Chicago, 1962/1970 (2nd edition, with postscript).

Latour, B., *Science in Action: How to Follow Scientists and Engineers through Society*. Open University Press, Milton Keynes, 1987.

Price, D.J. and Beaver, D., 'Collaboration In an Invisible College'. *American Psychlogist*. Vol. 21(11), 1966, pp. 1011-1018.

Price, D.J., 'Network of Scientific Papers'. *Science*. Vol. 149, 1965, pp. 510-515.

Raza, A., Kausar, R. and Paul, D., 'The Social Democratization of Knowledge: Some Critical Reflections on E-Learning'. *Multicultural Education & Technology Journal*. Vol. 1(1), 2007, pp. 64-74.

Santerre, L., 'From Democratization of Knowledge to Bridge Building between Science, Technology and Society'. *Communicating Science in Social Contexts*. Donghong, C., Claessens, M. et al. (eds), Springer, New York, 2008.

Shirokanova, A., *Prehistory of Distributed Research Teams*. 2010 (paper manuscript, used with author's permission).

Stehr, N., *Knowledge Societies*. Sage, London, 1994.

Василькова, В.В. и Басов, Н.В., *Интеллектуальный Ландшафт: Самоорганизация Знания в Сетевых Структурах* (неопубликованная рукопись, используется с разрешения авторов).

Степин, В.С., *Философская Антропология и Философия Науки*. Высшая Школа, Москва, 1992.

Шютц, А., 'Хорошо Информированный Гражданин. Очерк о Социальном Распределении Знания' в *Смысловая Структура Повседневного Мира*. ФОМ, Москва, 2003.

Part I

Intellectuals in Academia: Institutionalized Knowledge Creation

The Rationalization of Academia: From *Bildung* to Production

Jeroen van Andel

Abstract
Using Herbert Marcuse's rationalization paradigm this chapter aims to demonstrate that the ways in which academic knowledge is created and accumulated have become increasingly rational and one-dimensional. It is argued that the rationalization and one-dimensionality of knowledge creation and accumulation have far-reaching consequences for both academia and society. It is further argued that the on-going rationalization of academic knowledge seems to have resulted in (a further) erosion of the concept of *Bildung* in favour of a more instrumental approach towards knowledge and learning.

Key Words: Academia, Marcuse, rationalization, knowledge, *Bildung*.

*****

>Whether or not men can perceive the epochal themes and above all, how they act upon the reality within which these themes are generated will largely determine their humanization or dehumanization, their affirmation as Subjects or their education as objects. - *Paulo Freire*[1]

Throughout history academia has always been strongly involved in the creation and accumulation of knowledge. However, over the years, the character of knowledge creation (i.e., research) and accumulation (i.e., academic publications) appears to have become more and more 'rational.' That is, the creation and accumulation of 'academic' knowledge seems to have become means rather than ends. Means to economic (i.e., profitable) ends, characterized by a strong degree of individuality and one-dimensionality. This development is thought to have serious consequences for the way and extent to which academic knowledge will be shared, both within as well as outside academia.

Using the theoretical outlook of Herbert Marcuse, as provided in *One-Dimensional Man* (first published in 1964), combined with more contemporary perspectives (e.g., Lynch, Thompson) this chapter reflects on what is seen as the 'rationalization' of 'academic' knowledge.[2] By doing so this chapter aims to construe the dominant nature of the rationalization of academia, and address some of the consequences of this development for both the creation and accumulation of 'academic' knowledge as well as for the concept of *Bildung*.

1. **Rationalization of Society**

In his classical work, *One-Dimensional Man*, Herbert Marcuse provides a diagnostics of what he sees as an increasingly rationalized and one-dimensional society.[3] Although published over forty years ago Marcuse's analysis of the rationalization of society appears to have lost nothing of his strength and vigour. On the contrary, Marcuse's depiction of western society seems even more accurate today than it was then.

In his study Marcuse argues that through changes in production, consumption, culture and thought, 'advanced industrial society' has arrived at 'a state of conformity.'[4] A condition characterized by its one-dimensionality.

According to Marcuse the one-dimensionality of western society can be seen as the outcome of a process in which the universality of capitalist production and the omnipotent power of technological progress have created a culture in which rationality and reason have become primarily instrumental.[5] That is, rational thinking and reason have become instrumental in the sense that they allow for a greater control and domination over humanity, a domination which is exercised through administration.[6]

Although Marcuse emphasizes that critical reason has always been a source of both the individual's liberation and the advancement of society for the benefit of all social groups and interests, he argues that freedom of thought, speech and conscience, just as the free enterprise which they served to promote and protect, are in essence *critical* ideas designed to replace an obsolescent material and intellectual culture by a more productive and rational one.[7] He however concludes that the progression of society has resulted in an increasing demand for reason to '[...] accommodate the economic and social apparatus to such an extent that all contradiction seems irrational and all counteraction impossible.'[8] Thus emerges a pattern of one-dimensional thought and behaviour in which the ideas, aspirations and objectives that transcend the established universe of discourse and actions are either repelled or reduced to terms of this universe. According to Marcuse this has resulted in a sweeping definition of the function, content and essence of thought and knowledge.[9]

In the one-dimensional society Marcuse witnesses a widespread and far-reaching conformation to pre-existing norms and behaviour, in contrast to a more 'multidimensional' discourse which allows for possibilities that transcend the established state of affairs.[10] This conformation is defined by Marcuse as the process of *mimesis*: '[...] an immediate identification of the individual with *his* society and, through it, with the society as a whole [...].'[11] As all individuals (although often unaware) function as the spokesman of the institutions, influences and interests embodied in organizations, through their decisions the institution (e.g., the corporation, the university) is '[...] set in motion, pre-served, and reproduced - as a (relatively) ultimate, universal reality, overriding the particular institutions or peoples subjected to it.'[12]

2. Rationalization of Academia

When the outlook of Herbert Marcuse is used to reflect on current day academia there can be found several indications that academia has adopted some form of instrumental 'economic' rationality. Over the past decades academia has become increasingly preoccupied with concepts such as (the demands of the) labour market, the student as consumer, customer responsiveness, product quality, and efficiency to name just a few 'buzz words.' All over the world higher education institutes have adopted the 'model of the market' and its accompanying discourse which resulted in a move towards structured, consumable education through modularization, semesterization and self-directed learning in which education is being dealt with '[...] as a commodity.'[13] What is more, various kinds of 'performance indexes' have begun to determine the quality of institutions whereas the quality of scholarship is judged on the amount of 'external research users' and various sorts of 'impact indicators.'

Some therefore conclude that the university has changed from '[...] a centre of learning to being a business organization with productivity targets [...] to transfer its allegiance from the academic to the operational.'[14] A shift in focus from a more abstract idea to more practical and 'rational' functions. According to Lynch this development has resulted in a form of Orwellian surveillance of academics everyday work by the university institution that is paralleled in one's person life with a reflexive surveillance of the self, everything one does has to be measured and counted and only the measurable matters.[15]

It is thought that this development, here characterized as the 'rationalization of academia', has strongly affected the creation and accumulation of academic knowledge. In the following Marcuse's rationalization paradigm will be used to reflect on the relationship between the rationalization of academia and the creation and accumulation of 'academic' knowledge.

3. Rationalization and Knowledge Creation

With regard to knowledge creation, here defined as scientific research, Marcuse states that the rationality of science can be seen as, in essence, value free, a rationality which does not stipulate any practical ends, 'neutral' to any extraneous values that may be imposed upon it.[16] However, he emphasizes that the character of this neutrality is 'positive.'[17] He exemplifies this by stating:

[t]he stars which Galileo observed where the same in classical antiquity, but the different universe of discourse and action - in short the different social reality - opened the new direction and range of observation and the possibilities of ordering the observed data.[18]

Scientific rationality thus makes for a specific societal organization precisely because it projects mere form (or mere matter) which can be bent to practically all ends.[19] However, Marcuse underlines that the dominance of positivism should also be regarded as a struggle against all metaphysics, transcendentalism, and idealisms as obscurantist and regressive modes of thought.[20]

Marcuse asserts that authentic and critical investigation can only be expressed through a conscious methodological alienation from the entire sphere of business and industry, and from its calculable and profitable order.[21] If not, the analysis of reality will be locked, judgments confined within a context of facts which excludes judging the context in which the facts are made, man-made, and in which their meaning, development and function are determined.[22] Marcuse therefore emphasizes that critical analysis must dissociate itself from that what it strives to comprehend; the terms must be other than the ordinary ones in order to elucidate the full meaning of the latter.[23] He adds that 'true judgment' evaluates reality not in its own terms but in terms which envisage its subversion through which this subversive reality comes into its own truth.[24]

For academia to create authentic, critical and even subversive knowledge it thus has to 'alienate' itself from the context in which 'facts are made' and dissociate itself from what it strives to comprehend. However, throughout academia there can be witnessed a growing synthesis of commercial enterprise and research. This merging is presented as both desirable and necessary and university policies are increasingly directed towards rewarding such links.[25] Nevertheless, Lynch for instance argues that when universities become more and more dependent on contract research, this will leave little time to develop the critical and creative conceptual frameworks that follow after contracts are finished.[26] What is more, as a consequence of the growing entanglement of academia and business there can be found more and more cases in which judgment of contexts is confined and researchers are severely discredited due to the conclusions of their research, and are forced to withdraw or alter their conclusions.[27] In addition, with contract research, there is little time to publish about the project when it is in progress. According to Lynch this inevitably results in layers of silencing, and indeed of exploitation, which are built into the whole process.[28]

It is also thought that when academia becomes too reliant on industry-funded research or too beholden to the business-driven agenda of governments, the interests of the university can become synonymous with powerful vested interests which can strongly undermine the public interest function of the university, which is to serve the good of humanity in its entirety.[29] There are indications that this is already happening in areas such as food production, genetics, biotechnology and environmental protection.[30]

Besides the developments characterized above there can also be witnessed a growing decline in the funding of studies and research in Critical Theory, Sociology, Community Development, Critical Social Policy, Cultural Studies, Equality Studies, Disability Studies, Adult Education and Women's Studies as these do not provide short-term stakes and are often regarded as too costly.[31] However these are precisely the fields which have proven themselves able to be truly critical and subversive and allows academics to alienate themselves from the sphere of business and industry. A decline of studies in these fields can be seen as another step towards the creation of less critical and subversive, and more one-dimensional knowledge.

Finally, the rational approach towards knowledge creation also manifests itself in its restriction of cognition to rational (positivist) thought. Passions for instance are seen as irrational as they are lying 'beyond the dominion of the intellectual and the consciousness.'[32]

However, in *Part III* of this volume, Carlos D. G. Mancilla, Claire Heaney and Oleksandra Nenko demonstrate that (emotional) knowledge can be acquired through art (e.g., paintings and literature) as well.[33] This 'intuitive knowledge' goes beyond rational knowledge and discloses a message that deductive reasoning alone cannot discover.[34]

According to these three authors only the language of art is able to grab and approximate theories of the passions, to speak about something of which we cannot speak about, in a language that goes beyond the rational language. A language that tells us about the world as well as about ourselves and which can result in a deeper emotional involvement with our surrounding world whereas the more general approach of *abstrahieren* can easily result in a disconnection from the surrounding environment (of which a fine example is given by Heaney through the cognitive path of novel character, David Lurie).[35]

4. **Rationalization and Knowledge Accumulation**

With regard to the accumulation of academic knowledge, here defined as the accumulation of knowledge through academic publications, Marcuse concludes that in a one-dimensional society, one has to communicate one's thoughts in a language which is not one's own. Marcuse acknowledges that one is allowed to speak one's own language, but it must be a translatable language, and the language of the individual *will* be translated.[36] The language through which the subject is forced to communicate is a closed language which does not demonstrate and explain but rather communicates decision, dictum and command.[37] The unified functional language of the one-dimensional society is irreconcilably anti-critical and anti-dialectical.[38] Its operational and behavioural rationality absorbs the transcendent negative oppositional elements of reason.[39]

According to Marcuse thinking in the one-dimensional society (or at least its expression) is not only '[…] pressed into the straightjacket of common usage, but also enjoined not to ask and seek solutions beyond those that are already there.'[40] What is more, in speaking what they believe to be their own language, people also speak the language of their masters, benefactors, advertisers. Therefore they do not only express themselves, their own knowledge, feelings and aspirations, but also something other than themselves.[41]

To accumulate critical and non-rational knowledge, i.e., knowledge that transcends the boundaries of a particular time and place and which thus transcends the limitations and constraints imposed in the rational realm as well, academia has to communicate its thoughts in its own language which allows for the presentation of 'solutions that are not already there.' However, the fact of the matter is that academic knowledge is increasingly transmitted in a closed, conventional and one-dimensional language. Whether it is the use of academic English, the APA-standards or conformity to specific journal standards the language in which academic knowledge is shared has become ever more rational. By pushing academics to publish in peer-reviewed journals only academia actively discourages academics to share ideas with public in one's own society, with those outside the university and to engage in public debate in newspapers, popular books or the media.[42] What is more, the 'good' academic is forced to become a locally silent academic in his or her own country; silent in the public sphere and silent by virtue of engaging in dialogue only with academic peers outside one's own country.[43]

The developments outlined above are thought to have far-reaching effects for academia's role in the *Bildung* of students and its role in the *Bildung* of those outside academia. Through the rationalization of knowledge creation and accumulation academia seems to move away from *Bildung* and towards production.

5.   ***Bildung* and Rationalization of Academic Knowledge**
Over past years, the concept of *Bildung* has received new attention in various different countries (e.g., Germany, Sweden, the Netherlands). Often associated with so-called learning societies it has become a key-term in politics, representing the different competencies which are thought required for 'survival' in the learning society.[44] However, as the concept of *Bildung* has various different meanings and connotations (in policy documents as well

as in academic publications) this chapter aims to revisit the original idea behind the concept.

The notion of *Bildung* is often ascribed to Wilhelm von Humboldt (1767-1835) and the philosophical and pedagogical developments surrounding the Enlightenment.[45] The discourse of *Bildung* represented a countermovement to the more dominant utilitarian approach to education. Instead of 'merely' being prepared for a certain vocation (i.e., *Erziehung*), Von Humboldt postulated the necessity of '[...] the highest and most proportionate development of all talents to a whole' (i.e., *Bildung*).[46] *Bildung*, in the classical sense, represents the endless task of developing, unfolding, and enlightening the human mind to realize the independence of human will and action from natural and social determinations, coercion and constraints.[47] A social figuration which combines individuality and sociality, the endless voyage of an individual towards him-/herself as part of an ideal humanity.[48] *Bildung* therefore is about self-realization and self-elevation in all spheres of social reproduction and thus breaks through the more affirmative character of *Erziehung*.[49] *Bildung* thus represents a non-utilitarian approach towards education, aiming for an endless developing, unfolding, and enlightening of the human mind.

Although *Bildung* is about much more, knowledge and learning unmistakably play an important role in the *Bildung* of individuals.[50] Within universities the sharing of knowledge through teaching activities therefore plays an important role in the *Bildung* of students. However, Thompson for instance witnesses that *Bildung* of students has become strongly determined by an instrumental economic rationality.[51] Today it appears as if the majority of academics are suffering from some form of ephebiphobia: fear of young people. Instead of helping students develop, unfold and enlighten their minds to the fullest and challenging them with their latest findings they '[...] prepare notes for easy academic consumption and examine these notes rather than examine a subject.'[52] This is not surprising giving the fact that the incentive to teach or share findings is negligible and the academic is pushed to 'produce' scientific papers rather than syllabi.

Yet, students are not only obliged to examine mere notes, today they are also increasingly directed towards economic self-interest and credential acquisition. Harkavy for instance observes that as Universities openly and increasingly pursue commercialization, they legitimize and reinforce the pursuit of economic self-interest by students which contributes to the widespread sense that they are in college solely to gain career skills and credentials.[53] This development signifies a rather one-dimensional approach towards education and the complete opposite of what the concept of *Bildung* aims to achieve.

Besides the *Bildung* of its students, academia plays an important role in the *Bildung* of those outside academia as well. In *Part II* of this book

Sechaba Mahlomaholo and Vhonani Netshandama for instance show how academia can engage in struggles for equity, social justice, freedom, peace, hope and transformation and help strive for a more equitable and democratic society.[54] It seems however that today academia is, more than ever before, providing disincentives to share ideas with public in one's own society, to go outside the university, act as a public intellectual and engage in public debate in newspapers, popular books or the media.[55]

Over the years the university has begun to increasingly and systematically devalue dialogue with persons and bodies other than academics. As a consequence academia has effectively privatized learning among paid-up members (students and academics) of the academic community which has serious consequences for the democratization of learning and for the sharing of findings in more publicly accessible forums. Today, when there is no 'peer review' value in engaging in public debate, there is no incentive to engage in the public sphere, to challenge ill-informed absolutisms and orthodoxies. In effect there is no incentive to publicly dissent or engage within the very institutions that are charged with the task of dissent and engagement and thus fail in sharing knowledge which can be used by those outside academia to achieve their *Bildung*.

6. Rationalization and the Art of Resistance

From the analysis presented above one can conclude that contemporary 'academic' intellectuals seem entangled in a web of rationality which apparently leaves them with little choice but 'publish' (i.e., adopt the rational approach towards knowledge creation) or 'perish' (leave academia). Therefore, the question can be raised how and if the on-going rationalization of academia can be challenged and/or resisted. In *Part II* of this book both Tunde Adeleke and Olga Procevska address different approaches which can be related to 'the art' of resisting the on-going rationalization of academia.[56]

In her chapter, Olga Procevska argues that the creation and dissemination of knowledge is, in its essence, an ideological work. According to Procevska (academic) intellectuals find themselves struggling with either ignoring or acknowledging the ideological nature of his work. A struggle between either being an 'organic intellectual,' aware of his embodiment in a particular ideology or affiliation with a particular group or movement, or being an 'autonomous intellectual.' someone who is hiding his involvement into power creation and distribution structures under the claims of objectivity, universal values and truth. A struggle between someone like Walter A. Rodney regarded as being an armchair appendage of the ruling class or disseminating knowledge for the greater good of mankind and for the good of those from under- or working class in particular (see the chapter by Tunde Adeleke). In his chapter, Adeleke makes clear that men like Rodney felt strongly about the role of the intellectual as a public servant, someone who transformed knowledge into a weapon against domination and exploitation, and who committed knowledge to the cause of the underclass.

From the chapters of Adeleke and Procevska, two approaches can be derived which can be used to challenge or resist the on-going rationalization of academia. In his chapter, Adeleke shows that someone like Walter Rodney might advocate some form of 'guerrilla intellectualism' which would allow for an intellectual to be imbedded within an oppressive system to undermine or destroy it from within. Procevska, on the other hand, elaborates on a more nuanced approach and discusses the idea of the intellectual as a 'collaborator' taking into account concepts such as identity and functionality.

Based on the works of Procevska and Adeleke, one can conclude that not only does an intellectual have to be aware of his embodiment in the particular one-dimensional ideology of academia, but to challenge the dominant 'rational' approach towards academic knowledge the intellectual thus has to transcend the rational ways of knowledge creation and accumulation and find ways to disseminate this knowledge for it to play a role in the *Bildung* of those both in as well as outside academia.

Concerning the resistance against the on-going rationalization of society Marcuse himself has always been rather cynical.[57] He anticipated, that the more rational, productive, technical, and total the repressive administration of society would become - the more unimaginable the means and ways by which the administered individuals might break their servitude and seize their own liberation from the one-dimensional realm.[58] He predicted, that once the rational one-dimensional vocable had become official, constantly repeated in general usage, it would lose all its cognitive value and would 'merely' serve as recognition of an unquestionable fact.[59]

Contrary to Marcuse's pessimism, some silver linings can be seen. Today there can be found few initiatives which strive to resist and challenge the on-going rationalization of academic knowledge and academia. It seems that those who strive to challenge the one-dimensionality of academia use a more collaborative approach in order to use the potentiality of the system and transcend its economic rational approach towards the creation, accumulation and dissemination of knowledge. In the Netherlands for instance the Royal Netherlands Academy of Arts and Sciences in corporation with three research universities (Tilburg, Utrecht and Nijmegen) has initiated a project on 'rich publications.' The project, which started in January 2011, aims to widen the access to scientific publications, 'enrich' these publications with relevant illustrations, audio and video, add relevant links and allow access to source material such as raw data. By doing so, these publications not only become far more practical and insightful but also become more usable and understandable for those outside academia. Therefore these 'rich publications' could play an important role in the *Bildung* of those outside academia.

Another approach is explored by James Moir in the second chapter of this part.[60] In his chapter, Moir argues that the 'intellectual' nature of higher education has been devalued and academics often (have to) exclude rather than include others in (their) intellectual work. According to Moir 'the market' has come to dictate how we view the 'outputs' of higher education as well as that there has been too much focus on higher education to 'deliver' on employability. His plea for the return of the concept of the *Democratic Intellectual*, in which knowledge creation is seen as a participative and interactive process for the public good sounds both promising as well as convincing.

7. Conclusion

Based on the rationalization paradigm of Herbert Marcuse this chapter has aimed to explain that academia and its attitude towards knowledge creation and accumulation have become increasingly rational and one-dimensional. Although one could argue that the rationalization of academia has been going on for quite some time, it seems that over the past decades this process has reached a new level. Consequently, academia appears to have changed from a centre of learning to a business organization, an organization which uses 'productivity targets' and seems to have transferred its allegiance from the academic to the operational. More than ever before, both teaching and research 'output' is measured, and faculties and institutions are in a constant struggle to be 'cost-effective.' As a consequence knowledge creation and accumulation have been strongly influenced by this form of instrumental 'economic' rationality.

With regard to the creation of knowledge (i.e., research) there can be witnessed a growing entanglement between business and academia and a growing lack of truly critical and subversive studies. With regard to the accumulation of knowledge (i.e., academic publications) there can be witnessed the 'production' of peer-reviewed 'closed' publications by a small group of experts who have become more and more silent in the public sphere.

The rationalization of the creation and accumulation of academic knowledge appears to have strongly eroded the *Bildung* function of academia. Within the university there could be witnessed a shift from *Bildung* to *Erziehung*. Teaching has become less 'profitable' for academics as their 'quality' is defined by the number of peer-reviewed publications rather than by the quality of their teaching whereas student attitude towards education has become more and more utilitarian as it is often used to gain career skills and credentials rather than personal development. Moreover, the growing pressure to publish in academic, peer-reviewed journals seems to work as a strong disincentive to operate as a public intellectual and share knowledge with the wider public. This appears to have eroded the *Bildung* of those outside academia. Additionally, the knowledge that *is* shared seems to become more and more one-dimensional and more and more influenced by vested interests of certain sectors (e.g., food production and biotechnology).

Besides the erosion of the concept of *Bildung*, the cognitive costs of the rationalization of academic knowledge also include the growing inability to identify (an)other dimension(s) which can be used to perceive possibilities that transcend the rational economic and one-dimensional thinking. However, although the on-going rationalization of academia seems inevitable, there can be witnessed some initiatives developed by those who strive to resist the on-going rationalization. These often seem to use a more collaborative approach to develop or promote initiatives which challenge the one-dimensionality from within.

Notes

[1] P. Freire, *Education for Critical Consciousness*, Continuum, London and New York, 2010 [1974], p. 5.

[2] H. Marcuse, *One Dimensional Man*, Routledge Classics, London and New York, 2010 [1964]; K. Lynch, 'Neo-Liberalism and Marketisation: The Implications for Higher Education', *European Educational Research Journal*, Vol. 5(1), 2006, pp. 1-17; C. Thompson, 'Adorno and the Borders of Experience: The Significance of the Nonidentical for a Different Theory of Bildung', *Educational Theory*, Vol. 56(1), 2006, pp. 69-87.

[3] Marcuse, op. cit.

[4] Ibid.

[5] Ibid.

[6] Ibid.

[7] Ibid., p. 4.

[8] Ibid., p. 11.

[9] Ibid., p. 107.

[10] Ibid., p. xxvii.

[11] Ibid., p. 12.

[12] Ibid., p. 210.

[13] P. Gibbs, 'Higher Education as a Market: A Problem or a Solution', *Studies in Higher Education*, Vol. 26(1), 2001, pp. 85-94, p. 87.

[14] A. Doring, 'Challenges to the Academic Role of Change Agent', *Journal of Further and Higher Education*, Vol. 26(2), 2002, pp. 139-148.

[15] Lynch, op. cit., p. 7.

[16] Marcuse, op. cit., p. 160.

[17] Marcuse sees positivism as '[…] a struggle against all metaphysics, transcendentalism, and idealisms as obscurantist and regressive modes of thought,' Ibid., p. 176.

[18] Ibid., p. 161.

[19] Ibid., p. 160.
[20] Ibid., p. 176.
[21] Ibid., p. 62.
[22] Ibid., p. 119.
[23] Ibid., p. 197.
[24] Ibid., p. 136.
[25] Lynch, op. cit.
[26] Ibid., p. 8.
[27] A.J.F. Kobben and H. Tromp, *De onwelkome boodschap*, Mets & Schilt, Amsterdam, 1999.
[28] Lynch, op. cit., p. 8.
[29] Ibid.
[30] G. Monbiot, *Captive State*, Macmillan, London, 2000.
[31] Lynch, op. cit.
[32] C.D. Garcia Mancilla, 'Art and the Passion of Intellect', 2011, this volume.
[33] Ibid.; C. Heaney, 'Emotional Intelligence: Literature, Ethics and Affective Cognition in J.M. Coetzee's *Disgrace*', 2011, this volume; O. Nenko, 'Aesthetic Emotional Experience: From Eye Irritation to Knowledge', 2011, this volume.
[34] Garcia Mancilla, op. cit.
[35] Ibid.; Heaney, op. cit.
[36] Marcuse, op. cit., p. 196.
[37] Ibid., p. 105.
[38] Ibid., p. 100.
[39] Ibid.
[40] Ibid., p. 182.
[41] Ibid., p. 198.
[42] Lynch, op. cit., p. 9.
[43] See also J. Moir, 'The Democratic Intellect Reconsidered', 2011, this volume.
[44] J. Masschlein and N. Ricken, 'Do We (Still) Need the Concept of Bildung?' *Educational Philosophy and Theory*, Vol. 35(1), 2003, pp. 139-154.
[45] Thompson, op. cit.
[46] W. von Humboldt, *Schriften in 5 Bänden, Vol. 1*, K. Giel and A. Flitner (eds), Darmstad, Wissenschaftliche Buchgesellschaft, 2002, p. 64.
[47] N. Ricken, 'In den Kulissen der Macht: Antropologien als figurierende Kontexte pädagogischer Praktiken', *Vierteljahrschrift für wissenschaftliche Pädagogik*, Vol. 66, 2000, pp. 425-454.
[48] Masschlein and Ricken, op. cit.
[49] Ibid.

[50] C. Fritzell, *A Late Modern Concept of Bildung*, Paper presented at European Conference on Educational Research, University College Dublin, Ireland, 7-10 September 2005.
[51] Ibid., p. 74.
[52] D. McArdle-Clinton, *The Consumer Experience of Higher Education: The Rise of Capsule Education*, Continuum, New York, 2008, p. 3.
[53] I. Harkavy, *The Role of the Universities in Advancing Citizenship and Social Justice in the 21st Century*, Paper presented at the Citizenship Education and Social Justice Conference, Queen's University Belfast, Ireland, 25 May 2005, p. 15.
[54] S. Mahlomaholo and V. Netshandama, 'Post-Apartheid Organic Intellectual and Knowledge Creation', 2011, this volume.
[55] Lynch, op. cit.
[56] O. Procevska, 'Not a Sin, but a Side Effect: Collaboration and Knowledge Creation by Organic Intellectuals', 2011, this volume; T. Adeleke, 'Walter A. Rodney and the Instrumentalist Construction and Utilization of Knowledge', 2011, this volume.
[57] Marcuse, op. cit., p. 148.
[58] Ibid., p. 9.
[59] Ibid., p. 98.
[60] Moir, op. cit.

Bibliography

Doring, A., 'Challenges to the Academic Role of Change Agent'. *Journal of Further and Higher Education*. Vol. 26(2), 2002, pp. 139-148.

Freire, P., *Education for Critical Consciousness*. Continuum, London and New York, 2010 [1974].

Fritzell, C., *A Late Modern Concept of Bildung*. Paper presented at European Conference on Educational Research, University College Dublin, Ireland, 7-10 September, 2005.

Gibbs, P., 'Higher Education as a Market: A Problem or a Solution'. *Studies in Higher Education*. Vol. 26(1), 2001, pp. 85-94.

Harkavy, I., *The Role of the Universities in Advancing Citizenship and Social Justice in the 21st Century*. Paper presented to the Citizenship Education and Social Justice Conference, Queen's University Belfast, 25 May, 2005.

Kobben, A.J.F. and Tromp, H., *De onwelkome boodschap*. Mets & Schilt, Amsterdam, 1999.

Lynch, K., 'Neo-Liberalism and Marketisation: The Implications for Higher Education'. *European Educational Research Journal*. Vol. 5(1), 2006, pp. 1-17.

Marcuse, H., *One Dimensional Man*. Routledge Classics, London and New York, 2010 [1964].

Masschlein, J. and Ricken, N., 'Do We (Still) Need the Concept of *Bildung*?'. *Educational Philosophy and Theory*. Vol. 35(1), 2003, pp. 139-154.

McArdle-Clinton, D., *The Consumer Experience of Higher Education: The Rise of Capsule Education*. Continuum, New York, 2008.

Monbiot, G., *Captive State*. Macmillan, London, 2000.

Ricken, N., 'In den Kulissen der Macht: Antropologien als figurierende Kontexte pädagogischer Praktiken'. *Vierteljahrschrift für wissenschaftliche Pädagogik*. Vol. 66, 2000, pp. 425-454.

Thompson, C., 'Adorno and the Borders of Experience: The Significance of the Nonidentical for a 'Different' Theory of *Bildung*'. *Educational Theory*. Vol. 56(1), 2006, pp. 69-87.

Von Humboldt, W., *Schriften in 5 Bänden. Vol. 1*, Giel, K. and Flitner, A. (eds), Darmstad, Wissenschaftliche Buchgesellschaft, 2002.

The Democratic Intellect Reconsidered

James Moir

Abstract
This chapter revisits the notion of the democratic intellect in light of the current nature of knowledge production in the academy. The role of the intellectual has become that of a specialist knowledge-worker bound up with income generation. Gone is the notion of the intellectual being someone who shares their knowledge with the wider public. It has been suggested that the intellectual as a professional academic is much more in the business of excluding rather than including others in the activities of 'intellectual work.' As van Andel shows rational one-dimensional knowledge production from above has become the dominant epistemological *modus operandi*.[1] This has been exacerbated by the current economic situation in which universities have come to increasingly operate within a market-like structure vying with each other in terms of how they can maximize their commercial interests. This has also extended to considering the higher education as an investment in intellectual capital for the knowledge economy rather than for living in the knowledge society. These developments are discussed in terms of the role of knowledge production within the knowledge society and it is suggested how this needs to be reconnected with the democratic ideal of shared knowledge for the public good.

Key Words: Democratic intellect, citizenship, academia, knowledge society, knowledge economy.

*****

1. **Introduction**
This chapter argues the case for educators within higher education to consider themselves as 'transformative intellectuals,' who can promote 'critical literacy' within their students.[2] This is related to the much touted notion of 'citizenship' and is set within a revaluation of the Scottish tradition of 'democratic intellectualism' which was discussed by George Davie in his book *The Democratic Intellect* (1961).[3] The broad thrust of the arguments developed has been stimulated by the recent critical evaluations of the personal development planning and the notion of graduate attributes in higher education.[4] This has been extended to a critique of the 'Bologna Process' and the move towards a 'modernized' European higher education system.[5] Finally, the recent writings of Jean Barr have been drawn upon in her critical engagement of democratic intellectualism with regard to adult education.[6]

Davie examined the decline of a type of higher education offered in Scottish universities after the Enlightenment of the eighteenth century which encouraged breadth of study and a commitment to public engagement through the study of philosophy and broader concern with theoretical and conceptual issues. Even today, the notion of a broad higher education, at least to begin with in the early part of a program of study, is still within many of Scotland's four-year degree programs.

However, to return to Davie's historical account, the argument he advanced was that the democracy of the democratic intellect lay in the way in which the generalism of the Scottish philosophical tradition acted as a barrier to an individualistic notion of learning and in so doing bridged the gap between the expert few and lay majority. In so doing it was argued that this created a 'sort of intellectual bridge between all classes' in which the Scottish intelligentsia remained in touch with its popular roots, retaining a strong sense of social responsibility. In this way Davie argued that a 'common sense' developed in which the expert knowledge of individuals was enhanced by, and held accountable to, the understanding of the wider public. This was 'democratic' in as much as there was a social distribution of intellectual knowledge. This 'democratic intellect' therefore runs contrary to the notion of intellectual elites and rule by experts. It is a perspective on intellectuality in terms of the social function of the intellectual. However, this was very much a male experience and one in which there is more than a little mythology surrounding the relationship between the classes.

2. The Changing Nature of Knowledge Production in Academia

Academia is said to be in the process of transformation in terms of a shift from a 'knowledge-for-its-own-sake' paradigm to the one that stresses knowledge capitalization.[7] Universities have sought to exploit academic research in order to secure alternative streams of income within a more competitive environment.[8] This has resulted in, for example, collaborative research between university and industry, with an increased emphasis on using the commercialization of intellectual property as a means generating revenue.[9] Some scholars have argued that this institutional transformation is a positive organizational development for universities and have suggested that the growing convergence between academia and industry can be thought of as a 'new' mode of knowledge. It is argued that this links university, private enterprise and government together in a mutually beneficial and productive relationship.

Nevertheless, others are more critical of this emphasis on the commercialization of knowledge. In their view, 'academic capitalism' carries with it negative connotations in terms of an encroaching profit motive into academia.[10] This response is based upon what is considered to be a conflict of values and interests; between academic curiosity and strive for objectivity on the one hand, and entrepreneurialism and commercialization on the other. This is claimed not only to lead to divided loyalties and role conflict, but also, at its starkest, to represent an ideological assault on academic freedom and autonomy. Thus the transformation of academia towards a more market-facing presence represents a major challenge to core academic ideals and professional and intellectual identity.[11]

In parallel with this process towards the development of the entrepreneurial university there has been a shift in emphasis in undergraduate education. Universities are now charged with producing graduates who are able to meet the challenges of the knowledge economy. For example, in the context of European Union, much of this has been driven by the Bologna Process and the focus on modularization, accumulation of academic credit, and the possession of graduate attributes.[12] This was instituted following the Bologna declaration of 1999 which aims to create a European-wide higher educational area. These developments have intensified following the European Union Lisbon Treaty of 2007 and European Commission Lisbon Agenda for addressing the globalised knowledge economy. Aspects of this agenda are aimed at improving graduate employability and competitiveness.

This new vocationalist emphasis has been conceptualized as part of a neoliberal discourse in which 'the market' has come to dictate how we view the 'outputs' of higher education. This new rhetoric represents fundamental change in how higher education is legitimated; one in which knowledge content is relegated to that of the possession of attributes that equip graduates to respond to the changing nature of the labour market. Given the impact of the current global economic situation there is an imperative on higher education to 'deliver' on employability. However, as with the role of academic, the intellectual nature of higher education has arguably been devalued.

3. Bildung Revisited

In spite of this arguable devaluation, there has been a revival of the concept in higher education, namely that of the German concept of *Bildung*. As van Andel points out, this has led to a concern with the development of intellectual public engagement and engendering a critical consciousness in students.[13] We may take the view that the changed legitimation of knowledge has to some extent eroded the notion of its elevated status. The notion of an intimate or edifying connection between knowledge and the 'knower' is part of the neo-humanistic notion of formation or *Bildung*. In revisiting *Bildung* there is a sense in which the concept can be turned against the increasing relationship between user and supplier of knowledge in terms of commodity producers and consumers. The primary task of higher education is to make it possible for students to develop strategies for problem-solving and learning for the ability to connect one's own life to the socio-political processes in society gives the individual justification and means required for a lifelong process of *Bildung* and participation. This is just the very argument that is now being deployed in justifying higher education for the knowledge society rather than merely the knowledge economy.

There is a debate around the differentiation of the terms 'knowledge society' and 'knowledge economy' and the relevance of this for higher education.[14] The two terms tend to be used interchangeably but it is evident that although they are inter-related, there are differences between them. The term 'knowledge society' arose from the earlier term of 'information society' in order to move beyond the notion of technological change and to cover social, cultural, economic, political and institutional transformation. Some authors, notably Castells, refer to the information society, making the comparison between industry and industrial.[15] In this regard Castells draws attention to the ways in which his use of the term 'information' is indicative of a form of social organization in which information is fundamentally linked to productivity and power. Castells goes onto considering how informationalism reinforces control over the labour process and extends capitalism through a 'networked' *modus operandi* around the world.

However, whilst the position expressed by Castells has much to say about the reach of informationalism within the knowledge society, in which knowledge is aligned with production, he has less to say about knowledge as a potentially negotiable, conflicting and, perhaps, liberatory aspect of human activities and social relations. In other words, there is a conflation between the knowledge society and the knowledge economy that reduces the latter to the former. However, the knowledge society may also be viewed as distinct from the knowledge economy in the sense that it is more than a commodity or something to be managed. It can also be regarded as something that is a participative and interactive process that is for the public good.

For the purpose of this chapter, the position taken is not to become ensnared in debating the appropriateness of one term or another, but rather to consider how higher education can support both a transformative role as well delivering graduates who are able to develop both as citizens within the knowledge society and also in relation to their potential employment as part of the knowledge economy. Knowledge is based on information, but is always bound to persons and constructed by them.[16]

In returning to the concept of *Bildung* it can be claimed that knowledge bound up with persons is a fundamental condition for democracy but combining aligning it with critical thinking (what van Andel attempts to do in the previous chapter) is a complicated matter.[17] The process of *Bildung* is sometimes considered as an academic journey of cultivation, and often, with reference to Gadamer's description of personal growth, as seeking a home in the alien in order to become at home in it. The person who goes out into the world to acquire *Bildung* and to become an educated person returns home refreshed and more cultivated than when she or he left. The metaphor grasps how *Bildung* encompasses the relationship between the person and the world. However, it is a somewhat introspective conception and one that is in need of linkage with a more democratic orientation towards knowledge. There is a danger in treating *Bildung* as nothing more than self-development and this can blunt its critical edge. It is for this reason that we need to place the concept alongside another tradition in higher education: that of the democratic intellect.

4. A Resurgence of the Democratic Intellect?

Whilst higher education is in a state of transformation across the world as it responds to the growth of the knowledge economy, there has also been a realization that the process of globalization requires undergraduates to be exposed to an education that will develop citizenship. The 2009 synthesis report from the Global University Network for Innovation (GUNI) entitled *Higher Education at a Time of Transformation: New Dynamics for Social Responsibility* draws attention to the many challenges confronting the sector that stem from those of wider society: beyond the 'ivory tower' or 'market-oriented university' towards one that innovatively adds value to the process of social transformation. The report argues that this creation and distribution of socially relevant knowledge is something that needs to be core to the activities of universities, thereby strengthening their social responsibility.[18]

As the GUNI report puts so well, this calls for us to rethink the purpose of higher education; a purpose that is one of transformation rather than transmission.

> The central educative purpose of HEIs ought to be the explicit facilitation of progressive, reflexive, critical, transformative learning that leads to much improved understanding of the need for, and expression of, responsible paradigms for living and for 'being' and 'becoming,' both as individuals alone and collectively as communities.[19]

On the face of it, this notion of higher education as educating citizens with a sense of civic awareness may seem to chime with that of the democratic intellect. However, a note of caution needs to be sounded in that it is set within the context of ever increasing costs for those entering higher education and a legitimating rhetoric of 'employability.' There is little room here for notion of citizenship and the democratization of knowledge that involves, not simply the development of expertise, but also the importance of bringing in 'knowledge from below' in terms of forging a real connection with lived experience. To do otherwise might risk opening up new spaces for critical debate and alternative ideas and practices. As Lyotard put it in *The Postmodern Condition* we are left with an 'exteriorization of knowledge with respect to the 'knower,' at whatever point he or she may occupy in the knowledge process.'[20] And so as with academics in their research, what more than not transpires is an exclusion rather than inclusion of others in intellectual work.[21]

This can occur even in areas such as my own discipline of sociology, where despite a call for a public sociology, the rhetoric does not match up with the actual practice of the discipline. For example, it has been argued that it has become a 'hyper-professionalized' endeavour in which highly abstract explanatory theories are valued but at the expense of making the social world less comprehensible in terms of everyday experience.[22] This is the very opposite to that intended in the development of the 'sociological imagination.'[23]

5. Overcoming the Hurdles

At this point it is worthwhile drawing upon a Wittgensteinian-inspired analysis of the notion of education as involving practicing.[24] The notion of education as an initiation into practices can, on the face of it, appear to be somewhat conservative in that it emphasizes the reproductive functions of teaching and learning. However, this need not be the case and they note that different ways of learning or enacting are very much bound up with a sense of self and identity. It is learning through practicing which can lead to a transformation of self through interactions and relations with others in the learning process. Practices can therefore transform the self by encouraging certain interpretations but also may lead to subversions that distance the person from these. It is in Aristotelian terms the notion of 'praxis;' how one lives as a citizen and human being and is the personal, social and political embodiment of practice.

This more critical and reflective process of narrativization in relation to the learning process can be found in the recent attempts to encourage personalization as an aspect of the development of graduate attributes (GAs). The major pedagogical implication of such an approach is the adoption of measures designed to encourage students to be self-learning, self-actualizing and self-initiating. There is the view that a homogeneous offering is not sufficient in meeting students' needs. Yet, despite this latter emphasis, a major driver behind the move towards personalization is the recognition that mass higher education has also been accompanied by a concern regarding retention and motivation.

It is clearly the case that those who are actively engaged in the educational process both inside and outside the classroom are more likely to be successful than their disengaged peers.[25] Influential writers such as Barnett suggest that the 'will to learn' is a key aspect of the student experience that needs to be encouraged and nurtured.[26] According to this view it is not the subject of study or the acquisition of skills that educators need to focus on but rather personal aspects such as authenticity, dispositions, inspiration, passion and spirit (see later in this volume on the emotional aspects of knowledge). As he puts it,

> the fundamental educational problem of a changing world is neither one of knowledge nor of skills, but is one of being. To put it more formally, the educational challenge of a world of uncertainty is ontological in nature.[27]

Much of Barnett's focus is therefore directed towards how such qualities or attributes can be developed and in doing so this connects with related concepts such as personal development planning (PDP) and graduate attributes (GAs).[28] Simon Barrie's work has had a significant impact on thinking about the nature of generic GAs in higher education.[29] For example, in developing a conceptual framework for the development of GAs, Barrie notes a series of factors including, under the heading of participation, 'generic attributes are learnt by the way students participate and engage with all the experiences of university life.'[30]

The personalization of learning has been applied differently across and within subjects, but has effectively become a 'de rigueur' aspect of the higher education system.[31] However, this must also be accompanied by a shift from traditional knowledge production and transmission (mode 1 knowledge) to wisdom based on collaborative learning (mode 2 knowledge). Yet, the increasing bureaucratization of the learning process as a codified product is paradoxical when set aside the ways in which students are encouraged to engage with their curricula in a constructivist manner. Thus, as some have suggested, this has enabled a managerial model of learning to be surreptitiously substituted for the dialogic and critical model which characterizes the ideal of learning in higher education.[32]

To some this process is arguably more about the legitimation of PDP and GAs as a means of showing their operation within an audit-driven and accountable culture. This view has been most strongly put by Mary Evans in her book *Killing Thinking: Death of the Universities*, who writes that there has been

> a transformation of teaching in universities into the painting-by-numbers exercise of a hand-out culture [...] [in which] rich resources are increasingly marginalized by cultures of assessment and regulation [...]. Increasingly, students are being asked to pay for the costs of the regulation of HE rather than education itself.[33]

If the case for a focus on employability relies on the notion of adaptation to the global knowledge economy, then it can also be argued that a case can be made for defending the inclusion of the values that encourage a more global perspective in the curriculum. This is in accord with the notion of the democratic intellect.

It is also the case that GAs are often associated with notions of creativity and transformation. In this respect it is worth noting Mayo's invocation of Shaull's foreword to Friere's *Pedagogy of the Oppressed*.[34]

> Education either functions as an instrument that is used to facilitate the integration of the younger generation into the logic of the present system and bring about conformity to it, or it becomes the 'practice of freedom,' the means by which men and women deal critically and creatively with reality and discover how to participate in the transformation of their world.[35]

Although for some this polarization may seem heavily ideological, it can be argued that a vision of higher education as not only contributing to the sharing of values, but also the shaping of them is a desirable goal related to the notion of GAs. For a university education to be fit for purpose in a globalizing world, students need 'a set of values that transform them, both now and in the future.'[36]

This chimes with the recent focus on identity within higher education.[37] In other words, there is a concern with how the personal aspect of being a student in higher education is related to GAs in a more engaged and transformational sense. It is also interesting, that recent work points to the challenges of teaching and learning within the contradictions of increasing specialization, but also at the same time transdisciplinary contexts.[38] This raises the issue of the local-global dimension and how we can begin to encourage students to consider themselves and their relationship to their studies within this much broader context. Within the context of the rapidly changing nature of knowledge society and economy, the ability to adapt to change and to be able to evaluate different kinds of knowledge is crucial. In addressing this aspect it is worth returning to Ron Barnett who writes:

> In a world of liquid knowledge, where knowledge has become knowledges jostling and even competing with each another, there are knowledge spaces: universities can approach knowledge - and are doing so - in radically different ways.[39]

6. Conclusion

Whether or not the higher education can free itself from the relentless drive towards the mercerization of knowledge remains to be seen. However, based on the current drive towards the student rather than the state funding tuition, this may be more wishful thinking than a realistic assessment. The notion that university academics should consider themselves as 'transformative intellectuals' is one that appeals to many in terms of their pedagogic practice, and yet they are caught up in a bureaucratic audit-driven system both in terms of their teaching and research.

Nevertheless, there are signs that the spirit of the democratic intellect may indeed be something that can be cultivated, not in terms of knowledge as a means of social differentiation in terms of graduate attributes or employability, but rather in terms of a recognition that there is a strong cultural dimension to higher education in which knowledge is set within its social and political context. Perhaps the current economic situation may prompt some rethinking about how universities structure their curricula, how they engage with their students, and indeed there are already signs that this is so.

Notes

[1] J. van Andel, 'The Rationalization of Academia: From *Bildung* to Production', 2011, this volume.

[2] N.K. Denzin and Y.S. Lincoln, 'Introduction: Critical Methodologies and Indigenous Inquiry', *Handbook of Critical and Indigenous Methodologies*, N.K. Denzin, Y.S. Lincoln and L.T. Smith (eds), Sage, Los Angeles, 2008, p. 8.

[3] G.E. Davie, *The Democratic Intellect,* Edinburgh University Press, Edinburgh, 1961.

[4] J. Moir, 'Personal Development Planning in Higher Education: Localised Thinking for a Globalised World', *The Crisis of Schooling? Learning, Knowledge and Competencies in Modern Societies*, J.M. Resende and M.M. Vieira (eds), Cambridge Scholars Press, Newcastle upon Tyne, 2009.

[5] J. Moir, 'Bologna Bytes: Higher Education and Personal Development Planning', *The International Journal of Learning*, Vol. 16, 2009, pp. 367-373.

[6] J. Barr, 'Re-Framing the Democratic Intellect', *Scottish Affairs*, Vol. 55, 2006, pp. 23-46; J. Barr, *The Stranger Within: On the Idea of an Educated Public*, Sense Publishers Rotterdam, 2008.

[7] B.R. Clark, *Creating Entrepreneurial Universities,* Pergamon Press, Oxford, 1998; H. Etzkowitz, A. Webster, C. Gebhardt and B. Terra, 'The Future of University and the University of the Future: Evolution of Ivory

Tower to Entrepreneurial Paradigm', *Research Policy*, Vol. 29, 2000, pp. 313-330.

[8] S. Slaughter and L.L. Leslie, *Academic Capitalism: Politics, Policies, and the Entrepreneurial University*, Johns Hopkins University Press, Baltimore, 1997.

[9] P. D'Este and P. Patel, 'University-Industry Linkages in the UK: What Are the Factors Underlying the Variety of Interactions with Industry?', *Research Policy*, Vol. 36, 2007, pp. 1295-1313; D.S. Siegel, M. Wright and A. Lockett, 'The Rise of Entrepreneurial Activity at Universities: Organizational and Societal Implications', *Industrial and Corporate Change*, Vol. 16, 2007, pp. 489-504.

[10] S. Slaughter and G. Rhoades, *Academic Capitalism and the New Economy: Markets, State, and Higher Education*, Johns Hopkins University Press, Baltimore, 2004.

[11] J. Beck and M.F.D. Young, 'The Assault on the Professions and the Restructuring of Academic and Professional Identities: A Bernsteinian Analysis', *British Journal of Sociology of Education*, Vol. 26, 2005, pp. 183-197.

[12] K. Barkholt, 'The Bologna Process and Integration Theory: Theory, Convergence and Autonomy', *Higher Education in Europe*, Vol. 30, 2005, pp. 23-29.

[13] J. van Andel, op. cit.

[14] S. Sörlin and H. Vessuri (eds), *Knowledge Society vs. Knowledge Economy: Knowledge, Power, and Politics*, UNESCO Forum on Higher Education, Research and Knowledge, International Association of Universities, Palgrave Macmillan, New York, 2007.

[15] M. Castells, *The Rise of the Network Society*, Blackwell, Oxford, 2000.

[16] G.J.B. Probst, S.P. Raub and K. Romhardt, *Managing Knowledge: Building Blocks for Success*, John Wiley and Sons, Chichester, 2000.

[17] J. van Andel, op. cit.

[18] Global University Network for Innovation (GUNI), *Higher Education at a Time of Transformation: New Dynamics for Social Responsibility*, Palgrave Macmillan, Basingstoke, Hampshire, New York, 2009, p. 7.

[19] Ibid., p. 11

[20] J.F. Lyotard, *The Postmodern Condition: A Report on Knowledge*, Manchester University Press, Manchester, 1984, p. 4.

[21] E. Yeo, *The Contest for Social Science: Relations and Representations of Gender and Class*, River Orams Press, London, 1996.

[22] D. Noy, 'The Contradictions of Public Sociology: A View from a Graduate Student at Berkeley', *The American Sociologist*, Vol. 40, 2009, pp. 253-248.

[23] C.W. Mills, *The Sociological Imagination*, Penguin, Harmondsworth, 1970.
[24] P. Smeyers and N.C. Burbules, 'Education as Initiation into Practices', *Showing and Doing: Wittgenstein as a Pedagogical Philosopher*, Paradigm Press, Boulder, USA, 2010.
[25] S.R. Harper and S.J. Quaye (eds), *Student Engagement in Higher Education: Theoretical Perspectives and Practical Approaches for Diverse Populations*, Routledge, New York, 2009.
[26] R. Barnett, *A Will to Learn: Being a Student in an Age of Uncertainty*, McGraw-Hill/Open University Press, Maidenhead, 2007.
[27] R. Barnett, 'Graduate Attributes in an Age of Uncertainty', *Graduate Attributes, Learning and Employability*, P. Hager and S. Holland (eds), Springer, Drordrecht, p. 51.
[28] R. Barnett, 'Knowing and Becoming in the Higher Education Curriculum', *Studies in Higher Education*, Vol. 34(4), 2009, pp. 429-440.
[29] S.C. Barrie, 'A Research-Based Approach to Generic Graduate Attributes Policy', *Higher Education Research and Development*, Vol. 3, 2004, p. 261-275; S.C. Barrie, 'Understanding what We Mean by Generic Attributes of Graduates', *Higher Education*, Vol. 51(2), 2006, pp. 215-241; S.C. Barrie, 'A Conceptual Framework for the Teaching and Learning of Generic Graduate Attributes', *Studies In Higher Education*, Vol. 32(4), 2007 pp. 439-458.
[30] Barrie, 'A Conceptual Framework...', op. cit., pp. 444-449.
[31] S. Clegg and M.E. David, 'Passion, Pedagogies and the Project of the Personal in Higher Education in 21st Century Society', *Journal of the Academy of Social Sciences*, Vol. 1, 2006, pp. 149-167.
[32] B. Lambier and S. Ramaekers, 'The Limits of Blackboard are the Limits of My World: On the Changing Concepts of the University and its Students', *E-Learning*, Vol. 3, 2006, pp. 544-551.
[33] M. Evans, *Killing Thinking: The Death of the Universities*, Continuum Books, London, 2005, pp. ix-x.
[34] P. Mayo, 'A Rationale for a Transformative Approach to Education', *Journal of Transformative Education*, Vol. 1(1), 2003, pp 38-57, p. 42.
[35] P. Freire, *Pedagogy of the Oppressed*, Continuum Books, New York, 1970, pp. 13-14.
[36] D. Otter, 'Globalisation and Sustainability: Global Perspectives and Education for Sustainable Development in Higher Education', *Internationalising Higher Education*, E. Jones and S. Brown (eds), Routledge, London, 2007, pp. 42-53.
[37] R. Barnett and R. Di Napoli (eds), *Changing Identities in Higher Education: Voicing Perspectives*, Routledge London, 2007.

[38] C. Kreber (ed), *The University and Its Disciplines: Teaching and Learning within and beyond Disciplinary Boundaries*, Routledge, London, 2008.
[39] R. Barnett, *Being a University*, Routledge, Oxon., 2011.

Bibliography

Barkholt, K., 'The Bologna Process and Integration Theory: Theory, Convergence and Autonomy'. *Higher Education in Europe*. Vol. 30, 2005, pp. 23-29.

Barnett, R., 'Graduate Attributes in an Age of Uncertainty'. *Graduate Attributes, Learning and Employability*. Hager, P. and Holland, S. (eds), Springer, Drordrecht, 2006.

Barnett, R., *A Will to Learn: Being a Student in an Age of Uncertainty*. McGraw-Hill/Open University Press, Maidenhead, 2007.

—, 'Knowing and Becoming in the Higher Education Curriculum'. *Studies in Higher Education*. Vol. 34, 2009, pp. 429-440.

—, *Being a University*. Routledge, Oxon., 2011.

Barnett, R. and Di Napoli, R. (eds), *Changing Identities in Higher Education: Voicing Perspectives*. Routledge, London, 2007.

Barr, J., 'Re-Framing the Democratic Intellect'. *Scottish Affairs*. Vol. 55, 2006, pp. 23-46.

—, *The Stranger Within: On the Idea of an Educated Public*. Rotterdam, Sense Publishers, 2008.

Barrie, S.C., 'A Research-Based Approach to Generic Graduate Attributes Policy'. *Higher Education Research and Development*. Vol. 23, 2004, pp. 261-275.

—, 'Understanding What We Mean By Generic Attributes of Graduates'. *Higher Education*. Vol. 51, 2006, pp. 215-241.

—, 'A Conceptual Framework for the Teaching and Learning of Generic Graduate Attributes'. *Studies In Higher Education*. Vol. 32(4), 2007, pp. 439-458.

Beck, J. and Young, M.F.D. 'The Assault on the Professions and the Restructuring of Academic and Professional Identities: A Bernsteinian Analysis'. *British Journal of Sociology of Education.* Vol. 26, 2005, pp.183-97.

Castells, M., *The Rise of the Network Society.* Blackwell, Oxford, 2000.

Clark, B.R., *Creating Entrepreneurial Universities.* Pergamon Press, Oxford, 1998.

Clegg, S. and David, M.E., 'Passion, Pedagogies and the Project of the Personal in Higher Education in 21st Century Society'. *Journal of the Academy of Social Sciences.* Vol. 1, 2006, pp. 149-167.

David, M., 'Equity and Diversity: Towards a Sociology of Higher Education for the Twenty-First Century?'. *British Journal of Sociology of Education.* Vol. 28, 2007, pp. 675-690.

David, M. and Clegg, S., 'Power, Pedagogy and Personalization in Global Higher Education: The Occlusion of Second-Wave Feminism?'. *Discourse: Studies in the Cultural Politics of Education.* Vol. 29, 2008, pp. 483-498.

Davie, G.E., *The Democratic Intellect.* Edinburgh, University Press, Edinburgh, 1961.

Denzin, N.K. and Lincoln, Y.S., 'Introduction: Critical Methodologies and Indigenous Inquiry'. *Handbook of Critical and Indigenous Methodologies.* Denzin, N.K., Lincoln, Y.S. and Smith, L.T. (eds), Sage, Los Angeles, 2008.

D'Este, P. and Patel, P., 'University-Industry Linkages in the UK: What are the Factors Underlying the Variety of Interactions with Industry?'. *Research Policy.* Vol. 36, 2007, pp. 1295-1313.

Evans, M., *Killing Thinking: The Death of the Universities.* Continuum Books, London, 2005.

Etzkowitz, H., Webster, A., Gebhardt, C. and Terra, B., 'The Future of University and the University of the Future: Evolution of Ivory Tower to Entrepreneurial Paradigm'. *Research Policy.* Vol. 29, 2000, pp. 313-330.

Freire, P., *Pedagogy of the Oppressed.* Continuum Books, New York, 1970.

Gibbons, M., Limoges, C., Nowotny, H., Schwartzman, S., Scott, P. and Trow, M., *The New Production of Knowledge.* Sage, London, 1994.

'Global Network for University Innovation (GUNI)', *Higher Education at a Time of Transformation: New Dynamics for Social Responsibility.* Palgrave Macmillan, Basingstoke, Hampshire, New York, 2009.

Harper, S.R. and Quaye, S.J. (eds), *Student Engagement in Higher Education: Theoretical Perspectives and Practical Approaches for Diverse Populations.* Routledge, New York, 2009.

Henkel, M. 'Can Academic Autonomy Survive in the Knowledge Society? A Perspective from Britain'. *Higher Education Research & Development.* Vol. 26, 2007, pp. 87-99.

Kreber, C. (ed), *The University and its Disciplines: Teaching and Learning within and beyond Disciplinary Boundaries.* Routledge, London and New York, 2008.

Lambier, B. and Ramaekers, S., 'The Limits of Blackboard Are the Limits of My World: On the Changing Concepts of the University and its Students'. *E-Learning.* Vol. 3, 2006, pp. 544-551.

Lyotard, J.F., *The Postmodern Condition: A Report on Knowledge.* Manchester University Press, Manchester, 1984.

Mayo, P., 'A Rationale for a Transformative Approach to Education'. *Journal of Transformative Education.* Vol. 1, 2003, pp. 38-57.

Mills, C.W., *The Sociological Imagination.* Penguin, Harmondsworth, 1970.

Moir, J., 'Personal Development Planning in Higher Education: Localised Thinking for a Globalised World'. *The Crisis of Schooling? Learning, Knowledge and Competencies in Modern Societies.* J.M. Resende and M.M. Viera (eds), Cambridge Scholars Press, Newcastle upon Tyne, 2009.

Moir, J., 'Bologna Bytes: Higher Education and Personal Development Planning'. *The International Journal of Learning.* Vol. 16, 2009, pp. 367-373.

Noy, D., 'The Contradictions of Public Sociology: A View from a Graduate Student at Berkeley'. *The American Sociologist.* Vol. 40, 2009, pp. 253-248.

Otter, D., 'Globalisation and Sustainability: Global Perspectives and Education for Sustainable Development in Higher Education'. *Internationalising Higher Education.* Jones E. and Brown, S. (eds), Routledge, London, 2007.

Probst, G., Raub, S.P. and Romhardt, K., *Managing Knowledge: Building Blocks for Success.* Wiley, Chichester, 2000.

Siegel, D.S., Wright, M. and Lockett, A., 'The Rise of Entrepreneurial Activity at Universities: Organizational and Societal Implications'. *Industrial and Corporate Change.* Vol. 16, 2007, pp. 489-504.

Slaughter, S. and Leslie, L.L., *Academic Capitalism: Politics, Policies, and the Entrepreneurial University.* Johns Hopkins University Press, Baltimore, 1997.

Slaughter, S. and Rhoades, G., *Academic Capitalism and the New Economy: Markets, State, and Higher Education.* Johns Hopkins University Press, Baltimore, 2004.

Smeyers, P. and Burbules, N.C., 'Education as Initiation into Practices'. *Showing and Doing: Wittgenstein as a Pedagogical Philosopher.* Peters, M.A., Burbules, N. and Smeyers, P. (eds), Paradigm Press, Boulder, USA, 2010.

Sörlin, S. and Vessuri, H. (eds), *Knowledge Society vs. Knowledge Economy: Knowledge, Power, and Politics.* UNESCO Forum on Higher Education, Research and Knowledge, International Association of Universities, Palgrave Macmillan, New York, 2007.

Yeo, E., *The Contest for Social Science: Relations and Representations of Gender and Class.* River Orams Press, London, 1996.

Part II:

Intellectuals in the Public Sphere: 'Organic' Knowledge Creation

Post-Apartheid Organic Intellectual and Knowledge Creation

Sechaba Mahlomaholo and Vhonani Netshandama

Abstract
This chapter defines the concept of the organic intellectual along Gramscian lines as that 'contradictory space of production' where the privileges as well as the power of bourgeois academic position on the one hand and the gaping wounds of powerlessness and poverty of the underclass on the other meet.[1] Thus the notion of the 'organic intellectual' gives us the terminology to explore our roles as academics in the post-apartheid South Africa. The chapter therefore argues that because of our subaltern class origins we are unable to be objective in pursuing our work as researchers. All the time in our work we are subjective as we give due to the agenda for equity, social justice, freedom, peace and hope, hence, transformation of our still unequal social arrangement. Predicated by the above we then proceed to describe the principles and mechanisms of how, through research and the creation of knowledge, we bring the rich resources of academia to buttress further community cultural wealth of the underclass communities towards a more equitable democratic South Africa. Our contradictory position thus becomes the place for creative action and designing of new knowledge and practices based on the experiences of the subaltern.

Key Words: Post-apartheid, organic intellectual, knowledge creation, community cultural wealth, critical emancipatory research.

*****

1. **Subaltern Organic Intellectual: A Definition**
   The organic intellectual, in terms of our understanding of Gramsci's theorization, is not necessarily any singular person or thing, rather this concept refers to a place or space which is infinite and can be occupied by whomever, depending on how they are positioned in discourses.[2] Henriques, Hollway, Urwin, Venn and Walkerdine in their seminal book titled *Changing the Subject* assist us to see identity, such as that of the organic intellectual, not as inherent and intrinsic but as non-essentialist and based on one's positioning in discourse(s).[3] It is this very same notion of positionality, which Jacques Lacan in his reinterpretation of Freud's theorization of personhood, describes.[4] According to Lacan identity as 'the signifier' may even be seen as arbitrary and imagined before it is finally enacted. It is a role and not something which some people have while others do not. Therefore, if the organic intellectual is a role and a space it is possible to have it in multiple

forms. This idea of multiplicity makes variations and contradictions within this notion possible and even unavoidable.

It is on the basis of the above that we are encouraged to also see ourselves as organic intellectuals as we go about doing our work as academics. In fact in our view, any person who plays some or all of the following seven roles which we will describe below qualifies to be described as an organic intellectual. This description will differ from how the public intellectual is conceptualized because of a number of reasons which we will also provide. Whereas the public intellectual is seen in singular and centralist terms, the organic intellectual true to the postmodern project is multiple and diverse but is kept coherent by the transformative agenda which describes his/her role. Reading Simet's account of Hrant Dink and Adeleke's story of Walter Rodney, one gets the feeling of a public intellectual who is a national, ethnic, class and/or group hero to mention a few.[5] The standards which these public heroes set for qualification into this category seem to be extremely high for ordinary mortals as they involve a measure of self-sacrifice and martyrdom which we as organic intellectuals may never attain. The kind of intellectual described by Simet and Adeleke is the one who has to evince elements of bravado and thus be visible especially in the public domain and has to objectively pursue the 'truth' irrespective of the consequences. This public intellectual, it seems, also has to be antithetical to the ruling elite/government/party/status quo under all circumstances.

While we agree that some of these characteristics also do apply in describing the organic intellectual, in terms of our reading of Gramsci we come to the conclusion that there are other ways also of seeing this role and place. As such, our definition thus affirms that sometimes the organic intellectual may be vocal, loud and visible but this is not necessarily the *conditio sine qua non.* Sometimes, in fact most of the time, the organic intellectual is more discerning than that as he/she has to weigh the pros and cons of his/her actions more carefully. The criterion for action is whether it advances the transformative agenda or not. The organic intellectual may lie low for a while if it benefits the abovementioned agenda to do so. To come out in the open and fight the tanks, planes and the whole might of the regime bare-handed may be more counterproductive than gradually influencing public opinion against it.

In fact, the concerns which Procevska raises about the bravado and antics of some of the public intellectuals are valid as they adequately underlie our definition of what space and role constitute the organic intellectual.[6] For example, the organic intellectual who Gramsci refers to and who we are and attempt to be, is the one who is in the employ and thus on the payroll of the bourgeoisie or hegemonic institutions/companies and who has to tread very carefully lest he/she be fired from the comfort of his/her job.[7] Such an organic intellectual has for a very long time been co-opted, educated and generally nurtured in the knowledge, skills, values, culture and temperament of the middle class/oppressive system which he wants to rebel against or depose or destroy. Such an immersion is bound to take its toll on the organic intellectual's thinking, outlook and mode of operation. Our view therefore is that no matter how hard the organic intellectual may try 'to be' with the subaltern/underclass and the oppressed, the fact of the matter is that he/she is no longer one of them as he/she no longer has the same *habitus* as they do.[8] His/her material conditions have changed, as have all his/her capitals.[9] His/her social networks are different and in many instances more powerful than those of the underclass.

It is at this point where our definition of the organic intellectual inserts within itself the notion of a space and a role of contradictions because Gramsci makes us aware that the vantage position which now such a person inhabits should at the same time enable him/her to look back and bring to the agenda the plight of his/her less fortunate underclass compatriots.[10] The assimilation by privilege and elevated socio-economic/intellectual status should not be complete, but should leave at least the conscience intact. Such a conscientious intellectual may want to bring the totalitarian or repressive regime to its knees through a number of ways, one of which is to openly criticize and demonize it as the public intellectual defined elsewhere in this chapter does, or he/she may choose to engage in less overt operations which are sustainable in pursuance of the same stated objective.

For us in the post-apartheid democratic South Africa, we take our cues from the legislative and policy contexts which are all out in favor of the underclass in spite of the shadows of our horrific racist apartheid past still lingering in practice and, as such, holding progress towards full transformation captive.[11] Our intentions as organic intellectuals are thus different from those of our ilk in non-democratic contexts, as instead of militating against the regime, we actually support the operationalization of its declared agenda for equity, social justice, freedom, peace and hope.[12] We thus see ourselves as organic intellectuals who are defined by our roles and spaces as the *mediators* for transformation, the *designers* of contexts for the attainment of a better life for all, effective and impartial *administrators* of our community's cultural wealth, *scholars* of repute in service of the national transformation agenda who are charged with the responsibility of providing *pastoral care* for those less fortunate of our people and as monitors and *assessors* of progress towards total freedom as well as becoming internationally renowned *experts* on our local knowledge.[13]

As organic intellectuals who are mediators, we use our knowledge and skills acquired from both the privileged and the subaltern classes to enable the latter to access the former and the former to take cognizance of the latter towards mutual knowledge, respect and enrichment of each other's community cultural wealth.[14] The contradictory space which we occupy thus becomes the arena for productivity, growth and development of all. Based on the above we also assist in the designing of a better life for all through 'being there' with the disadvantaged, experiencing their plight with them and together experimenting with ways of transforming their lives for the better.[15] We are not imposing, with respect we allow the people we work with to determine their agenda while we provide advocacy and advisory roles.[16] Our research, our community engagement and our teaching are inextricably intertwined with the agenda for social transformation of the plight of the less privileged communities, informed and supported by the resources of the privileged bourgeoisie institutions we work at.[17] Because of the contexts of mutual trust between ourselves and the communities of the underclass with which we work we have found ourselves 'appointed' as administrators of their community cultural wealth.[18] They have allowed us into their very private spaces to document their experiences, their fears and aspirations through research which valorises and amplifies their voices.[19] They have even appointed us to support their men, women and children as they design development strategies for their municipalities and neighbourhoods as well as safely keep their valued cultural artefacts that celebrate their lives, their tribulations and their achievements.[20] All the above we have tried to do with due care and respect but at the same time with the rigor required of scientific research. We have become the scholars of the subaltern, the people's academy. Every bit of research we have done have been discussed and informed by their concerns and needs. We have gone through the interpretative phase of the research with them.[21] We have allowed them to dictate and determine the direction of our research. They have been there as we analysed the data together and we even had to justify for them every bit of conclusion and recommendation of such studies. Even at the final educative stage or implementation phase of much of our research, the agenda was determined by them while in terms of our expertise we provided the materials which enabled them to make informed decisions.[22] Sometimes the findings of our research were not palatable as they mirrored the experiences of exclusion and marginalization. Even under such circumstances we were always there to counsel and to provide encouragement and the strength which we found reciprocated in many instances by our communities.[23] Their community structures, such as school governing bodies, local municipality councils, etc., are always there to ask for our input and facilitation skills as they prepare their annual strategic plans as an example.[24] All these we have not done solely for altruistic intents as we also have benefitted in many ways from these interactions. We have become experts on what makes our communities function.[25] We have put their stories on the national and international agenda and we have also grown in the process.[26] We have monitored the progress which we are making collectively. We have benchmarked this along with other communities' progress.

In our view the above details have graphically indicated what we have come to see as the place and role that define an organic intellectual. Procevska is right that our collaborating so closely with communities has removed the innocence of objectivity, reliability, predictability, universal laws, generalizability, external validity.[27] However as she contends this overt subjectivity is not a sin but 'a side effect of intellectual's function.' In fact this overt leaning in favour of the subaltern is not 'a side effect' as we see it; instead it is the centrepiece of how we function as organic intellectuals. What informs our work and guides the quality of our research is not necessarily the aforementioned positivistic criteria, but rather, the criteria of good transformative processes of knowledge production which we describe below.

2. Periodization of Knowledge Production

In order to describe, justify and develop a better understanding of this 'good transformative processes of knowledge production' which we engage in as organic intellectuals, it is important to demonstrate how it is similar and/or different from some of the dominant epistemological lenses that have gained currency over the years. Once this has been done it will therefore be easier to show how in terms of its principles and mechanisms it is unique and more appropriate for our emancipatory agenda.

To initiate the debate, Auguste Comte contends that the development of knowledge and its production goes through three distinct stages.[28] The first stage he calls the *Theological*. During this stage, faith and belief are the sole mechanisms of knowing the truth. According to Comte true knowledge during this theological stage is about the canonized version of what is regarded as the divine revelation. However, Comte argues that because of the many inherent contradictions within this approach, philosophers of epistemology and practitioners of research realized that perhaps reason and logical deductions and not faith constituted the best approach to knowledge production. This second stage where reasoning and logical argumentation became the dominant approach, Comte calls the *Metaphysical* stage.[29]

Later on, another group of philosophers of research including Francis Bacon realized that reasoning though logical deduction alone was not always accurate because sometimes practically and empirically the findings differed from what logic and reasoning alone dictated.[30] Thus, for true knowledge to be produced a closer look of the phenomena was required. This closer look Comte called observation. Anything that could not be directly observed could thus not be true, or in existence, irrespective of the researcher's faith and/or logical reasoning. In fact, as Charles Darwin and Francis Bacon noted, research has to proceed from a hypothesis (an assumption about what is true) followed by intensive and extensive empirical observation of all individual cases and instances and then on the basis thereof a valid conclusion can be drawn.[31] This approach of using observations in combination with both the deductive and inductive reasoning, Comte called the Positive approach, proclaiming the respective (third) stage as the *Positive* stage. The Positive approach became popular and dominant around the turn of the 19th century. The main reason for this popularity was the achievements of the Industrial Revolution which gave credit to the power of positive approaches in its massive material and machinery inventions as well as productions that occurred then.

However, the greatest tragedy of all was unfortunately to befall human kind in 1914 and 1939 when people were killed in large numbers during World War I and II in spite of their seemingly superior methods of accessing true knowledge proclaimed by positivism.[32] As a result the human being was again called upon to question him or herself. Jean Paul Sartre in the tradition of Edmund Husserl and Brentano, as well as many other thinkers of the existential phenomenological persuasion including Van den Bergh with his metabletics, jumped onto the bandwagon to usher in a new era of doing research at that time because the old positivistic approach was found inadequate to answer to the questions of knowledge and its production especially about the meaning of life as well as those issues which were uniquely human.[33] In fact, debates centred on how knowledge production could still rely on positivism for understanding issues that were typically human if it could unleash destruction on such a scale as evidenced by the two world wars.[34]

Phenomenology was thus born to respond to this need as an interpretative and hermeneutic approach, which gives due to language and intersubjectivity, the primary modes of knowing about human beings' fears, experiences and aspirations.[35] Through this approach, the dictum *a human as a speaking being* became popular and famous.[36] This meant that useful research on humans was to be phenomenological and as such very cautious when it came to humans because they could not be truly understood using positive methods alone.

3.   **Critical Emancipatory Research as Transformative**

Given the contextualization above, Habermas, Adorno, Horkheimer and the Frankfurt School of 1924 agreed with the phenomenologists that researching typically human experiences required typically human research methodologies and strategies.[37] However, they felt that research should go further and deeper and be more critical of the human condition. They thus described their approach to research as Critical Theory (CT) because they criticized the excesses of power seemingly inherent in social formations containing human beings, such as communism, especially under Stalin. They also criticized the inhumanity of capitalism. Their main concern was why people who were oppressed and marginalized were compliant to the injustices they were subjected to by both systems.[38] Habermas found the answer in the concept and process of ideology which corresponds directly with Gramsci's notion of hegemony.[39] He figured it out that ideology, especially distorted ideology as inherent in the workings of the hegemonic interests, was making people to be subservient and to allow themselves to be abused. He argued that they behaved like they were possessed or blackmailed because they could feel the uneasiness of oppression due to the contradictions, especially in regard to their physical conditions but they were not questioning or subverting that hold of ideology because they had internalized their own oppression to the extent that it appeared natural for them to be oppressed.[40]

It is at this juncture that as organic intellectuals we found CR to be an approach containing principles and mechanisms addressing our concerns for a transformative agenda as described earlier. Our approach to knowledge production takes the critique of a distorted ideology as its starting point. Our argument is that apartheid was such an ideology, which has crippled us and our communities and has truncated our efforts towards a better life in spite of the demise of statutory apartheid. For us to rid ourselves of its hold and thus facilitate the creation of a counter hegemonic dispensation we need to start first with a thorough critique and interrogation thereof.

To elaborate the point further Habermas has identified three objectives or basic cognitive interests that define three different kinds of research, namely: work, language and power.[41] Each of these three categories corresponds to ways in which society is organized. As people we come together to produce through *work* for the continued existence of the human species. All natural sciences which are also known as positive sciences (positivism) are as a result of knowledge which is aimed at improving and facilitating *work*. This kind of knowledge is produced mainly by means of controlling what are called confounding variables so that the researcher can determine what impact or effect a predictor variable has on the outcome or dependent variables. It is the question of causality which is paramount in this mode of research. The argument is that if researchers could control for these extraneous and confounding variables, it would be easy for them to predict what the outcome was going to be when the cause is known, and also to know what the cause was if they knew what the effect or outcome was. If they can determine the cause, then they can predict what the outcome is going to be. They can even draw general and universal rules. They thus quantify, they talk about verifiability, validity and reliability and this is what Comte described as the positive approach.[42]

In our approach to knowledge production as organic intellectuals, while we do not reject the value of positive research, we, however, feel that we need to go beyond merely formulating general laws and predictions because most of the time human behaviour is not easily amenable to laws and predictions. We use such positivistic strategies primarily for diagnostic purposes in order to attempt to measure broad patterns before we look more closely at the individual and deeper meaning construction of the researched/participant as shaped by the ideology.

Furthermore, our view as informed by CT is that language is another pillar of society, hence research and knowledge production. The argument is that human society is organized on the basis of inter-subjectivity, communication and hermeneuticism, where the latter is also as interpretative as phenomenological research. As organic intellectuals we also acknowledge the value of understanding the human being as the speaking subject who, just as us as researchers, makes sense of the world and as such we see our research as being about interpreting other people's interpretations.[43] We regard it as a singular privilege to be allowed by other human beings to understand their world, their fears, their experiences and their aspirations with them. For us this is a humbling experience that causes us to be forever grateful and respectful of the participants in our research whom we never describe as a sample as it is the case with objects of study in the natural sciences laboratory.

The last basic cognitive interest identified by Habermas through Critical Emancipatory Research affirms that human society is also organized on the basis of power, which regulates interactions, roles and identities among its members.[44] Unfortunately, power corrupts, especially when it is excessive. Power, yes, can be productive as Michel Foucault notes, but power is most of the time oppressive.[45] Excessive power produces ideologies of superiority and inferiority and, thus, it has to be confronted and subverted. Habermas continues to say that Critical Emancipatory research is important because it thematizes power and ideology.[46] It enables the marginalized and oppressed people to question their status in life and want to change it.

This basic cognitive interest, more than any other, is the one that describes our work more as organic intellectuals than any other. Through it we are made consciously aware of the power of the apartheid ideology and of our horrific past that apportioned privilege and power unequally among our communities. It is our intention and practice as mentioned earlier in this chapter to deconstruct these unequal power relations. The communities and individuals who are on the margins need to be brought into the centre of economic participation and productivity where they also can enjoy together with everyone else a better life that includes, for example, access to quality education, descent housing, good health facilities and other such basic resources. Again, as we interact with the less powerful subaltern communities, we are also made aware of the overwhelming privileges and power which we as intellectuals hold because we are beneficiaries of the bourgeoisie institutions we live and work at. This awareness enables us to attempt at all times to temper our possible arrogant interactions with caution, respect and humility, a kind of de-powering approach dictated by our role as organic intellectuals.

It may be that the subaltern communities seem powerless but the theoretical lens provided by critical emancipatory research also enables us to see the strengths which these same communities have. Yosso argues very strongly that cultural capital which Bourdieu ascribes to the middle and affluent communities is also found among the subaltern classes, albeit in a different form and this he calls community cultural wealth.[47] This kind of wealth is explained as the accumulated richness of experiences, knowledge, skills, abilities and contacts possessed and utilized by the subaltern communities to survive and to resist macro and micro-forms of oppression.[48]

The subaltern communities seem to have had aspirations that had sustained them through the harsh periods of oppression and marginalization. Their hope for a better future insulated them when everything else had failed. Even their social skills helped them to navigate their way around the myriad of problems and potential social and political mine fields. The resilience which seemed built-in from within enabled them to resist oppression in all its forms. They had survived the worst. Through their social networks they could tap into all forms of support and help.[49] Their families cushioned their pain and their linguistic abilities enabled them to know even more languages than their oppressor communities. The positive outcome was that their lives were going on and intact although under very difficult circumstances. They could still eke out an existence in spite of their poverty. Through these *capitals* they managed to create a life out of almost nothing and these Yosso collectively refers to as the community cultural wealth of the underclass communities which as organic intellectuals we unearth, valorise, validate and amplify.[50] It is this knowledge which has been marginalized which we bring into the foreground and highlight through critical emancipatory research.

4. Mechanisms for a Transformative Knowledge Production

One of the criticisms levelled against critical emancipatory research is that it theorizes without providing practical strategies.[51] However Patti Lather argues that Critical Emancipatory Research is the most practical of research approaches because it talks about praxis as being very central to its operations.[52] As explained earlier, the first step in the application of this kind of research is what Lather calls the *interpretative phase.* Here, the researcher has to be immersed in the community he wants to research, for him to be able to understand the community's ethos, their fears, experiences and aspirations. In short, the research that we do is determined by the people we want to research on and with.[53] Doing Critical Emancipatory Research involves being sensitive and mindful of the participants we work with. At this interpretative phase, as researchers we are attempting to be on the same wavelength as those researched. We are trying to be reciprocal, democratic, relevant and responsive.

From the interpretative phase then we move to the *analytic phase* where we can go back into history, into the internet, the library, etc. with the intention of investigating and analysing the problem/topic we heard from the community. On the basis of this process, then we arrive at the findings, conclusion and results which compel us to go back to the communities for cross-checking whether our analysis and understanding go with that of the researched themselves. These conversations are also conducted so as to facilitate reciprocity and mutual respect that will result in *praxis* where the researched are taught and they interrogate the report for their own empowerment and transformation.[54] Such an approach to research enables us as organic intellectuals as well to learn and understand afresh from the other perspective which we may not have been formally initiated into.

Critical Emancipatory Research thus aims at emancipating those researched and the researchers from distorted consciousness engendered through a distorted ideology which is hereby deliberately subverted.[55] Critical Emancipatory Research as practiced today is not one homogenous approach, but it includes many schools of thought brought together by the common concern to transform society and to give power to those who have been excluded and marginalized. Among these we can mention feminism from its version of cultural feminism to post-modern feminism.[56] These are researchers objecting to excessive power as exercised by our assumed patriarchal society. This brand of Critical Emancipatory Research has alerted us to the fact that, even in language, women are excluded. For example, we should always use both he/she when the gender of a person is not known. Most of the time men are given unfair privileges in research, and stereotypes of females as inferior and as the fairer and weaker sex are perpetuated through research. Feminism has brought female stories to the table and the advances we see of attempts by all to be sensitive to gender discrimination are embedded in our discursive practices. We can also mention *post-colonialism* as another strand within Critical Emancipatory Research informed by the likes of Steve Biko, Stuart Hall, Homi Bhabha to mention a few.[57] Post-colonialism, like Post-Apartheid, criticizes the hold that the previous colonial and apartheid regimes still have on the subaltern communities. No matter how hard we try to move from the past, our efforts are not useful if we do not have post-colonial and critical emancipatory tools to liberate ourselves from the hegemonic interests of the past.

At the practical operational level we have already indicated that in a Critical Emancipatory Research we collect mainly qualitative data through individual interviews and/or focused group interviews that serve the purpose of creating spaces and opportunities for reflection among the researchers and the researched as equal human beings in normal conversations but directed towards some mutually identified goal(s).[58] The role of the researcher throughout the data/information gathering stage is to facilitate consciousness-raising conversations that could be audio or videotaped for purposes of analysis at a later stage. One technique which we found useful was designed by Ineke Meulenberg-Buskens, called the Free Attitude Interview (FAI) Technique which has similar theoretical origins as Carl Rogers' non-directive interview technique.[59] The FAI is easy but very effective to use because as researchers we ask one question (which is similar to the research question of the project) in order to generate the discussions which we follow up with *clarifying questions* to encourage further discussions, as well as *reflective summaries* in order to focus the participants' responses.[60]

There are many other techniques similar to this one and others, which are different, which enable the process of knowledge production to be human and humane without alienating and undermining the integrity of the research participants as full-fledged human beings. The number of respondents in this kind of research does not really matter because the aim is to do an in-depth understanding of each conversation thoroughly. To have many respondents does not increase the value of the findings because we are not aiming at quantifying or developing broad patterns or generalizing the findings beyond the researched. As researchers, we are interested in the depth of the *meaning making* and *meaning construction* of each participant.

The information or data thus collected are subjected to further analytical processes such as the ones suggested by Norman Fairclough and/or Teun Van Dijk's Critical Discourse Analysis.[61] Through this analytic tool we use *texts*, that is the spoken words by the researched as evidence to the interpretation we bring to them.[62] This interpretation is done also at the *discursive practice* level because it is understood that what we speak is a reflection of our practices or context-bound behaviours engendered over a period of time.[63] Our analysis using Critical Discourse Analysis technique comes to a climax when we conduct it at the third deepest level of meaning construction, which Fairclough and Van Dijk call the *social structural* level.[64] The point is that what participants and researchers say is authored also by their participation in particular social arrangements, societies, social classes, categories and groupings, or states, etc. To use Jacques Lacan's phrase, language speaks through us.[65] Therefore, to understand what people say we need to analyse that which predates them/us and informs our meaning and construction, which is the context of our existence as given to us through the symbolic order of language. In line with the research question(s) which were unpacked by the research objectives and prescribed as to which literature to be reviewed, which in turn guided the choice of appropriate methods for data collection and the analysis, we report our findings and make our recommendations in conjunction with those researched, who have been with us from the beginning of the study, who are our friends, our parents and our children with whom we share similar experiences, fears and aspirations.

5. Conclusion

In this chapter we have attempted to demonstrate that quality in research, just like the truth, is not one thing, but that it is multifaceted and dependent on the paradigm or theoretical framework which one uses to do research. As organic intellectuals, informed and guided by the Critical Emancipatory lens, we believe that quality of research is determined by its social usefulness. Research is of a high quality because it empowers and restores respect to the researched and the researcher and because it advances the agenda for equity, social justice, freedom, peace and hope. The knowledge production procedures described above are not objective because we agree with Patti Lather that objectivity does not exist in any research, that any researcher talking about objectivity is either not aware that he/she is not objective, or that he/she is just plainly lying.[66] Research is political and biased all the time and like in all human conditions it is shaped in the eye of the beholder, which the French call *méconnaissance*, or misrecognition.

The process of knowledge creation as described above clearly defines who we are as organic intellectuals occurring at the interstices between privilege and power of the hegemonic interests on the one hand and the exclusion and marginalization of the subaltern on the other. Our role seems to be that of reconciling these seemingly contradictory forces into productive spaces of transformation praxis. These objectives of our research which define our work as organic intellectuals serve as criteria for quality and make the knowledge creation processes from the described perspective unique, special and effective.

Notes

[1] A. Gramsci, *Selections from the Prison Notebooks*, Q. Hoare and G.N. Smith (ed), International Publishers, New York, 1977.
[2] S. Gill (ed), *Gramsci, Historical Materialism and International Relations*, Cambridge University Press, Cambridge, 1993, pp. 27-50.
[3] J. Henriques, W. Hollway, C. Urwin, C. Venn and V. Walkerdine, *Psychology, Social Regulation and Subjectivity*, Routledge, New York, 1988, pp. 80-138.
[4] B. Fink, *Écrits: The First Complete Edition in English*, Norton & Company, New York, 2006, pp. 36-59.
[5] G.F. Simet, 'Possibilities and Risks of Influencing Public Knowledge: The Case of Hrant Dink', this volume; T. Adeleke, 'Walter A. Rodney and the Instrumentalist Construction and Utilization of Knowledge', this volume.

[6] O. Procevska, 'Not a Sin, but a Side Effect: Collaboration and Knowledge Creation by Organic Intellectuals', 2011, this volume.

[7] A. Davidson, *Antonio Gramsci: Towards an Intellectual Biography*, Merlin Press, London, 1977, pp. 67-79.

[8] P. Bourdieu, 'Forms of Capital', *Handbook of Theory of Research for the Sociology of Education*, J.E. Richardson (ed), Greenwood Press, New York, 1986, pp. 38-49.

[9] T.J. Yosso, 'Whose Culture has Capital? A Critical Race Theory Discussion of Community Cultural Wealth', *Race, Ethnicity and Education*, Vol. 8(1), 2005, pp. 69-91.

[10] L. Flank, *Hegemony and Counter-Hegemony: Marxism, Capitalism, and Their Relation to Sexism, Racism, Nationalism, and Authoritarianism*, Red and Black Publishers, Florida, 2007, pp. 105-109.

[11] Department of Education, *National Education Policy Act 27*, Government Gazette, Pretoria, 1996, pp. 11-19.

[12] M.G. Mahlomaholo, 'A Framework for University and Provincial Education Department's Collaborative Research Towards the Creation of Sustainable Empowering Learning Environments: An Overview', *Praxis Towards Sustainable Empowering Learning Environments in South Africa*, D. Francis, M.G. Mahlomaholo and M.M. Nkoane (eds), Sun Media, Bloemfontein, 2010, pp. 1-27.

[13] V.O. Netshandama and M.G. Mahlomaholo, 'The Role of Community Engagement in Higher Education: Focus on the Discourse Relating to Knowledge Development', *The Intellectual: A Phenomenon in Multidimensional Perspectives*, N. Basov, G.F. Simet, J. van Andel, M.G. Mahlomaholo and V. Netshandama (eds), Interdisciplinary Press, Oxford, 2010.

[14] M.G. Mahlomaholo and V. Netshandama, 'Sustainable Empowering Learning Environments: Conversations with Gramsci's Organic Intellectual', in Ibid.

[15] M.G. Mahlomaholo, op. cit., pp. 9-13.

[16] M.G. Mahlomaholo, et al., *Attrition and African Learner Under-Representation in the Grade 12 top 20 List of the North West Education Department*, Commissioned Investigation by the MEC for Education in the NWED, 2010.

[17] V.O. Netshandama and M.G. Mahlomaholo, op. cit.

[18] M.G. Mahlomaholo and V.A. Hongwane, *Strategic Plan for 2009-2010 for the Ngaka Modiri Molema Education District of the North West Government*, Commissioned by the North West Education Department, 2009.

[19] M.G. Mahlomaholo, op. cit., pp. 10-11.

[20] Ibid.

[21] M.G. Mahlomaholo and V.A. Hongwane, *Strategic Plan for 2009-2010...*, op. cit.

[22] M.G. Mahlomaholo and V.A. Hongwane, *Analysis and Interpretation of the Data Gathered through the Monitoring Tool for All Schools in the Dr Ruth Mompati Education District of the North West Province*, Commissioned by the North West Education Department, 2009.

[23] M.G. Mahlomaholo, 'Can the Subaltern Speak an African Language?' *Did Africa Speak? A Colloquium of the African Studies, North-West University at the Vaal Campus*, Vanderbijlpark, 2009.

[24] M.G. Mahlomaholo and V.A. Hongwane, *Analysis and Interpretation of the Data...*, op. cit.

[25] M.G. Mahlomaholo, *In Search of Education Excellence in a Rural Setting: Reflections on Challenges Facing Stakeholders in Education in Rosendal and its Environments*, Motivational Workshop for Learners and Teachers at Rosendal and Its Environment, 20 March 2001, The Taung High School hall, 2001.

[26] M.G. Mahlomaholo, 'Empire Talks Back: Interrogating Indigenous Knowledge System and its Implications for Postgraduate Curriculum', *Proceedings of the Research and Postgraduate School Seminar*, L.O.K. Lategan (ed), May 2004, pp. 23-30.

[27] See: O. Procevska, 'Not a Sin, but a Side Effect: Collaboration and Knowledge Creation by Organic Intellectuals', 2011, this volume.

[28] O. Haac, *The Correspondence of John Stuart Mill and Auguste Comte*, Transaction Publishers, London, 1995, pp. 29-54.

[29] G. Lenzer, *Auguste Comte and Positivism: The Essential Writings*, Harper, New York, 1975, pp. 18-34.

[30] B. Farrington, *The Philosophy of Francis Bacon*, University of Chicago Press, Chicago, 1964, pp. 35-50.

[31] R.B. Freeman, *The Works of Charles Darwin: An Annotated Bibliographical Handlist*, Wm Dawson & Sons Ltd, Folkestone, 1977.

[32] T. Pytell, 'The Missing Pieces of the Puzzle: A Reflection on the Odd Career of Viktor Frankl', *Journal of Contemporary History*, Vol. 35(2), 2000, pp. 281-306.

[33] A.D. Schrift, *Twentieth-Century French Philosophy: Key Themes and Thinkers*, Blackwell Publishing, Oxford, 2006, pp. 160-174.

[34] T. Pytell, op. cit., 284-289.

[35] D.W. Smith and A.L. Thomasson (eds), *Phenomenology and Philosophy of Mind*, Oxford University Press, New York, 2005, pp. 29-51.

[36] A.D. Schrift, op. cit.

[37] G. Ritzer, *Sociological Theory, From Modern to Postmodern Social Theory (and Beyond)*, McGraw-Hill Higher Education, New York, 2008, pp. 567-568.
[38] T. McCathy, *The Critical Theory of Jürgen Habermas*, MIT Press, Cambridge, 1978, pp. 48-66.
[39] B. Flyvbjerg, 'Habermas and Foucault Thinkers for Civil Society?', *British Journal of Sociology*, Vol. 49(2), 1998, pp. 200-224.
[40] T. McCathy, op. cit., pp. 50-61.
[41] A. Edgar, *The Philosophy of Habermas*, Montréal, McGill-Queen's UP, 2005, pp. 10-49.
[42] O. Haac, op. cit., pp. 34-51.
[43] N.K. Denzin and Y.S. Lincoln, 'Introduction: Entering the field of Qualitative Research', *Handbook of Qualitative Research*, N.K. Denzin and Y.S. Lincoln (eds), Sage Publications, Thousand Oaks, 1994, pp. 1-17.
[44] B. Flyvbjerg, op. cit., pp. 210-221.
[45] A. Milchman, 'Foucault and Heidegger', *Contradictions*, Vol. 16, University of Minnesota Press, Minneapolis, 2003, pp. 143-182.
[46] B. Flyvbjerg, op. cit., pp. 200-223.
[47] P. Bourdieu, op. cit., pp. 40-49.
[48] Ibid.
[49] Ibid.
[50] Ibid.
[51] H. Piper and J. Piper, 'Reflections on Educational Research and Transformation', *Educational Transformation in South Africa*, H. Piper, J. Piper and M.G. Mahlomaholo (eds), Lynnwood Ridge, Science Africa Publishers, 2009, pp. 95-106.
[52] P. Lather, 'Research as Praxis', *Harvard Educational Review*, Vol. 56(3), 1986, pp. 257-278.
[53] M.G. Mahlomaholo, op. cit., pp. 9-11.
[54] M.G. Mahlomaholo and S.T. Matobako, 'Service Learning in South Africa Held Terminally Captive by Legacies of the Past', *Alternation*, Vol. 13(1), 2006, pp. 203-217.
[55] M.G. Mahlomaholo, 'Critical Emancipatory Research and Academic Identity', *Africa Education Review*, Vol. 6(2), 2009, pp. 224-237.
[56] L. Alcoff, 'Cultural Feminism versus Structuralism: The Identity in Feminism Theory', *Signs: Journal of Women in Culture and Society*, Vol. 13(3), 1988, pp. 405-436.
[57] J. Lavia and M. Moore (eds), *Cross-Cultural Perspectives on Policy and Practice: Decolonising Community Contexts*, Routledge, New York, 2010, pp. 122-150.

[58] M.G. Mahlomaholo, *Re-Membering the Organic Intellectual in the Mirror*, Inaugural Lecture, August 21. Faculty of Education Sciences in Potchefstroom, 2009, pp. 1-37.

[59] I. Meulenburg-Buskens, *Free Attitude Interview Technique: Qualitative Research Reader*, Human Sciences Research Council, Pretoria, 1993, pp. 19-28.

[60] Ibid.

[61] N. Fairclough, *Discourse and Social Change*, Polity Press and Africanwell Publishers, Cambridge, 1992, pp. 20-77.

[62] Ibid.

[63] Ibid.

[64] T.A. Van Dijk, 'The Study of Discourse: An Introduction', *Discourse Studies*, T.A. Van Dijk (ed), Sage, London, 2007, pp. 18-56.

[65] B. Fink, op. cit., pp. 36-59.

[66] P. Lather, 'Research as Praxis', op. cit., pp. 259-270.

Bibliography

Alcoff, L., 'Cultural Feminism versus Structuralism: The Identity in Feminism Theory'. *Signs: Journal of Women in Culture and Society*. Vol. 13(3), 1988, pp. 405-436.

Bhabha, H.K., *The Location of Culture*. Routledge, London, 1994.

Biko, S., *I Write what I Like*. San Francisco, Harper & Row, 1986.

Bourdieu, P., 'Forms of Capital'. *Handbook of Theory of Research for the Sociology of Education*. Richardson, J.E. (ed), Greenwood Press, New York, 1986.

Carr, D., *The Crisis of European Sciences and Transcendental Philosophy*. Northwestern University Press, Evanston, 1970.

Chisholm, R.M. and Simons, P., 'Brentano, Franz Clemens'. *Routledge Encyclopedia of Philosophy*. Craig, E. (ed), Routledge, London, 1998.

Davidson, A., *Antonio Gramsci: Towards an Intellectual Biography*. Merlin Press, London, 1977.

Denzin, N.K. and Lincoln, Y.S., 'Introduction: Entering the Field of Qualitative Research'. *Handbook of Qualitative Research.* Denzin, N.K. and Lincoln, Y.S. (eds), Sage Publications, Thousand Oaks, 1994.

Department of Education, *National Education Policy Act 27.* Government Gazette, Pretoria, 1996.

—, *National Curriculum Statement.* Government Gazette, Pretoria, 2003.

Edgar, A., *The Philosophy of Habermas.* Montréal, McGill-Queen's UP, 2005.

Fairclough, N., *Discourse and Social Change.* Cambridge, Polity Press and Africanwell Publishers, 1992.

Farrington, B., *The Philosophy of Francis Bacon.* University of Chicago Press, Chicago, 1964.

Fink, A., *Écrits: The First Complete Edition in English.* Norton & Company, New York, 2006.

Flank, L., *Hegemony and Counter-Hegemony: Marxism, Capitalism, and Their Relation to Sexism, Racism, Nationalism, and Authoritarianism.* Red and Black Publishers, Florida, 2007.

Flyvbjerg, B., 'Habermas and Foucault Thinkers for Civil Society?'. *British Journal of Sociology.* Vol. 49(2), 1998, pp. 200-224.

Freeman, R.B., *The Works of Charles Darwin: An Annotated Bibliographical Handlist.* Wm Dawson & Sons Ltd, Folkestone, 1977.

Gill, S. (ed), *Gramsci, Historical Materialism and International Relations.* Cambridge University Press, Cambridge, 1993.

Gramsci, A., *Selections from the Prison Notebooks.* Hoare, Q. and Smith, G.N. (ed), International Publishers, New York, 1977.

Haac, O., *The Correspondence of John Stuart Mill and Auguste Comte.* Transaction Publishers, London, 1995.

Hall, S., 'Notes on Deconstructing the Popular'. *People's History and Socialist Theory.* Routledge, London, 1981.

Henriques, J., Hollway, W., Venn, C. Walkerdine, V. and Urwin, C., *Psychology, Social Regulation and Subjectivity.* Routledge, New York, 1988.

Kruger, D. (ed), *The Changing Reality of Modern Man: Essays in Honour of Jan Hendrik van den Berg.* Duquesne University Press, Pittsburg, 1985.

Lather, P., 'Research as Praxis'. *Harvard Educational Review.* Vol. 56(3), 1986, pp. 257-278.

Lavia, J. and Moore, M. (eds), *Cross-Cultural Perspectives on Policy and Practice: Decolonising Community Contexts.* Routledge, New York, 2010.

Lenzer, G. (ed), *Auguste Comte and Positivism, The Essential Writings.* Harper, New York, 1975.

Mahlomaholo, M.G., *In Search of Education Excellence in a Rural Setting: Reflections on Challenges Facing Stakeholders in Education in Rosendal and its Environments.* Keynote Address to a Motivational Workshop for Learners and Teachers at Rosendal and its Environment, March 20, 2001 in the Taung High School Hall, 2001.

——, 'Empire Talks Back: Interrogating Indigenous Knowledge System and its Implications for Postgraduate Curriculum.' *Proceedings of the Research and Postgraduate School Seminar.* Lategan, L.O.K (ed), Central University of Technology, Bloemfontein, May 2004.

——, 'Critical Emancipatory Research and Academic Identity'. *Africa Education Review.* Vol. 6(2), 2009, pp. 224-237.

——, 'Can the Subaltern Speak an African Language?' *Did Africa Speak? A Colloquium of the African Studies, North-West University at the Vaal Campus*, Vanderbijlpark, 2009.

——, 'Remembering the Organic Intellectual in the Mirror'. *Inaugural Lecture August 21 at the North-West University's Faculty of Education Sciences.* Platinum Press, Potchefstroom, 2009.

—, 'A Framework for University and Provincial Education Department's Collaborative Research towards the Creation of Sustainable Empowering Learning Environments: An Overview'. *Praxis towards Sustainable Empowering Learning Environments in South Africa.* Francis, D., Mahlomaholo, M.G. and Noane, M.M. (eds), Sun Media, Blomfontein, 2010.

—, 'Towards Sustainable Empowering Learning Environments: Unmasking Apartheid Legacies through Scholarship of Engagement'. *South African Journal of Higher Education.* Vol. 24(3), 2010, pp. 8-13.

Mahlomaholo, M.G. and Hongwane, V.A., *Strategic Plan for 2009-2010 for the Ngaka Modiri Molema Education District of the North West Government.* A Plan Commissioned by the North West Education Department, Platinum Press, Potchefstroom, 2009.

—, *Analysis and Interpretation of the Data Gathered through the Monitoring Tool for All Schools in the Dr Ruth Mompati Education District of the North West Province.* A Study Commissioned by the North West Education Department, Platinum Press, Potchefstroom, 2009.

Mahlomaholo, M.G., Mamiala, T., Hongwane, V.A., Ngcongwane, S., Itlhopheng, K., Fosu-Amoah, Y., Mahlomaholo, R., Kies, M. and Mokgotsi, M., '*Attrition and African Learner Underrepresentation in the Grade 12 top 20 list of the North West Education Department*'. A Study Commissioned Investigation by the MEC for Education in the NWED, 2010.

Mahlomaholo, M.G. and Matobako, S.T., 'Service Learning in South Africa Held Terminally Captive by Legacies of the Past'. *Alternation.* Vol. 13(1), 2006, pp. 203-217.

Mahlomaholo, M.G. and Netshandama, V.O., 'Sustainable Empowering Learning Environments: Conversations with Gramsci's Organic Intellectual'. *The Intellectual: A Phenomenon in Multidimensional Perspectives.* Interdisciplinary Press, Oxford, 2010.

McCathy, T., *The Critical Theory of Jürgen Habermas.* MIT Press, Cambridge, 1978.

Meulenburg-Buskens, I., *Free Attitude Interview Technique: Qualitative Research Reader.* Human Sciences Research Council, Pretoria, 1993.

Milchman, A., 'Foucault and Heidegger'. *Contradictions.* Vol. 16. University of Minnesota Press, Minneapolis, 2003, pp. 143-182.

Netshandama, V., 'Community Development Approach to Community Engagement in Rural Based Higher Education Institutions in South Africa'. *South African Journal of Higher Education.* Vol. 24(3), 2010, pp. 50-55.

Piper, H. and Piper, J., 'Reflections on Educational Research and Transformation'. *Educational Transformation in South Africa.* Piper, H., Piper, J. and Mahlomaholo, M.G. (eds), Lynnwood Ridge, Science Africa Publishers, 2009.

Pytell, T., 'The Missing Pieces of the Puzzle: A Reflection on the Odd Career of Victor Frankl'. *Journal of Contemporary History.* Vol. 35(2), 2000, pp. 281-306.

Ritzer, G., *Sociological Theory, From Modern to Postmodern Social Theory (and Beyond).* McGraw-Hill Higher Education, New York, 2008.

Schrift, A.D., *Twentieth-Century French Philosophy: Key Themes and Thinkers.* Blackwell Publishing, Oxford, 2006.

Smith, D.W. and Thomasson, A.L. (eds), *Phenomenology and Philosophy of Mind.* Oxford University Press, New York, 2005.

Van Dijk, T.A., 'Critical Discourse Studies: A Sociocognitive Approach'. *Methods of Critical Discourse Analysis.* Wodak, R. and Meyer, M. (eds), Sage, London, 2009.

—, 'The Study of Discourse: An Introduction'. *Discourse Studies.* Van Dijk, T.A. (ed), Sage, London, 2007.

Yosso, T.J., 'Whose Culture has Capital? A Critical Race Theory Discussion of Community Cultural Wealth'. *Race, Ethnicity and Education.* Vol. 8(1), March 2005.

Walter A. Rodney and the Instrumentalist Construction and Utilization of Knowledge

Tunde Adeleke

Abstract
Few intellectuals in the annals of the Black experience argued as passionately and intensely for the instrumentalist construction of knowledge as the late West Indian activist-intellectual, Walter A. Rodney (1942-1980). Not only did Rodney theorize about the intellectual as a public servant, who transformed knowledge into a weapon of resistance against domination, but also, he set the example by immersing himself in the struggles against colonialism and neo-colonialism in Africa, and the working class struggles of his native Guyana. Rodney urged black intellectuals to commit knowledge to the cause of liberating the underclass. An organic intellectual in the true Gramscian sense, Rodney privileged the commission of class suicide. A truly revolutionary or 'Guerrilla' intellectual, must identify intimately with the challenges of the underclass. The 'Guerrilla intellectual' is embedded within an oppressive system and seeks to destroy it from within. He suggested two approaches. First, the intellectual must deconstruct ideas of the ruling class. Second, the black intellectual must consciously 'ground' with the underclass. This 'grounding' allows the intellectual greater insights into their challenges. In this chapter, I hope to analyse Rodney's ideas and writings on the notion of 'guerrilla intellectualism' and his attempts to merge theory with praxis.

Key Words: Rodney, Cabral, guerrilla intellectual, grounding, Nyerere, Eric Williams, Dark Continent, Africa, Diaspora blacks, Gramsci, underclass, subaltern.

*****

1. Introduction

Historically, education (access to knowledge) has been manipulated and restricted to reinforce European hegemony. From the colonization of the New World and institutionalization of slavery, to the expansion and entrenchment of imperialism in Africa and other parts of the world, knowledge had been manipulated to reinforce hegemony. To justify and solidify domination and exploitation, education, or the absolute denial of access to it (ignorance), was use to implant debasing, self-abnegating ideas and values in the colonized and enslaved respectively. As Frantz Fanon, Albert Memmi, Carter G. Woodson and others have demonstrated, European imperialists used education in Africa and America to shape a docile, compliant, mis-educated and misinformed population. Alienated from their history and culture, Africans and black Americans were socialized to regard Europeans values as universal and normative.[1]

European scholars depicted Europe as the cradle of civilization. They constructed Africa as a 'Dark Continent' of barbarism and heathenism; a static, ahistorical environment. According to this genre, civilization and history came to Africa with the arrival of Europeans. Even when European scholars later acknowledged the historical heritage of Africa, they portrayed that heritage in all its ramifications, as fundamentally negative and evil. Africa, they insisted, made no significant contributions to human development. Renowned Oxford historian Hugh Trevor Roper reflected this worldview in his response to a British Broadcasting Corporation (BBC) interview question on African history. Rebutting angrily, Roper declared that there was nothing historical in pre-colonial Africa. What existed, he declared, was, 'the unrewarding gyrations of barbarous tribes on picturesque but irrelevant corners of the globe.'[2]

The rejection and caricaturing of African history was meant to legitimize Europe's rape and denouement of the continent. The alleged backward and primitive character of pre-colonial Africa justified the enslavement and transplantation of Africans across the Atlantic. To strengthen slavery in the New World, Europeans again invoked history to facilitate the mental and psychological domination of the enslaved. The portrait of Africa as the 'Dark Continent' was deeply and indelibly imprinted into the consciousness of enslaved blacks. When slavery ended and Europeans embarked upon what some called 'the second great enslavement,' (that is, Colonialism), history again became a prized weapon of justifying and strengthening Europeans rule. Indeed, history became part of a broader repertoire of control and domination. Education was carefully structured, strictly controlled and used to create and nurture in Africans and Diaspora blacks mental and psychological dependency and inferiority complex. In its coverage of Africa, therefore, colonial historiography denied and denigrated African history and culture. As the late J.M. Blaut argued, Europeans perceived the world through a Eurocentric diffusionist prism that situated Europe at the epic centre of the universe, and non-Europeans as peripheral recipients of 'superior' European values and influences.[3] History was used to circumscribe the epistemological horizon of Africans/blacks. The dominant narrative among European scholars portrayed colonialism as a civilizing force, designed to bring Africans into the orbit of civilization and history. Thus, during both slavery and colonialism Europeans used knowledge as a means of destroying the self-esteem of Africans and ridding them of any positive self-deterministic and potentially subversive consciousness.

Recognition of the role of knowledge construction/deconstruction in reinforcing European hegemony compelled African and Africanist intellectuals in the post-colonial era to assume responsibility for challenging and reversing Eurocentric knowledge. They envisioned themselves as public intellectuals responsible for deconstructing entrenched Eurocentric misinterpretations and misrepresentations of African and Black Diaspora historical experiences. Some assumed a more proactively revolutionary role of re-educating the masses about the mechanisms, contents and repertoire of intellectual repression and hegemony. William E.B. Du Bois was among the earliest to articulate the critical role of the intelligentsia in the black struggle. As he explained it, '[t]he Negro race, like all races, is going to be saved by its exceptional men. The problem of education, then, among the Negroes must first of all deal with the Talented Tenth [...] the best of this race that they may guide the Mass.'[4]

Counteracting and destroying the stranglehold of epistemological racism required the development of revolutionary anti-hegemonic counter-narrative. The Guinean revolutionary intellectual Amilcar Cabral (1924-1973) deemed reversing this culture of imperial mis-education through a sound knowledge of historical reality fundamental to the attainment of freedom from colonial exploitation and domination.[5] As he insisted, 'Every people possessed the inalienable right [...] to have its own history.'[6] Rescuing African history from imperialist manipulation was, in Cabral's judgment, critical to liberation. He assigned revolutionary intellectuals a leadership role in helping to produce and shape this anti-hegemonic epistemology.[7] However, in a colonial context in which education was strictly controlled to reinforce hegemony, members of subordinated and marginalized groups who were fortunate to gain education had two options. First, either use the knowledge acquired to escape from marginalization to middle class status or second, use that knowledge to subvert the entrenched system of oppression. Put differently, the choice was between becoming, in the Gramscian sense, a 'traditional intellectual,' in cohort with the ruling and exploiter class, or an 'organic intellectual,' who renounced the values of the ruling class, and identify instead with, and help to advance, the interests and aspirations of the exploited and subaltern group.[8]

In Africa, the decades of the 1960s and 1970s witnessed sustained intellectual counter-attacks against Eurocentric ethnocentrism. The explosions of anti-colonial sentiments and movements in the late 1950s, and early 1960s in Africa, and concomitant radicalization of nationalist sentiments among blacks in America bolstered demands for a countervailing historiography which both challenged and invalidated prevailing racist and paternalistic assumptions about Africa. Consequently, African and black Diaspora intellectuals seriously took up researching and studying African history and culture. Determined to wrest control of interpretations of African history from Europeans, these scholars began systematically to chip away at the edifice of Eurocentric historiography. They sought not only to debunk the myths and misconceptions of Eurocentric historiography, but also to infuse Africans with a new outlook and consciousness that would empower them to both question and reject the self-abnegating and denigrating *Weltanschauung* that had oppressed them for centuries. To develop this revolutionary historical epistemology and mobilize the people, black intellectuals in Africa and abroad invoked history. Few intellectuals assumed this revolutionary responsibility as fervently and as passionately as Walter Anthony Rodney (1942-1980).

2. Walter Rodney: Background and Education (The Making of a Revolutionary Intellectual)

Rodney was born into a working class family in Georgetown, Guyana, on the 23rd of March 1942. His father was a tailor and an independent artisan, and his mother a housewife and part-time seamstress. In this society, one's racial background shaped one's life experiences, and also determined one's economic and social stations. Blacks were confined to the lowest of the social, economic, and political strata. In comparison, whites enjoyed affluence and privileges.[9] There were few escape valves for blacks from this 'prison-house' of misery and degradation. Education, which was restricted and controlled, offered the only escape avenue for those lucky to break through the barriers. But, this was not always the case. The hopes and expectations of those fortunate to acquire education were soon shattered as they quickly discovered, in the words of Rodney, 'there is not much room at the top to accommodate them.'[10] In Guyana, there were few opportunities for upwardly mobile blacks. Many therefore turned overseas (to the United States, Canada, and Britain) in search of greener pastures. Education became, according to Rodney, a 'conduit that led out of society,' transplanting many blacks into 'the wider capitalist world.'[11] Thus, Rodney grew up in a society in which intellectuals were socialized to envision education as a means of escaping poverty and gaining entry to middle class bourgeois culture. He witnessed educated West Indians desperately pursue this goal. For them, the primary purpose of education/knowledge was personal enrichment and empowerment. Rodney challenged this worldview and insisted that education conferred tremendous social responsibility.

Rodney was among those fortunate to gain access to education. He entered the University of the West Indies (UWI) at Mona in 1960 to study history, and graduated in 1963 with a first class honours degree, a distinction that earned him a UWI scholarship for post-graduate Studies in African History at the School of Oriental and African Studies (SOAS), the University of London.[12] As a graduate student, Rodney immediately confronted an existential dilemma about the relationship of the intellectual to revolution. According to him, it was exposure to Marxism, specifically his study of Lenin and the Russian Revolution that compelled him to confront this dilemma.[13] He began to question the purpose of his education. What would be his role as an intellectual? Is being an intellectual consistent and compatible with revolutionary activism? One of his teachers suggested that intellectualism and revolutionary activism were mutually exclusive. They were simply incompatible. One could not combine both.[14] Rodney was, however, not convinced. He was sure they were compatible and envisioned himself in that composite capacity. As he put it, 'I felt that somehow being a revolutionary intellectual might be a goal to which one might aspire, for surely there was no real reason why one should remain in the academic world, that is, remain an intellectual and at the same time not be revolutionary. So I bore this in mind.'[15] In London, Rodney joined a discussion group that formed around C.L.R. James and his wife Selma James. The discussions seemed to reinforce his decision to combine intellectualism and activism, and helped broaden his understanding of Marxism, as well as sharpen his analysis of social issues. As he explained it, 'Getting together in London and meeting over a period of two to three years on a fairly regular basis afforded me the opportunity that I, and a number of other people were seeking to acquire knowledge of Marxism, a more precise understanding of the Russian Revolution, and of historical formulation.'[16] Even in this early phase of his career, it was clear that Rodney wanted to utilize his knowledge in pursuant of the peoples' cause. In his view, the intellectual is useless if not revolutionary. What legitimizes an intellectual is the ability and willingness to use knowledge to transform society for the good of the underclass.

Undoubtedly, Rodney was drawn to African History partly by the need to develop a counter-narrative to the dominant Eurocentric epistemology. As he underscored, Europeans had 'already implanted numerous myths in the minds of black people: and those have to be uprooted, since they can act as a drag on revolutionary action.'[17] Black intellectuals had to apply precisely the same weapon in resisting and uprooting those entrenched myths. He insisted that liberation should be the driving force of education. As he put it, the intellectual's quest for, and acquisition of, knowledge of African history is relevant but, 'secondary to the concrete tactics and strategy which are necessary for our liberation.'[18] Knowledge of African history was, therefore, prerequisite for any meaningful and effective confrontation with Eurocentric historiography and worldview. Rodney rejected the doctrine of 'knowledge for knowledge sake,' and denounced what he termed 'false distinction between reflection and action, because the conquest of power is our immediate goal.'[19] In other words, the intellectual cannot afford to assume a detached, 'objective' posture, but must engage the production of critical knowledge that would empower the people. Thus, for Rodney, African history became a means of producing and disseminating this critical knowledge for combating what he termed, 'European cultural egocentricity.'[20]

As a graduate student, Rodney confronted yet another dilemma: that of studying and researching the African historical experience under the tutelage of some of the leading European historians whose writings had contributed to creating the myths he sought to challenge. In other words, Rodney found himself in an intellectually ambivalent milieu.[21] He advanced two fundamental rationalizations of this ambivalence. First, any aspiring critical scholar ought to engage seriously the writings and thoughts of other scholars, even those with whom he/she disagrees ideologically. This critical engagement with opposing ideas would equip one, intellectually, to understand, and thus effectively be able to debunk erroneous ideas and theories. Second, Rodney stressed the importance of adhering to, and satisfying, whatever academic standards were established as prerequisites for his degree program, regardless of personal misgivings about those standards. Failure to adhere to, and satisfy, those standards would, he reasoned, erode ones moral authority as an intellectual.[22] As he underscored, it is by legitimizing oneself first within the standards of academic excellence recognized in one's discipline that an intellectual is able more effectively, authoritatively, and creditably to engage opposing and erroneous ideas.[23] Though Rodney urged black intellectuals to embrace and satisfy standard set by the 'bourgeois' establishment in order to gain legitimacy as a scholar, he cautioned against making those standards 'as encompassing as one's existence'.[24] He advised black intellectuals to approach those standards critically. They should not constitute the all-encompassing standard of scholarship. In Rodney's view, critical anti-hegemonic scholarship must speak directly to the needs and challenges of the people, and not be hamstrung by the quest for establishment validation. The black intellectual must consciously communicate with the people and render his/her writings accessible to them.

Determined not to be faulted in any way, and seeking informed knowledge of the underpinnings of what he derisively tagged 'bourgeois scholarship,' Rodney devoured all 'bourgeois' literatures and theories presented to him in graduate school. He worked diligently to satisfy the academic standards established for his program, earning the Doctor of Philosophy (Ph.D.) degree in 1966 with a dissertation titled '*A History of the Upper Guinea Coast, 1545-1800.*'[25] Almost immediately, Rodney gave clear notice that he intended his scholarship specifically for uprooting the edifices of Eurocentric historiography and empowering the black masses in Africa and abroad. He would use his research and publications to unearth the true nature of African history and heritage. Most critically, he would focus on identifying and exposing the nature and sources of the problems bedevilling Africans and Diaspora blacks. He would address such questions as: who has been, and still is, responsible for African/black subordination and exploitation? What was the *modus operandi* of imperialism? What strategies would best guarantee a speedy liberation of blacks? In Rodney's view, knowledge creation for the public good has to consciously be anti-hegemonic. He emphasized rooting such knowledge within established and recognized canons of scholarship without compromising the intellectual's counter-hegemonic role. In other words, while it is important for the intellectual who is consciously constructing anti-hegemonic knowledge, and seeking to influence public awareness, to be validated by established intellectual standards, Rodney insisted however that in order to be truly anti-hegemonic, such intellectual must do so from a very critical perspective. The prevailing standards are not sacrosanct and inviolable.

3.   Rodney and the Production/Dissemination of Instrumentalist Knowledge: The Intellectual as Guerrilla
Rodney's preoccupation with redeeming the African historical experience and developing a combative countervailing African historiography led him even deeper into broadening his knowledge of, and familiarity with, Africa and Africans. As he observed, 'I also felt that one of the ways in which one could mobilize was by picking up a certain amount of information within an experience on the African continent itself.'[26] Consequently, upon completion of his PhD, Rodney accepted a teaching position at the University of Dar-es Salaam in Tanzania. This was a time of rapid political changes in Africa. In Tanzania, President Julius Nyerere was experimenting with radical socialist reforms. Across the continent, intellectuals debated the role of the university in emerging post-colonial states. In Tanzania, as in other former British colonies, and consistent with the British tradition, the university was conceptualized within an aristocratic intellectual milieu, as an institution that reinforced and complemented, rather than challenge, the status quo. In other words, the University was a bastion of privilege for the middle and upper strata of society.[27] At Dar-es Salaam, Rodney immediately joined a small group of radical left-leaning intellectuals who organized lectures and symposia about issues and challenges confronting Tanzania and other emerging post-colonial African states.[28]

Rodney, however, quickly realized that challenging Eurocentric historiography would not be easy given the control that Europeans exercised over the nature and dissemination of knowledge. To be successful in this endeavour, therefore, the black intellectual must become a guerrilla. Rodney consequently introduced the concept of the 'Guerrilla intellectual' (GI) to underscore what he termed 'the initial imbalance in power in the context of academic learning' between blacks and whites.[29] Given the fact that whites controlled and manipulated all aspects of education (books, reference materials, and theoretical assumptions), the black intellectual had no choice but to adopt guerrilla tactics. Rodney urged black intellectuals to embrace the 'first and major struggle,' that is, the struggle over ideas, by using their positions within the academy to challenge Eurocentric ideas.[30] As a product of bourgeois education, the GI must consciously and forcefully renounce bourgeois culture; indeed resist entrapment into bourgeois culture, and aggressively escape from what Rodney termed 'Babylonian captivity' of bourgeois society.[31] Rodney suggested three ways of accomplishing this escape. First, the GI should vigorously attack those distorted ideas within his/her discipline that were used to legitimize European domination and hegemony. Second, the GI should transcend his/her disciplinary boundary and challenge the dominant social myths in society, particularly those that were used to mask the ugly realities of society. Third, the GI should fully commit himself/herself to the masses by getting closer to, and grounding with them. This proximity to, and grounding with, the masses would provide the GI useful insights into the true character of society and culture and, in the process, undergo what Cabral called 'A spiritual reconversion of mentalities.' This 'reconversion' or 're-Africanization' is a prerequisite for liberation.[32] Accomplishing these three functions became, for Rodney, the litmus test for ascertaining the depth of the intellectual's commitment to the liberation of the people. In other words, the GI must create a linkage between the theoretical underpinnings of his/her education and convictions, and the practical realities of the experiences of the masses. He/she must become fully immersed in, and actively partake of, their daily experiences. This grounding would result in a dual process of exchange of valuable experiential lessons. The GI would learn from the masses, getting to know them better, and appreciate their needs and interests; while they in turn would benefit from the GI's knowledge of historical issues and critical perspective.[33] Rodney firmly believed that unless, and until, a black intellectual was willing and able to undertake this kind of transcendence, he/she would remain enemy of the people. As he declared, 'all of us are enemies to the people until we prove otherwise.'[34]

Rodney identified two prototypes of the GI. First, the one who merged theory with praxis and performed subversive functions within the academic establishment, and the other who was driven to adopt violence as a revolutionary strategy in the traditions of Cabral and Che Guevara. Merging of theory with praxis was critical to both. Notwithstanding, Rodney did not believe that the GI could effectively subvert the system primarily from within the confines of the university. However subversive ones ideas and writings, working within the ivory tower would not fundamentally subvert the system. The GI must actively merge theory with praxis by committing class suicide and grounding with the people. In other words, the existence of zones of intellectual subversion within academia was productive only if complemented by actively bridging the social and cultural gap with the underclass. Thus, the GI must be actively engaged in subversion also from the external front by working among the people. In other words, the academy is only one-half of the GI's terrain of activism. The other half is the world of the subaltern. Transitioning into this world required the commission of class suicide. As Rodney constructed it, the GI occupies what Mahlomoholo and Netshandama call 'contradictory space of production,' which essentially is a confluence of the privilege and power of bourgeoisie academic status and the powerlessness of the subaltern. Caught between, and perhaps reflective of, both worlds, the GI, according to Rodney, cannot afford a neutralist, 'objective' posture. The GI must take a stand alongside the people, and he/she must consciously produce and propagate subversive ethos of empowerment, knowledge that challenged and exposed the ugly realities of society. He/she must be willing to give up middle class privileges in order to fully and effectively embrace, and be immersed in, subaltern culture.[35] Such immersion and proximity would enable the GI more effectively function in the interest of the people. This is the vantage point of effective grounding. As Rodney explained it, grounding is not a linear one-way flow of influences from the GI to the people.[36] It is a two-way counter-hegemonic, knowledge creation process. First, it enables the GI to enlighten the people about their history and culture, debunk every misinformation, myths and misconceptions used to keep them in subjugation. Second, it puts the GI in position to learn from the people as well. Despite deficiency in western education, the masses are not ignorant. In Rodney's view, the GI must have the patience and humility to reach out to, and learn from, the people. In the process, the GI would acquire better understanding of the challenges, interests and aspirations of the people, and thus be better prepared and equipped to lead. The fundamental role of the GI is to challenge the self-abnegating knowledge implanted in the people's consciousness, and help them realize the hegemonic and self-destructive nature of such knowledge. In essence, as an organic intellectual, the GI is effective only if he/she is successful in clearly illuminating the contradictions between the people's interests, values and aspirations and those entrenched in their mis-education. Thus, the public knowledge the GI attempts to transmit to the subaltern is one that directly contradicts the values embedded in the Eurocentric knowledge that had been used for mental and psychological subjugation. In this respect, Rodney focused on reinterpreting African history, and developing critical understanding and knowledge of prevailing realities, while exposing the true nature and character of European domination. In his view, this would enhance the people's awareness of the structural and cultural contradictions in society by underlining how the interests of the dominant class contradicted those of the people. This would also empower the people to become more self-deterministic, and able to resist, and not permanently internalize, self-destructive values. As Rodney and Cabral theorized, the ultimate result is the preparedness and willingness of the people to become more actively and fully involved in self-liberation. This disposition would erode the force and conviction of the hegemonic state.

Rodney theorized about the critical importance of contextual/ cultural compatibility to the effectiveness of the GI. The GI is most effective when culturally rooted. In Rodney's view, it would be difficult for a GI to successfully and effectively merge theory and praxis working within an alien/foreign cultural context. He believed strongly that a GI is most effective within his/her cultural environment. Consequently, being a West Indian working in Africa, Rodney found his role as a GI severely constrained by the alien cultural environment. He could function effectively within the university, but only at the level of theory, by engaging other intellectuals. He was not able to ground with the Tanzanian masses. Despite his proficiency in Swahili, Rodney felt handicapped in the mastery of the cultural ethos that would have facilitated his grounding effectively with the common people.[37] As he underscored,

> [m]y political role in that institution was fairly well-defined: to stay within the university walls, first and foremost, to develop and struggle at the level of ideas, to relate to the student population. For me, being a non-Tanzanian, it meant that I had to relate to the indigenous intellectuals and students, within the university, and only secondarily to relate to Tanzanians outside the walls of the university. I draw that distinction [...]. One must recognize certain limits in any given political situation: limits of culture, limits of one's legal and citizenship status, limits that come from the fact that we are speaking in the university in one language, which is English, and the peoples of Tanzania were speaking Swahili.[38]

The effectiveness of the GI, therefore, depended on this contextual/cultural dynamics. Culture was the critical factor. As Rodney explained further,

> [o]ne must know that society, that environment. One must have a series of responses and reflexes that come from having lived a given experience. One must be able to share a joke because of a nuance in language and pronunciation. One must be able to go into the marketplace, in the case of Tanzania, and bargain in the Swahili manner without being perceived as an outsider.[39]

Since, according to Rodney, 'It would take virtually a lifetime to master that language and then master the higher level of perception that normally goes with a culture,' his days in Africa seemed numbered.[40] In this respect, as academics in South Africa, Mahlomoholo and Netshandama exemplify a typology of Rodney's GI: subversive GIs encased within a hegemonic intellectual environment. More importantly, they also perfectly illustrate Rodney's concept of contextual and cultural compatibility. As he emphasized, intellectuals with strong roots in the domestic culture are better able to perform subversive roles. However, Rodney is not convinced that subversive functions should be confined to the ivory tower. In a sense, therefore, by privileging subjectivity, Mahlomoholo and Netshandama are able to perform a kind of 'grounding' as they engage in producing knowledge to advance subaltern interests. Yet, the challenge for them is that subaltern-rooted intellectuals with their depth of cultural grounding must transverse dual spaces of subversion: the university and the community. They offer the perfect prototype of Rodney's culturally rooted GI who is 'qualified' academically and culturally to function effectively within a given context. Rodney was convinced that a successful revolution has to have a strong domestic cultural foundation. Such a revolution 'has to be made by people who are going to be grounded in that situation, who are going to stay there, who are going to make it part of their lives.'[41] Consequently, going to Africa was, for Rodney 'never an end in itself. It was always a means to an end, to me anyway. It was always with the understanding that I would return to the Caribbean.'[42]

Rodney felt constrained in Tanzania. There, he was 'in a fixed political role.'[43] Yet, he felt 'there was another culture from which I derived into which I could project myself with greater ease.'[44] Rodney's years in Africa, therefore, were preparatory to the substantive role he would assume as a GI in the West Indies, specifically his native Guyana where, culturally and linguistically, he felt adaptable, and culturally 'qualified' not only to work within the university but also to assume the role of praxis by grounding with the common people. It did not surprise anyone therefore when early in 1968 Rodney accepted a position at the University of West Indies, Kingston, Jamaica.[45] Upon arrival in Jamaica, Rodney immediately began to engage in activities beyond his professorial calling. He began to frequent the 'dungles' and 'rubbish dungs' of Kingston, to meet and 'ground' with the ordinary people. He began to offer free lessons on African history to the masses, while also learning from them.[46] As Pierre-Michel Fontaine contends, Rodney's objective was to free these people 'of the self-abasing and self-defeating attitudes fostered by centuries of colonialism followed by a thriving neo-colonial era.'[47] His actions, however, proved threatening to the Jamaican government and, in October of 1968, while attending a Congress of Black Writers in Montreal, Canada, Prime Minister Hugh Shearer barred Rodney from returning to Jamaica.[48]

Expelled from Jamaica, Rodney returned to his old job in Tanzanian. He resumed his critical engagement with the radical intelligentsia community at Dar-es Salaam. More importantly, this return marked the beginning of a productive intellectual career. He utilized Marxist methodology to dissect and expose the excesses of European imperialism in Africa. He ascribed his Marxist orientation to the influence of C.L.R. James, especially the discussion group discussed above.[49] Knowledge of Marxism provided Rodney with a platform for constructing a revolutionary ideology. However, he refused to acknowledge Marxism as an ideology uniquely fitted for a European context, emphasizing instead its flexibility and susceptibility to domestication and adaptation. In his view, the materialist interpretation of history offered a critique of imperialism and capitalism that was adaptable to different geographical and cultural contexts. Marxism thus acquired relevance to the African situation, especially since Africa had become fully incorporated into the global capitalist system.[50] Knowledge and understanding of the inner workings of capitalism became fundamental to its overthrow, and Marxism became the tool for disseminating this knowledge. Consequently, Rodney commended Cabral's efforts in merging the epistemological and revolutionary dimensions of Marxism, and in adapting the ideology to the situation in Guinea Bissau. Cabral, in Rodney's judgment, had ensured that, 'Marxism does not simply appear as the summation of other people's history, but appears as a living force with one's history.'[51]

In Tanzania, Rodney preoccupied himself with critical examinations of aspects of ancient and contemporary African history and political economy. True to his convictions, Rodney's writings reflected a conscious desire to address both the academic community and the masses within Africa and the Caribbean. First, there are the books and articles he wrote to challenge and debunk the ideas and erroneous historical theories of the leading European historians.[52] Second, there are publications he meant for wider and general public consumption that spoke directly to the people, and written in a style that was easily accessible and digestible to any lay person. Included in the latter category was perhaps his most important publication *How Europe Underdeveloped Africa* (1972), as well as *The Groundings with My Brothers* (1969).[53] Rodney chose slavery as one subject that required critical reassessment. This focus on slavery underscored his determination to contribute his perspective on a subject that, up to that time, European scholars had enjoyed a monopoly of interpreting. Drawing upon his doctoral study of the Upper Guinea Coast, Rodney began systematically to challenge established interpretations of slavery in Africa.[54] Although Rodney acknowledged and lamented both the participation of Africans in the slave trade and the existence of relationships of subordination and exploitation among Africans prior to the coming of the Europeans, he insisted, however, that slavery, in its trans-Atlantic character, was alien to Africa; introduced to

African societies via the Atlantic trade and it subsequently corrupted elements of indigenous African institutions and values.[55] Rodney also drew a direct correlation between slavery and the beginning of the underdevelopment of Africa. In his words 'under-developing tendencies can uniquely be identified with slavery.'[56]

Rodney's study of imperialism in Africa was perhaps the most combative of his scholarship and also best illustrative of anti-hegemonic genre. Utilizing a Marxist philosophical paradigm, Rodney offered a scathing indictment of European activities in Africa. His most popular publication, *How Europe Underdeveloped Africa*, was written, according to him, not for an academic audience, but specifically for the common people, those who, in his judgment, deserved to have knowledge of the true character of European imperialism and its impacts on the daily lives of Africans. As he acknowledged, the book was prompted by

> concern with the contemporary African situation [...]. In search for an understanding of what is not called 'underdevelopment' in Africa [...]. The phenomenon of neo-colonialism cries out for extensive investigation in order to formulate the strategy and tactics of African emancipation and development.[57]

With hindsight, it seems plausible to suggest that he intended this book as a stepping stone into the consciousness and world of the underclass of African and Diaspora blacks. He was successful. Since *How Europe* was not aimed primarily at an academic audience, but to the general reader, its influence spread rapidly inspiring and nurturing radical consciousness among African and Third World students. It quickly attained iconic status among generations of African/black students, community activists, ordinary people, and intellectuals. In *How Europe*, Rodney located the roots of African and black underdevelopment and dependency in the two major encounters with Europe - Slavery and Colonialism. Both encounters were marked by haemorrhages of African manpower and economic resources for the development of Europe, and the attendant rapid and systematic underdevelopment of Africa. Prior to both encounters, Rodney demonstrated that Africa was economically and culturally wealthy, with politically viable, stable states and empires.[58] The colonial era graphically illustrated the relationship of domination and exploitation. Colonialism, in Rodney's analysis, wrought unmitigated havoc on the African economy, leaving desolation in its wake.[59] Responding to some who proposed a 'balanced' assessment of colonial legacy in Africa, suggesting that though colonialism may have taken from Africa, it did give something back in return, Rodney characterized this interpretation as having 'some sentimental persuasiveness' albeit 'completely false.' In his words, 'Colonialism had only one hand-it was a one-armed bandit. It gave nothing to Africa in return.'[60] In thus situating Africa's underdevelopment squarely within Europe's imperial expansion, Rodney amplified a theme expanded upon earlier by fellow West Indian, Eric Williams, in his classic study *Capitalism and Slavery*.[61] In numerous other publications, Rodney highlighted the antiquity of civilization in Africa. He stressed the wealth and accomplishments of ancient and classical Africa civilizations and the superiority of African moral and ethical values.

In his writings, Rodney also criticized the philosophy of imperial education in Africa, and among West Indians. Since Europeans determined both the curricula and philosophy of education, Eurocentric education constituted an arm of the white power structure, designed to produce acquiescent blacks who would support and defend mainstream Eurocentric values. The ultimate goal of this education was to nurture self-denigrating and self-abnegating consciousness and, in the process, co-opt black intellectuals as appendages and apologists of the white power structure. They became what he called 'white-hearted blacks,' willing collaborators in the oppression of their people.[62] Challenging this mind-set, Rodney urged the GI to develop what he called, 'concrete tactics and strategy necessary' for black liberation.[63] He enjoined black intellectuals to re-evaluate themselves and redefine the world from 'out own standpoint.'[64] There is a strong echo of Afrocentrism in Rodney's thought: redefining African history from an African perspective, as a countervailing pedagogy in the struggles against Eurocentric scholarship and education. Rodney, in essence, enjoined the African and West Indian intelligentsia to choose between the people and the exploitative state. Choosing to serve the underclass implied a commitment to the destruction of the exploitative state. Education became a means to black empowerment, and the GI's role is to use his privileged intellectual resources for re-evaluating and redefining the world from a black perspective. Though Rodney emphasized the importance of challenging and debunking established Eurocentric ideas and theories, he cautioned the black intellectual against a blind adherence to a binary analysis that simplistically constructs the challenges confronting Africans/Diaspora blacks as externally rooted, and racially conditioned.[65] He warned the GI against being 'trapped in a pernicious moment of history' in which his/her scholarship reflected a racial binary (Europe-Africa, White-Black), and entrapped in this 'grand singular' discourse.[66] True to his Marxist convictions, Rodney suggested a critical interrogation of class as well. The GI must not be so focused on Europeans as to ignore domestic African factor. It was equally critical for the GI to move beyond race to interrogation of the internal class contradictions in Africa.[67]

Rodney mapped out a landscape of struggle that transcended intellectual posturing. It was just not enough to write about, and reinterpret, the black experience from a black perspective. The black intellectual has to translate his reflections and critical consciousness into concrete actions designed to attain national liberation. The intellectual, as a member of the petit bourgeoisie, to use Cabral's favourite appellation, has to rally the people against the system and values that had nurtured his own consciousness. In Rodney's judgment, it is the ability and willingness to use knowledge to advance the cause of freedom that distinguishes a GI from an armchair philosopher. He urged black intellectuals to transcend arm-chair philosophizing.[68] Rodney himself set the example. He left Tanzania in 1974 to assume the position of Professor and Chair of the History Department at the University of Guyana. The decision to leave Tanzania was very much against the pleas of his revolutionary and progressive African colleagues. This move reflected Rodney's acknowledgment of the limitations of his role as a West Indian intellectual engaged in counter-hegemonic knowledge production in an alien environment. As he explained, in any environment indigenous intellectuals were better equipped, culturally, to 'ground' with their own people.[69] Despite his knowledge of African history and proficiency in Swahili, Rodney felt ill-equipped to ground effectively with native Tanzanians. Being West Indian, he had no choice but to return to a terrain where he felt better suited to function. Rodney's action should, however, not have surprised anyone. After all, he clearly hinted earlier that his objective in going to Africa was to sharpen his knowledge and understanding of Africa in order to serve, more effectively, the cause of liberation in the West Indies.[70] In other words, he was drawn to Africa by the need to gain experience within Africa, and to acquire the type of practical knowledge of Africa that would facilitate his work in the West Indies.

The cultural domestication of the role of the GI reflects yet another of Rodney's debt to Cabral. The quintessential GI, Cabral has been described as 'a supreme educator in the widest sense of the world.'[71] He theorized extensively on the character and *modus operandi* of imperialism in Africa. Beyond that, however, he set the example by living his life in strict conformity with his ideas. Although a petty bourgeoisie himself, Cabral committed class suicide by 'grounding' with the masses of his native Guinea Bissau and Cape Verde, and committing his intellectual resources to the cause of their liberation. He refused to compromise with Portuguese imperialism, believing strongly that only armed confrontation would dislodge the imperialist from his native land. As the leader of *'Partido Africano da Independencia da Guinea Cabo Verde'* (PAIGC), Cabral adopted armed confrontation as the effective weapon of freeing his people from Portuguese colonialism. This confrontation ended with his assassination by agents of Portuguese fascism in 1973.[72]

Rodney's ideas bore the imprints of Cabral's revolutionary philosophy. He greatly admired Cabral, and read his works, from which he quoted copiously. In fact, Rodney's concepts of the GI and 'grounding' reflect Cabralian materialism. Rodney shared Cabral's conception of the role of history and culture as foundations for building a successfully liberation struggle. Culture, Cabral had argued,

> plunges its roots into the humus of the material reality of the environment in which it develops, and it reflects the organic nature of the society - History enables us to know the nature and extent of the imbalances and the conflicts (economic, political, social) that characterizes the evolution of society. Culture enables us to know what dynamic synthesis have been formed and set by social awareness in order to resolve these conflicts at each stage of evolution of that society.[73]

Accurate knowledge of history and culture, therefore, became for Cabral *sine qua non* for liberation. As he maintained, 'It is with the cultural factor that we find the germ of challenge which leads to the structuring and developing of the liberation movement.'[74] And as Cabral himself demonstrated, the revolutionary intellectual who is knowledgeable in the history of his/her society should also master that culture. This understanding of culture comes from the 'reconversion' of the GI's mentality as he/she engages the world of the subaltern, or to use Rodney's concept 'commits class suicide.'

Rodney's analysis suggests two prototypes of the GI. The first, which he exemplified, is the more moderate GI whose activities are confined to grounding with the masses and subverting the system of oppression from within, adopting every available means short of violence. The second is the Guevaran/Cabralian model, the one who not only commits class suicide by grounding with the people, but violently engages the power structure. Both Cabral and Che Guevara were revolutionary intellectuals who took up arms in furtherance of the national liberation of their people. Rodney had tremendous respect for Cabral and others who embraced armed struggle. As he declared, 'I have the greatest respect for those intellectuals who have taken up the gun.'[75] Although Rodney avoided armed confrontation, his strategy was no less courageous. He eventually suffered a similar fate. His return to Guyana was his final act in the commission of class suicide. Almost immediately, it became clear to the government of Prime Minister Forbes Burnham that Rodney was not going to confine his activities to the university, but that he was determined to become more politically engaged, particularly in the task of raising the social consciousness of the masses.

Considering what happened in Jamaica in the 1960s, Prime Minister Burnham of Guyana quickly revoked Rodney's teaching appointment at the university. Though he received numerous teaching offers from abroad, Rodney declined all, insisting on remaining in Guyana, to ground with the masses, as well as engage in political activism. Sensing the dangers ahead, several of his close friends urged him to consider the offers from abroad. But this was not an option for Rodney. As a GI, he chose to remain in Guyana, in proximity to the people whose cause he had pledged his life.[76] Rodney seemed to believe it was possible to affect change peacefully through the political process. He helped to organize a progressive political movement, the Working Peoples' Alliance (WPA). Along with revolutionary activists live Clive Thomas, Eusi Kwayana, Josh Ramsammy, Moses Baghwan, and Malcolm Rodriguez, Rodney began to lecture, organize and mobilize the masses, exposing the corrupt and exploitative nature of government policies. They also succeeded in discrediting the socialist and populist pretensions of Burnham and his People's National Congress (PNC).[77] The growing popularity of the WPA posed a threat to the government. On numerous occasions, Rodney and his comrades in the WPA were intimidated, arrested, and incarcerated. They were, however, too determined and committed to the people's struggle to be deterred. If Rodney was not mobilizing rice growers on the East coast, he was at Linden organizing the Bauxite workers. Government propaganda began to lose its steam as the masses, conscientized and mobilized, began to flock to WPA rallies.[78] Paradoxically, while Rodney sought revolutionary changes through non-violent means, the political establishment in Guyana saw him as a threat which only violence could extinguish. Rodney's activities were becoming too threatening to, and subversive of, governmental programs to be ignored. On the 13th of June 1980, Rodney died as a result of injuries sustained from the explosion of a two-way radio that had earlier been given to him by one Gregory Smith, later identified as 'a government plant.'[79]

Contrary to the insinuations of some observers following his assassination, Rodney did not openly seek martyrdom. He never embraced violence, his uncompromising opposition to government policies notwithstanding. According to Clive Thomas, a close comrade in the WPA,

> Rodney was no martyr, and in fact recognized that whatever else it represented, martyrdom is a self-defeating political act. He, therefore, did not court his death [...]. He prized being alive as necessary to continuing political struggle.[80]

Rodney himself acknowledged the 'severe limitations' of violent confrontation. As he noted, 'it is not everybody who will become a Che Guevara. That kind of image could even become destructive.'[81] He defined a major task of the GI as 'to operate within the aegis of the *institution* and the *structure* and to take from it and to transform it *over time*' (Emphasis added).[82] By *institution* and *structure*, Rodney meant the university and society. The GI has to function from within both to bring about change *over time* (i.e., gradually). Rodney successfully tied the conceptual dimension of his struggle to the praxis, establishing that he was not just another revolutionary theoretician. His faith in the potency of the ideas he preached led him to champion the revolutionary application of those ideas. His message was clear and simple: the black intellectual should never maintain a purely philosophical posture, however critical the perspective; but should endeavour to tie consciousness and reflection to 'our immediate goal,' which is 'the conquest of power.'[83]

4. Conclusion

Public intellectuals who undertake to 'make knowledge public' as Georg Simet underscores engage in a risky and potentially deadly function.[84] In the process of 'making knowledge public' these intellectuals are able to shape public discourse on subjects such as race, colonialism neo-colonialism (Rodney), the Armenian problem (Hrant Dink), poverty, race, inequality and injustice (Mahlomoholo/Netshandama).[85] Depending on the nature of the subject and the circumstances, such efforts could have deadly consequences (Rodney, Dink) Thus, regardless of context and ideological persuasion, intellectuals who attempt to shape public knowledge are engaged in a risky provocative venture. The intellectual's ability to shape and inform public opinion is a powerful tool, one with the potentiality to destabilize the State. Knowledge creation and dissemination, therefore, are a function of ideology and power (Olga Procevska), and intellectuals, as Antonio Gramsci argued, must take a stand.[86] The intellectual can choose either to be collaborative or subversive. The latter role could take the form of producing and disseminating of counter-hegemonic knowledge or, from a more activist and revolutionary standpoint, the expansion of the parameters of subversion by committing class suicide and siding with the people against the oppressive state (Rodney). Rodney exemplified the latter. For him, knowledge was useless if not put to public service. He was the public intellectual *par excellence*. In his view, education is a first and major step in the production and transformation of knowledge for public use. The intellectual must use his/her knowledge to shape public discourse about problems confronting the subalterns. Whether one actively engages in the production and propagation of anti-hegemonic knowledge, or one simply attempts to shape public understanding of a subject (Dink), the intellectual, in both contexts, is exercising power that potentially could generate negative hostile reactions.

Rodney's recognition of the role of education in the sustenance of colonial and post-colonial structures of domination led him to devote his entire life, scholarship, and struggle to articulating, and forcefully propagating, a combative, revolutionary epistemology; one that was capable, in his judgment, not only of reversing the debilitating impact of Eurocentric historiography on black consciousness, and loosening the death grips of the Europeans on the political economy of African and black Diaspora societies, but also undermining and subverting an entrenched neo-colonial, exploitative state. His counter revolutionary epistemology entailed the emergence of theory and praxis: the revolutionary intellectuals must transcend intellectual theorizing and posturing. Rodney thrust two fundamental responsibilities on such intellectuals. First, they had to function as public intellectuals who propagate revolutionary, counter-establishment cultural values, and consciousness among the masses, and second, position themselves in the vanguard of the struggle to free the masses from exploitation. His writings and activities clearly mapped out, and demarcated, these two fundamental levels of engagement for the revolutionary intellectual. A central theme of his revolutionary epistemology, therefore, is the transformation of the revolutionary theoretician into a revolutionary activist. Rodney's career manifested this transformation.

Rodney consequently lived the experience he wrote and theorized about, grounding with the brothers and sisters in the dark alleys and shanty towns of Jamaica and Guyana. Refusing to be shackled and hamstrung by considerations of his petit bourgeois class and training, Rodney, in essence, escaped the 'Babylonian Captivity' of his class, becoming a formidable weapon against, and a threat to, the very class that would have afforded him comfort, and shielded him from the ugly and painful experiences of the common people. As George Lamming aptly surmised, 'he (i.e., Rodney) lived to survive the distortions of his training and the crippling ambivalence of his class.'[87] Besides the struggle that defined, shaped, and ultimately took his life, Rodney left behind a rich intellectual legacy. No discussion of the Atlantic slave trade, European imperialism/colonialism in Africa, and the crises of development and underdevelopment in Africa, is complete without considerations of his contributions. Published posthumously, his last book, *A History of the Guyanese Working People, 1881-1905*, highlights the materialist and other complex external forces that shaped working class history and experience in Guyana.[88] Three decades after his death, scholars are still grappling with several of the theoretical underpinnings of his scholarship. Relative to the challenge of knowledge creation, Rodney's writings underscore two imperatives. First, the creation of anti-hegemonic knowledge has to engage critically the prevailing intellectual standards and values. This is indeed paradoxical. For the GI to dismantle hegemonic knowledge, Rodney seems to suggest, he/she must be validated by acknowledged intellectual standards. In other words, to be functional, the revolutionary intellectual has to engage and deconstruct hegemonic knowledge from a position of intellectual strength, and this strength, in Rodney's view, comes partly from being validated by established intellectual canons. Second, knowledge creation is not a one-way traffic. The GI is not all-knowing, western education notwithstanding. To be effective in creating the kind of knowledge that would advance the people's liberation, the GI must also be willing to become fully embedded with, and learn from, the people. Rodney represented the GI as a 'public intellectual' whose role specifically dictated challenging and deconstructing the values of the ruling and dominant class, one who, therefore, in the Gramscian sense, is also an organic intellectual. Implicit here is a distinction between a 'public intellectual' whose role is simply to shape and influence public knowledge which could possibly advance hegemonic interests (such as Black Conservative intellectuals), and an organic intellectual who consciously and aggressively creates and mobilizes anti-hegemonic knowledge while fully and publicly embedded with the subaltern. In Rodney's view, therefore, an organic intellectual is a public intellectual, but a public intellectual is not necessarily an organic intellectual. Rodney was indeed a rarity, a public intellectual who insisted on using his knowledge for the good of society, but an organic intellectual as well who insisted on immersing himself in the people's struggles and experiences, and creating anti-hegemonic knowledge to destabilize and upstage the exploitative and oppressive state. For him, therefore, knowledge had just one *raison d'être*: liberation of the people from the shackles and stranglehold of oppression. Rodney did not compromise on this point, even when the circumstances seemed overwhelmingly to his disadvantage, and was presented with the opportunity to safely and comfortably advance his own personal fortunes elsewhere. He would not abandon the people, his people, whose struggles he fully embraced. If there is one fundamental lesson Rodney's life taught is that knowledge production and dissemination for the public good is a deadly preoccupation, unless, of course, if such exercise is meant to serve and advance the interests of the hegemonic and exploitative state/power.

Notes

[1] F. Fanon, *The Wretched of the Earth*, Presence Africaine, Paris, 1963; F. Fanon, *Black Skin, White Masks*, Editions du Seuil, Paris, 1952; A. Memmi, *The Colonizer and the Colonized*, Beacon Press, Boston, 1991 (originally published in 1965); A. Memmi, *Racism*, University of Minnesota Press, Minneapolis, 2000; C.G. Woodson, *The Mis-education of the Negro*, Africa World Press, Trenton, 1990 (originally published in 1933).

[2] A. Afrigbo, *The Poverty of African Historiography*, Afrografrika Publishers, Idanre, 1977, p. 4, originally quoted in 'The Rise of Christian Europe', *Listener*, London, November 28, 1963.

[3] J.M. Blaut, *The Colonizer's Model of the World: Geographical Diffusionism and Eurocentric History*, The Guilford Press, New York, 1993, pp. 1-43.
[4] A.G. Paschal (ed), *A W.E.B. Du Bois Reader*, Collier Books, New York, 1971, p. 31.
[5] R. Handyside, *Revolution in Guinea: Selected Texts by Amilcar Cabral*, Monthly Review Press, New York, 1969, pp. 90-111.
[6] Ibid., p. 102.
[7] Ibid., pp. 90-111.
[8] A. Gramsci, *Selections from the Prison Notebook*, Lawrence & Wishart, London, 1971; see also S. Jones, *Antonio Gramsci*, Routledge, London, 2006.
[9] R. Hill (ed), *Walter Rodney Speaks: The Making of an African Intellectual*, Africa World Press, Trenton, 1990, pp. 1-5; R.C. Lewis, *Walter Rodney's Intellectual and Political Thought*, Wayne State University Press, Detroit, 1998, chapter 1.
[10] Hill (ed), *Walter Rodney Speaks*, op. cit., p. 3.
[11] Ibid.
[12] Lewis, *Walter Rodney's Intellectual and Political Thought*, op. cit., chapter 2.
[13] Hill, *Walter Rodney Speaks*, op. cit., p. 19.
[14] Ibid.
[15] Ibid.
[16] Ibid., p. 28; see also Lewis, *Walter Rodney's Intellectual and Political Thought*, op. cit., chapter 2.
[17] W. Rodney, 'African History in the Service of Black Revolution', *The Groundings With My Brothers*, Bogle L'Ouverture, London, 1969, pp. 51-59.
[18] Ibid., p. 51.
[19] Ibid.
[20] Ibid., p. 56.
[21] Hill, *Walter Rodney Speaks*, op. cit., pp. 23-24.
[22] Ibid., pp. 22-27.
[23] Ibid.
[24] Ibid., p. 25.
[25] Lewis, *Walter Rodney's Intellectual and Political Thought*, op. cit., pp. 41-45.
[26] Hill, *Walter Rodney Speaks*, op. cit., p. 33.
[27] Ibid., pp. 37-38; see also B. Swai, 'Rodney on Scholarship and Activism - Part 1'. *Journal of African Marxists*. Vol. 1, 1981, pp. 31-43.
[28] Ibid.; see also R. Lewis, *Walter Rodney's Intellectual and Political Thought*, op. cit., chapter 6.
[29] Hill, *Walter Rodney Speaks*, op. cit., p. 111.

[30] Ibid., pp. 112-113.
[31] Rodney, *The Groundings With My Brothers*, op. cit., p. 62.
[32] Ibid.; see also A. Cabral (ed), *Unity and Struggle: Speeches and Writings*, Heinemann, London, 1980, p. 145.
[33] Rodney, *The Groundings With My Brothers*, op. cit., pp. 63-64.
[34] Ibid., p. 65.
[35] Ibid.
[36] Ibid., pp. 63-65.
[37] Hill, *Walter Rodney Speaks*, op. cit., p. 39.
[38] Ibid.
[39] Ibid., p. 42.
[40] Ibid., pp. 43-44.
[41] Ibid., p. 44.
[42] Ibid., p. 33.
[43] Ibid., p. 43.
[44] Ibid., pp. 42-43.
[45] Lewis, *Walter Rodney's Intellectual and Political Thought*, op. cit., chapter 5.
[46] Ibid.; see also P-M. Fontaine, 'Walter Rodney: Revolutionary & Scholar in the Guyanese Political Cauldron', *Walter Rodney: Revolutionary and Scholar: A Tribute*, University of California Press, Los Angeles, 1982, pp. 15-36.
[47] Ibid.
[48] Ibid., pp. 17-18; Lewis, *Walter Rodney's Intellectual and Political Thought*, op. cit., pp. 99-102; see also Swai, 'Rodney on Scholarship and Activism', op. cit.
[49] Hill, *Walter Rodney Speaks*, op. cit., p. 28.
[50] W. Rodney, *Marx in the Liberation of Africa*, Typed Transcript of a Speech Delivered at Queens College, New York, 1975; see also W.E. Ferguson, 'Walter Rodney's Application of Marxist Theory to the African Past and Present', *Walter Rodney: Revolutionary and Scholar. A Tribute*, op. cit., pp. 99-118.
[51] Rodney, *Marx in the Liberation of Africa*, op. cit., p. 10.
[52] W. Rodney, *A History of the Upper Guinea Coast, 1540-1800*, Clarendon Press, Oxford, 1970; W. Rodney, 'African Slavery and Other Forms of Social Oppression in the Upper Guinea Coast in the Context of the Atlantic Slave Trade', *Journal of African History*, Vol. 7(3), 1966, pp. 431-443; W. Rodney, 'A Reconsideration of the Mane Invasion of Sierra Leone', *Journal of African History*, Vol. 8(2), 1967, pp. 219-246; W. Rodney, *West Africa and the Atlantic Slave Trade*, East African Publishing, Nairobi, 1967; W. Rodney, 'European Activities and African Reaction in Angola', *Aspects of Central*

African History, T.O. Ranger (ed), Heinemann, London, 1968, pp. 49-70; W. Rodney, 'The Imperialist Partition of Africa', *Monthly Review*, Vol. 21(11), April, 1970, pp. 103-114; W. Rodney, 'The Guinea Coast', *The Cambridge History of Africa*, R. Gray (ed), Vol. 4, c.1600-c.1790, Cambridge University Press, London, 1975, pp. 223-324; W. Rodney, 'Africa in Europe and the Americas', *The Cambridge History of Africa*, R. Gray (ed), op. cit., pp. 578-622; W. Rodney, 'The Political Economy of Colonial Tanganyika, 1890-1930', *Tanzania Under Colonial Rule*, M.H. Kaneki (ed), Longman, London, 1980, pp. 128-163; W. Rodney, 'The Colonial Economy', *Africa Under Colonial Domination, 1880-1935*, A. Boahen (ed), Heinemann & UNESCO, California, 1985, pp. 153-161.
[53] W. Rodney, *How Europe Underdeveloped Africa*, Bogle L'Ouverture, London, 1972.
[54] Rodney, *A History of the Upper Guinea Coast*, op. cit.; Rodney, *West Africa and the Atlantic Slave Trade*, op. cit.; Rodney, 'African Slavery and Other Forms of Social Oppression ...', op. cit.; W. Rodney 'Upper Guinea and the Significance of the Origins of Africans Enslaved in the New World', *Journal of Negro History*, Vol. LVI(4), October, 1969, pp. 327-345.
[55] Rodney, *West Africa and the Atlantic Slave Trade*, op. cit.
[56] W. Rodney, 'Slavery and Underdevelopment', *Historical Reflections*, Vol. 6(1), 1979, pp. 275-286.
[57] Rodney, *How Europe Underdeveloped Africa*, op. cit., p. 7.
[58] Ibid., chapters 1-5.
[59] Ibid., chapter 6; see also Rodney, 'The Colonial Economy', op. cit.
[60] Rodney, *How Europe Underdeveloped Africa*, op. cit., p. 205.
[61] E. Williams, *Capitalism and Slavery*, Andre Deutsch, London, 1964.
[62] Rodney, *The Groundings With My Brothers*, op. cit., pp. 32-34; Rodney, *How Europe Underdeveloped Africa*, op. cit., pp. 239-240; Hill, *Walter Rodney Speaks*, op. cit., pp. 112-114.
[63] Rodney, *The Groundings With My Brothers*, op. cit., p. 51.
[64] Ibid.
[65] Hill, *Walter Rodney Speaks*, op. cit., pp. 69-70.
[66] Ibid.
[67] Ibid.
[68] Ibid., p. 113-115; see also Rodney, *The Groundings With My Brothers*, op. cit., pp. 50-51; Swai, 'Rodney on Scholarship and Activism - Part 1', op. cit.
[69] Hill, *Walter Rodney Speaks*, op. cit., pp. 39-42.
[70] Ibid., p. 33.
[71] B. Davidson, 'Introduction', *Unity and Struggle: Speeches and Writings*, op. cit., p. ix-xvii, p. x.

[72] Ibid.; see also: Handyside, *Revolution in Guinea: Selected Texts by Amilcar Cabral*, op. cit.; R.H. Chilcote, *Amilcar Cabral's Revolutionary Theory and Practice: A Critical Guide*, Lynn Reinner Publishers, London, 1991; J. McCulloch, *In the Twilight of Revolution: The Political Theory of Amilcar Cabral*, Routledge & Kegan Paul, London, 1983; K. Opoku, 'Cabral and the African Revolution', *Presence Africaine*, Vols. 105/106, 1978, pp. 45-60.
[73] Handyside, *Revolution in Guinea: Selected Texts by Amilcar Cabral*, op. cit., p. 142.
[74] Ibid.
[75] Hill, *Walter Rodney Speaks*, op. cit., p. 113.
[76] Fontaine, 'Walter Rodney: Revolutionary & Scholar in the Guyanese Political Cauldron', op. cit., pp. 15-36.
[77] C.Y. Thomas, 'Walter Rodney and the Caribbean Revolution', *Walter Rodney: Revolutionary and Scholar. A Tribute*, op. cit., pp. 119-132.
[78] Ibid.; see also J. Ohiorhenuan, 'Walter Rodney: His Life and Work', *And Finally They Killed Him*, Positive Review, Ile-Ife, Nigeria, 1980, pp. 1-6.
[79] Fontaine, 'Walter Rodney: Revolutionary & Scholar in the Guyanese Political Cauldron', op. cit., p. 29.
[80] Thomas, 'Walter Rodney and the Caribbean Revolution', op. cit. p. 130.
[81] Hill, *Walter Rodney Speaks*, op. cit., p. 113.
[82] Ibid.
[83] Rodney, *The Groundings With My Brothers*, op. cit., p. 51.
[84] G.F. Simet, 'Possibilities and Risks of Influencing Public Knowledge: The Case of Hrant Dink', 2011, this volume.
[85] Ibid.; S. Mahlomaholo and V. Netshandama, 'Post-Apartheid Organic Intellectual and Knowledge Creation', 2011, this volume.
[86] O. Procevska, 'Not a Sin, but a Side Effect: Collaboration and Knowledge Creation by the Organic Intellectuals', 2011, this volume.
[87] G. Lamine, 'Forward', *A History of the Guyanese Working People, 1881-1905*, The Johns Hopkins University Press, Baltimore, 1981, p. xxx.
[88] Rodney, *A History of the Guyanese Working People, 1881-1905*, op. cit.

Bibliography

Afigbo, A.E., *The Poverty of African Historiography*. Afrografrika Publishers, Idanre, 1977.

Alpers, E. and Fontaine, P.M. (eds), *Walter Rodney: Revolutionary and Scholar: A Tribute*. University of California, Los Angeles, 1982.

Blaut, J.M., *The Colonizer's Model of the World: Geographical Diffusionism and Eurocentric History*. The Guilford Press, New York, 1995.

Cabral, A., *Unity and Struggle: Speeches and Writings*. Heinemann, London, 1980.

Chilcote, R., *Amilcar Cabral's Revolutionary Theory and Practice: A Critical Guide*. Lynn Reinner Publishers, London, 1991.

Davidson, B., 'Introduction'. *Unity and Struggle: Speeches and Writings*. A. Cabral, Heinemann, London, 1980, p. ix-xvii.

Fanon, F., *Black Skin, White Masks*. Editions du Seuil, Paris, 1952.

——, *The Wretched of the Earth*. Presence Africaine, Paris, 1963.

Gramsci, A., *Selections from the Prison Notebook*. Lawrence & Wishart, London, 1971.

Handyside, R., *Revolution in Guinea: Selected Texts by Amilcar Cabral*. Monthly Review Press, New York, 1969.

Hill, R. (ed), *Walter Rodney Speaks: The Making of an African Intellectual*. Africa World Press, Trenton, NJ, 1990.

Jones, S., *Antonio Gramsci*. Routledge, London, 2006.

Lewis, R.C., *Walter Rodney's Intellectual and Political Thought*. Wayne State University Press, Detroit, 1998.

McCulloch, J., *In the Twilight of Revolution: The Political Theory of Amilcar Cabral*. Routledge & Kegan Paul, London, 1983.

Memmi, A., *The Colonizer and the Colonized*. Beacon Press, Boston, 1991.

——, *Racism*. University of Minnesota Press, Minneapolis, 2000.

Ohiorhenuan, J., 'Walter Rodney: His Life and Work'. *And Finally They Killed Him*. Positive Review, Ile-Ife, Nigeria, 1980.

Opoku, K., 'Cabral and the African Revolution'. *Presence Africaine*, Vols. 105/106, 1978, pp. 45-60.

Paschal, A.G., *A W.E.B. Du Bois Reader*. Collier Books, New York, 1971.

Rodney, W., *A History of the Guyanese Working People, 1881-1905*. The Johns Hopkins University Press, Baltimore, 1982.

——, *A History of the Upper Guinea Coast, 1540-1800*. Clarendon Press, Oxford, 1970.

——, 'A Reconsideration of the Mane Invasion of Sierra Leone'. *Journal of African History*. Vol. 8(2), 1967, pp. 219-246.

——, 'Africa in Europe and the Americas'. *The Cambridge History of Africa, Vol. 4, c.1600-c.1790*. Gray, R. (ed), Cambridge University Press, London, 1975.

——, 'African History in the Service of Black Revolution'. *The Groundings with My Brothers*. Bogle-L'Ouverture, London, 1969.

——, 'African Slavery and Other Forms of Social Oppression in the Upper Guinea Coast in the Context of the Atlantic Slave Trade'. *Journal of African History*. Vol. 7(3), 1966, pp. 431-443.

——, 'European Activities and African Reaction in Angola'. *Aspects of Central African History*. Ranger, T.O. (ed), Heinemann, London, 1968.

——, *How Europe Underdeveloped Africa*. Bogle L'Ouverture, London, 1972.

——, *Marx in the Liberation of Africa*. Typed Transcript of a Speech Delivered at Queens College, New York, 1975.

——, 'Slavery and Underdevelopment'. *Historical Reflections*. Vol. 6(1), 1979, pp. 275-286.

——, 'The Colonial Economy'. *Africa Under Colonial Domination, 1880-1935*. Boahen, A. (ed), Heinemann & UNESCO, California, 1985.

——, *The Groundings with My Brothers*. Bogle L'Ouverture, London, 1969.

——, 'The Guinea Coast'. *The Cambridge History of Africa, Vol. 4, c.1600-c.1790.* Gray, R. (ed), Cambridge University Press, London, 1975.

——, 'The Imperialist Partition of Africa'. *Monthly Review.* Vol. 21(11), April, 1970, pp. 103-114.

——, 'The Political Economy of Colonial Tanganyika, 1890-1930'. *Tanzania Under Colonial Rule.* Kaneki, M.H. (ed), Longman, London, 19803.

——, 'Upper Guinea and the Significance of the Origins of Africans Enslaved in the New World'. *Journal of Negro History.* Vol. LVI(4), October 1969, pp. 327-345.

——, *West Africa and the Atlantic Slave Trade.* East African Publishing, Nairobi, 1967.

Swai, B., 'Rodney on Scholarship and Activism - Part 1'. *Journal of African Marxists.* Vol. 1, 1981, pp. 31-43.

Thomas, C.Y., 'Walter Rodney and the Caribbean Revolution'. *Walter Rodney: Revolutionary and Scholar: A Tribute.* Alpers, E. and Fontaine, P-M. (eds), University of California Press, Los Angeles, 1982.

Williams, E., *Capitalism and Slavery.* Andre Deutsch, London, 1964.

Woodson, C.G., *The Miseducation of the Negro.* Africa World Press, Trenton, NJ, 1990 (originally published in 1933).

Possibilities and Risks of Influencing Public Knowledge: The Case of Hrant Dink

Georg F. Simet

Abstract
The making of knowledge public counts on intellectuals who welcome the opportunity to express themselves, as they are interested in making their implicit knowledge explicit by sharing their point of view with others. In the following, the case of Hrant Dink will be used as a paradigmatic example to demonstrate the interest of journalists in expressing their political opinion - firstly, as an individual and to some respect as part of a community. Dink's intention was to make Armenians and the Armenian point of view visible. It will be shown, how intellectuals such as Dink interact with the public in this regard and the possibilities they have to influence and maybe change public opinion. As such actions need intercultural sensibility, *change management* is an important, but difficult task in this context. Therefore, it will be investigated, how such a dialogue could succeed and why Dink did not. Furthermore, it will analyse how Dink's subsequent murder impacted further discussions.

Key Words: Armenia, Dink, Ergenekon, Gökçen, public intellectual, Pamuk, Şafak, Turkishness, İpekçi.

*****

1. **Dink's Motivation for Becoming a Public Intellectual**
In order to understand Dink's motivation and his decision of becoming a journalist and a critical *public* intellectual, we have to recapitulate the main facts of his biography.[1]

Hrant Dink was born on 15 September 1954 in Malatya. In the age of seven, the marriage of his parents broke down and Dink was sent to Istanbul, where he was grown up in an Armenian orphanage. He met his wife Rakel in a summer camp in Tuzla that was set up and functioned as a meeting centre for the Armenian youth. Dink came there first time, when he was eight years old and worked there for 20 years. Hrant and Rakel married in 1977. They managed the youth camp until the putsch on 12 September 1980, when the land was confiscated. This was justified by the claim that the Armenian Church bought the land illegally. The event left a lasting impression on the 25-year old Dink: 'This moment I became aware of what it means to be an Armenian in Turkey. I decided to fight for my identity.'[2]

The decision to conduct this fight in public by writing articles and talking at conferences critically and provocatively came much later, in 1994.

First Dink worked two years for the Marmara Armenian newspaper. Then he founded his own weekly newspaper 'Agos.' This term means in Turkish and Armenian a 'ploughed furrow' and indicates the place in which the seed (of words) falls which later bears the *fruit*.[3] Agos is Turkey's first and only bilingual newspaper, published in Turkish and Armenian. In total, Dink wrote 19 columns for Agos.[4]

In view of the above it is important to state that Dink acted in order to express himself. He established and used Agos only as a means. Dink is a *public* intellectual (at least by definition of Thomas Sowell, as Dink's work began and ended with the idea to overcome the ethnic conflict).[5] He also is an *organic* intellectual (who works not independently, but with others), but only in so far as he acted in and with the relatively small Agos team. Dink was a political intellectual only as he tried to encourage the Armenian citizens to become self-confident. Dink was not a 'Guerrilla intellectual' as Rodney or a revolutionary intellectual as Che Guevara. Dink concentrated on the strengthening of the individuality, as in modern Turkey the concept of a pure Turkish, Sunni unity dominates and rules the whole public life. From Dink's case we can learn about the difficulties to change the concept of society from a unity centred very traditional way of living to the (post-) modern individual centred understanding and approach of acting.

2. Dink's Legal Disputes

Dink was tried several times for 'insulting' and/or 'denigrate' Turkishness' by reference to Article 301 of the Penal Code that was introduced with the legislative reforms of 1 June 2005.[6] The first paragraph of this article stipulated:

> [a] person who publicly denigrates Turkishness, the Republic or the Grand National Assembly of Turkey, shall be sentenced a penalty of imprisonment for a term of six months to three years.

The first time Dink was accused of this crime was for statements he made at a conference held in Urfa in 2002. He provoked the Turkish public by saying: 'I was not a Turk but from Turkey and an Armenian.'[7] For these words Dink was sentenced to six months in prison (suspended for good behaviour).[8] This was the first conviction from the Turkish highest judicial authority on the interpretation of Article 301 of the new Criminal Code. Lastly, on 12 July 2006, he was again given a half year suspended prison sentence in connection with statements that were made, primarily in the following two columns published in the Agos on February 2004.

On 6 February 2004 Dink published an article about Sabiha Gökçen saying that she is an Armenian by birth. This threw the whole of Turkey into commotion, as Gökçen - born in Bursa on 21 March 1913; and died in Ankara on 22 March 2001 - is an adopted daughter of Mustafa Kemal Atatürk, the first girl student of the Turkish Civil Aviation School and Turkey's first female combat pilot. The statement that this lady adopted by Atatürk, the 'father of all Turks,' an aviation pioneer and hero could be an Armenian was shocking.

Nevertheless, the bone of contention was Dink's *suggestion*, written in Agos on 13 February 2004: To 'replace the poisoned blood associated with the Turk, with fresh blood associated with Armenia.'[9] The sentence expresses a radical change of meaning and perspective: to see Armenians not as people who poison the unity and ethnic purity, but instead to bring in *fresh blood*, to enrich and make the society more colourful.

In his last article in Agos published on 10 January 2007, Dink documents the blatant failure of large parts of the Turkish judiciary which sentenced him.[10]

A few days later he wrote: 'For me, 2007 is likely to be a hard year.'[11] He was unfortunately right. On Friday, 19 January he was gunned down in front of his office in a city street in Şişli, a vibrant downtown neighbourhood of Istanbul, at 3 p.m., in the middle of the day.

3. Dink's Interrelationship with the Public

Dink's only interest in becoming a public figure and acting in public, as we saw, was to make the interrelationship between Armenians and Turks a subject of discussion. His intention is based on his own biographical, existential background: he was born as an Armenian, but grown up and living in Turkey; and so he experienced personally - throughout his life - the impact of this problematic constellation, of being 'merely a Turkish citizen.'[12] In opposite to the most other Armenians living in Turkey, he intended to (1) make the Turkish-Armenian relationship visible, (2) reformulate the Armenian question, and (3) overcome the conflict. In order to make his perspective visible and to introduce his perspective, he had to provoke the public. Dink became a public intellectual as he had to address 'the general public.'[13] He created knowledge as he (1) made others aware of the social problem, (2) analysed and discussed it and (3) gave thought-provoking impulses for solutions. However, it is to be noticed that the social problem that Dink focused is first of all his *own* very existential problem. He acted as he was directly affected.

In this context Dink also took a position on other countries and thought about how they could and should help to overcome the strained ethnic and national Turkish-Armenian relations. Dink formulated very ambitious, almost unrealistic expectations, in particular from the European Union. So, Dink demanded the prospect of full membership not only for Turkey, but also for Azerbaijan, Armenia and Georgia.[14]

Nevertheless, the Turkish public saw in Dink entirely an Armenian who opposed Turks and Turkishness. This picture was considerably determined and underpinned by the trials. Unfortunately, the litigation achieved its purpose. Dink became an object of hatred among nationalists and Islamists. Although Dink's murderer, a 17-year-old man he had never met, was heard to shout 'I have killed the infidel,' he acted not as driven by his own conviction, but as an executor of the will of the prosecution and the nationalists.[15] The acceptance of the murder as an executor and *hero* appeared, when the media published photos and a video on which security officials posed with the teenage murder suspect after his arrest.[16] In reaction to the reported 'hero treatment' of the suspect, the government launched at least a half-hearted inquiry into the footage.[17]

The latter shows that Dink was killed by the national jurisdiction rather than a single young man and his beliefs. Dink was seen by the public as someone who exposed himself as different to the Turkish community.

4. Dink's Fight against Nationalism

Turkishness is for Turks most of all a feeling; it is not an abstract, mainly rational term. It is therefore not and cannot be defined scientifically (and juridically, respectively). Modern Turks have a strong feeling of being part of their *own* community. They perceive themselves as a family and so they distance themselves from others (who are not part of their family). If Turks speak to each other, they often use terms like *brother, sister, daughter, son, uncle, aunt*, etc.[18]

This common consciousness of the Turkish nation as a family (that includes all Turks wherever they live) was politically created by the Young Turks and in this tradition used by Mustafa Kemal Atatürk.[19] The surname Atatürk, meaning the father (Turkish *ata*) of the Turks, was given to him by the Grand National Assembly on 24 November 1934, as he made the former 'Sick Man of Europe' proud of itself again (as Turkey was during the heyday of the Ottoman Empire).[20] Atatürk's main important sentence in this regard is: '*Ne mutlu Türküm diyene*' (*How happy is he/she who calls himself/herself a Turk*), a sentence which welcomes travellers at the entrance of almost all cities in Turkey.[21]

The self-confidence of Turkey as a nation is still seen as the endeavour to build a unity in familial solidarity. This political belief, for instance, is clearly expressed in the famous speech of Recep Tayyip Erdoğan, the current prime minister of Turkey, given in Köln, on 10 February 2008:

> [m]y dear brothers and sisters, we in Turkey are happy and stilled insofar as you here are happy and stilled. Your problems are our problems. Be ensured that your concerns are our concerns, too. It is important that we do not give up

hope, that we never allow derogations from the spirit of solidarity, that we are unitary, strong and vital.[22]

It is still one of the unsolved questions in Turkey, whether the unity of Turkish society can allow for diversity or not. All political movements and parties in Turkish society operate under state control. This is the main reason that there is little room for *organic* intellectuals. All initiatives to make the country's ethnic diversity public (e.g. the Ebru Project by Attila Durak) are initiatives of individuals.[23]

Dink's intention was to fight as 'honest intellectual' against nationalism on all sides.[24] He acted as an individual, a public (but not organic) intellectual against the nationalism of the Turks, the Armenians, the Kurds, etc.[25] He was convinced that peace needs to focus on community. His criticism was clear: 'Today the Western world moves from cultural uniformity, but we [...] are running in the other direction.'[26] In his article 'Questions to My Teacher' Dink quoted a schoolbook on national security that says: '95 % of the population of Turkey share since thousands of years the same destiny, the same culture and the same wishes and are merged together.'[27] So, Dink asked: 'Is it right, that 95 % are first-class and 5 % are second-class citizens? My teacher, I apologise, but do such questions fall under separatism?'[28]

Separatism is the greatest fear of the military, the state and the majority of the Turkish people still today. (This is the main reason for the on-going war against PKK). Dink became the most important target of the nationalists who attacked him by Article 301 of the Penal Code. A cartoon of Sever Selvi shows this in a paradigmatic way. The number 301 is written in red against a black backdrop. Inside the oval that forms the number '0' Dink's face appears like a trophy released for discharge.[29]

The murder of Hrant Dink did and does not keep the public prosecutors from prosecution.[30] Their power is based on the term *Turkishness* (*Türklük*). Bülent Algan comments rightly: 'Many definitions can be found for 'nation,' 'Turkish Nation,' and 'Turkishness.' Vagueness is the common character for all.'[31] In because of its vagueness, Article 301 is a powerful, adaptable weapon in the hands of the supreme prosecutors and judges for fighting against all who express different opinions.

For the most part, two movements are opposing each other in modern Turkey. On one hand, the dominant national movement which built the country claims to be not only the most but the only party which guarantees the continuation of the nation. Its values are homogeneity and a more or less quasi-militarily order. Homogeneity is defined for them by Atatürk's principle to build one, coherent *Turkish* nation, a principle which culminates in the already cited credo *Ne mutlu Türküm diyene*. All beliefs, behaviour and acts have to be subordinated to this sentence. On the other hand, there are intellectuals, whom Dink calls 'honest intellectuals', who refuse to subordinate themselves of whatever reasons.

Nevertheless, all social and political controversies are still being led under the question of what Turkishness means, a dispute which is being led judicially by the nationalists' movement. Intellectuals from the non-'nationalist' side counter more creatively. So, Extramücadele (*Extrastruggle*) published a poster which shows the face of the murdered Dink titled '*Ne ölü 'Ermeniyim' diyen*' (*How dead is he who says 'I am an Armenian'*).[32]

However, as long as Turkey does not accept diversity in its society, it is not possible to join the European Union, as 'unity in diversity' is the 'motto' (Article I-8) and the 'heart' of its constitution.[33]

5. Dink in Comparison with Elif Şafak and Orhan Pamuk

Intellectuals are seen by the Turkish state in principal as suspicious, as the state's representatives assume that intellectuals in general tend to the left, and that the left tend to communism, and that such communists intend to destroy the state. So, the state authorities are convinced that they have to see intellectuals as their *natural* enemies and to treat them as such.[34]

In order to estimate Dink as the main target of the state and all nationalists, his case is to be reflected in comparison to the estimated 60 other intellectuals who were persecuted by the state authorities of having insulted the Turkish national identity.[35] The two most famous cases of Elif Şafak and Orhan Pamuk will be reflected representatively.

Let us start with Elif Şafak, 'Turkey's most famous female writer.'[36] Her case is remarkable, as it was the first time that Article 301 had been used against a work of fiction.[37] Nevertheless, the nationalistic stubborn prosecutors failed. The judges acquitted Şafak on 21 September 2006 soon after the trial opened, citing a lack of evidence.[38]

In *Baba ve Piç* (literally translated 'Father and Bastard'), Şafak's sixth novel, the enmeshment of Turkish and Armenian relationships is reflected from both, the Armenian and Turkish sides. Thanks to the accusation, 'The Bastard of Istanbul' - as the book is titled in the English edition - 'has officially gone from 'novel' to 'cultural touchstone.''[39] It became a best seller in Turkey.[40]

The most objected excerpt from the book is the following sentence spoken by Armanoush Tchakhmakhchian, one of main protagonists (who, by the way, are all female):

> I'm the grandchild of genocide survivors who lost all their relatives at the hands of Turkish butchers in 1915, but I myself have been brainwashed to deny the genocide because I was raised by some Turk named Mustafa!"[41]

This little sentence is very insightful, as it contains first of all two important words. The first is the term *genocide*. The Turkish state tried and still tries very hard to prevent even other states such as France for naming the massacres of Armenians in 1915 (in the context of the war of the Young Turks against Russia) as 'genocide.'[42] So, the use of this term marks the breach of a national taboo. The second word the prosecutors complained about is the designation of Turkish soldiers as 'Turkish butchers.' This as well marks a breach of a national taboo. It is the military which built modern Turkey. So, Turkish soldiers can't be bad. In the book *Şu Çılgın Türkler* ('Those Mad Turks') by Turgut Özakman, published in April 2005 which achieved 292 editions by March 2006, the Turkish War of Independence is seen as 'a holy war.'[43] (The same belongs to the battles against PKK. In all reports of the Turkish press, the roles of the good, the soldiers, and the bad, the terrorists, are *a priori* defined.) Last but not least, the third breach of taboo is that the protagonist Armanoush, an Armenian, was raised by 'some Turk named Mustafa.' She doesn't know, but the readers know, that the protagonist Mustafa is a raper. The clue of the novel is that the Armenian Armanoush travels from the diaspora in the USA to Turkey, the homeland of the genocide, and becomes a friend of Asya, the Turkish bastard.

The most famous intellectual who was accused for having 'offended the Turkish identity' was Orhan Pamuk. His offence was that he said in an interview in *Das Magazin*, a weekly supplement to a number of Swiss daily newspapers, that 'we Turks are responsible for the death of 30 thousand Kurds and a million Armenians and no-one in Turkey dares speak about it, except me.'[44]

The interview was conducted on 6 February 2005. At that time, Pamuk had published seven novels and was already a famous writer in Turkey. His statements and all what he was doing in public were therefore monitored with close attention. Since the announcement of the Nobel Prize in Literature on 12 October 2006, Pamuk evoked an even larger degree of publicity. However, this does not mean that the Turkish people are proud of Pamuk. On the day of the announcement, the daily newspaper *Hürriyet* ('freedom') headlined: 'An Armenian shadow falls on Nobel.'[45] According to survey results published in *Milliyet* ('Nationality') on 4 December 2006, only 20.9 % take the view that Pamuk received the prize rightly.[46]

In opposite to his statement in *Das Magazin*, Pamuk's novels do not reflect politically charged ethnic themes as the Armenian or Kurdish conflict. Although the plot of his seventh novel *Kar*, published in 2002 (English translation, 'Snow,' published in 2004) is set in Kars, none of his protagonists is either Armenian or Kurdish. This is amazing, as Kars is a city close to the border to Armenia with Armenian and Kurdish influences. In this respect, there is a certain discrepancy between Pamuk's political statements in public and his literary work. The personal of Pamuk's novels is always and exclusively Turkish. A debate with Armenians does not take place.

Turkey's intellectuals concentrate primarily on individual freedom rights, not on ethnic rights. Dink's demand that Turkey has to 'put an end to coercive assimilation of all minorities' remains a task for the future.[47] It is no accident that Dink was the only one of the accused who was sentenced under Article 301.

6. The Involvement of the 'Deep State'

The complaints against Dink, Şafak and Pamuk were almost exclusively presented by Kemal Kerinçsiz. This lawyer founded the 'Great Union of Jurists' which he heads. Kerinçsiz and his association represent, as Ionnis N. Grigoriadis states, 'a new wave of nationalist mobilization against liberal intellectuals and minorities.'[48] The legal battle is fought between these two parties. At least in the legal area, the non-nationalistic intellectuals were bolstered up. On 26 January 2008, Kerinçsiz was arrested in simultaneous police raids against the Ergenekon *gang*.[49] Then nationalistic movement came under suspicion of conspiracy (nevertheless, it seems that the investigation is just another 'government's suppression mechanism against its opposition').[50]

The Ergenekon gang, named after the legendary retreat of the *Göktürk* ('Sky Turks'), was blamed to plan 'a coup d'état for 2009' with 'the purpose of creating chaos in the country and thus an atmosphere suitable for a military takeover.'[51]

In this context, it is important to remember that the Turkish republic is built by the military in a War of Independence. The importance of the military as the guarantee of the state is still visible even in the expression of non-military associations. Just one example: a poster of the Aydın Chess District Representative in 2009 shows Atatürk in front of marching soldiers saying 'The Turkish nation loves its armed forces; and regards it as the preserver of its ideals.'[52]

The fear of the nationalists and the military as well as the bulk of the population is still that Turkey could be split and fall apart. This scenario is worked out in the novel *Metal Fırtına* ('The Metal Storm'), published in winter/spring 2004/2005 by Orkun Uçar and Burak Turna. In this paradigmatic fiction, US forces invade Turkey in 2007 in order to 'divide Turkey between Greece and Armenia and also allow for the emergence of a Kurdish state.'[53] The importance and effect of the book on the public is shown by the fact that it 'sold about 500,000 copies.'[54]

It is obvious that the year 2005 marks a turning point in the debate between the nationalists and their opponents. On the one hand Dink and his supporters (as Şafak and Pamuk) published columns and novels and gave interviews. Concomitant with this, they challenged the powerful. On the other hand, the nationalists faced the challenge and reacted. They wanted to prosecute these *crimes* and discovered a powerful ally, the law. The increase of the liberality in the group of intellectuals of the more left-leaning opposition resulted in even more accentuated expressions of the nationalist movement.

7. Dink - A Tragic Hero

In the hours after Dink's murder, hundreds gathered spontaneously in Istanbul's central Taksim Square. In the evening they marched from there to Dink's office in Şişli chanting: 'We are all Armenians! We are all Hrant Dink!' On 23 January 2007, more than 100,000 people escorted Dink's coffin repeating the same slogans 'We are all Armenians! We are all Hrant Dink!'

The solidarity Dink did not receive in his lifetime was shown for him after his death. Taner Akçam, one of Dink's close friends, is convinced that the intellectuals marched as they felt ashamed. Pamuk expressed his concern in a similar way. One day after his murder, he visited Dink's family to express his condolences.

Dink's death did not change the fundamental convictions. The clash within the Turkish society, described by Şafak as 'a collision between those who are state-oriented and those who are civil-society oriented' is going on.[55]

Looking at Dink's life, it becomes clear that he played the role of a tragic hero. The conflict between the state and its authorities and the intellectuals who demand individual minority rights manifested itself in his person.

At the first time, Dink rebelled against the putschists. Referring to Emile Zola - who wrote on 13 January 1898 an open letter to the President of the French Republic, Félix Faure, in which he used several times the phrase 'J'accuse!' - Dink wrote in 1999 in an article in which he remembered his post-putsch experiences of 1980.[56]

> I accuse! We have been expelled from the model city which we had built. 1,500 children were robbed of their work and our island, our Atlantis, has been taken away.[57]

Dink opposed against the military, the most nationalistic part of the Turkish state. Since Atatürk, the military still understands itself as guardian of the state and the nation. The term nation is connected to Islam. Although the state is based on laicism in public life, Islam is the preferred religion in private life. As nearly all Turks are Muslim, the affiliation to Islam guarantees unity, but the permission of non-Islamic beliefs and conceptions could generate separatism. This is the reason, why '*Turkish*ness' (*Türk*-lük) plays such an important role in the Penal Code (instead of the term *Türkiye*-lilik, 'affiliation to *Turkey*' as a country, as Dink preferred).[58]

Dink was an intellectual by occupation.[59] He used his newspaper and his status to make his opinions public as editor, journalist and speaker at human rights conferences. In this regard he acted as a public intellectual. His intention was to make the public aware of the fact that (1) in Turkey not only Turks are living, but also people of other ethnic origin, religion, etc., and (2) that these people, although they are different from Turks, feel as Turkish citizens. Dink expressed this opinion mostly as a single individual. Dink did not feel and act as an 'organic intellectual.'[60] He looked at the world almost exclusively from an ethnic point of view and did not concentrate on social aspects. Ethnic and religious minorities in Turkey feel themselves intimidated and repressed. Only brave individuals like Dink dare to rebel. These individuals live in danger (as the Dink case shows).[61] They have to act mostly isolated, as they can build only on solidarity of other individuals, e.g. 'traditional intellectuals' (as Antonio Gramsci would call them), but cannot build on solidarity of well-organized communities within the country.[62]

Another case is the murder of Abdi İpekçi on 1 February 1979 in Nişantaşı, Istanbul. İpekçi (like Dink) acted as editor in chief and journalist.[63] As he 'turned away from nationalistic intolerance to help build bridges between Turkish and Greek journalists [...., he] became honoured among journalists in both countries.'[64] In 2000 he received the title of 'World Press Freedom Hero.'[65] Nevertheless, for a lot of people in Turkey (state authorities included), İpekçi was no hero, this honour was given to his murder. So, Mehmet Ali Ağca who killed İpekçi and became well known as the assassin of Pope John Paul II (on 13 May 1981) was invited for an interview on TRT - that calls itself 'Turkey's 'first' and 'only' public broadcasting corporation' - on 15 November 2010.[66] Ağca was introduced as 'innocent' - the murder of İpekçi was not even mentioned - and was offered the possibility to tell his side of the story of the assassination without any critical word of objection. According to Ağca the assassination was ordered by the Vatican itself. Commentator Karen Krüger concludes rightly: TRT 'has made Christian conspiracy theories circulating in the country socially acceptable.'[67] Nationalistic campaigns are still not only tolerated, but supported and (sometimes) also forced by the state. Even Prime Minister Erdoğan justified the invitation and interview of Ağca.[68]

Reflecting the last eight years from the perspective of the anti-nationalistic intellectual movement, the year 2005 can be marked as the year of confrontation between Turkish nationalists who insist on the ideal of homogeneity and intellectuals who see the reality and future of Turkey more diverse. Two years later, the confrontation turned to hate. The murder of Dink in 2007 happened on hatred and desire for vengeance. In retrospect, the year 2007 can be called the year of shame.

8. Possibilities for Change

On the occasion of the 10th anniversary of the founding of Agos, Dink listed the following five achievements: (1) 'the problems of our [Armenian] community became problems of the Turkish public;' (2) 'Armenians in Turkey can express their identity without fear;' (3) whenever our history is 'wrongly presented, we correct it;' (4) we make it abundantly clear that 'we, as all other people, have the right on politics;' and (5) we are 'recognized by the democracies of other countries.'[69]

In retrospect it is to say that Dink was too optimistic, as we worked out in this article.

Nevertheless, the year 2009 can be seen as a year of possible change. On 6 September 2008, President Abdullah Gül went to Yerevan to watch a football match between Turkey and Armenia in order to qualify for the 2010 FIFA World Cup. Despite of all historical grievances and against the opposition's resistance, Gül accepted an invitation by the president of Armenia, Serge Sargsyan.[70] It was the first ever visit of a president of Turkey to Armenia.

In December 2008 a group of at first 200 Turkish intellectuals published the following apology:

> [m]y conscience does not accept the insensitivity showed to and the denial of the Great Catastrophe that the Ottoman Armenians were subjected to in 1915. I reject this injustice and for my share, I empathize with the feelings and pain of my Armenian brothers and sisters. I apologize to them.[71]

By March 2009, this petition has been signed already by over 30,000 Turks around the world.[72]

Gül's *football diplomacy* achieved at least some concrete political results. On 10 October 2009, the foreign ministers of Turkey and Armenia signed two protocols on establishing diplomatic ties and developing relations between the two countries.[73]

These protocols could be an important step towards the fulfillment of one of Dink's dreams. As Taner Akçam reported about his last talks with Dink, it was Dink's wish to open the borders in order to bring the people together. He believed that the offsetting of misconduct (in the past) is not as important as a mutual understanding (now). Today, Armenians do not know much about Turkey and Turks know almost nothing about Armenia. This is to be changed. The Islamic politicians from the AKP and the anti-nationalistic intellectuals try this challenging way. They deserve our support.

9. Dink's 'Public Intellectual:' Importance of the Personal Route

Comparing to other concepts of intellectuals working in public and producing applied knowledge, Dink's case shows a unique way to form novelty in public views and transform the existing discourse.

In this part of the book other authors elaborate different concepts of public intellectuals influenced by the contexts wherever they appear to act. Thus, Sechaba Mahlomaholo and Vhonani Netshandama present a public intellectual who is placed in the shaky crossroad position in-between class interests: privileges of bourgeois academic position on the one hand and powerlessness and poverty of the underclass on the other.[74] Dink occupied an individual position, and he didn't openly acknowledge his work as ideological and overtly political. Moreover the 'subaltern' public intellectuals do not lead, as Mahlomaholo and Netshandama state, to such risks to personal well-being as Dink's private initiative caused, for their research work is in tandem with the intents of the national agenda.

Tunde Adeleke's paper is relevant for more comparison with Dink's case, for he has worked out another personified image of a public intellectual, i.e. Walter Rodney as a 'Guerrilla intellectual' (GI) based on the conviction that a 'black intellectual' has to consider 'the experiences of the masses.'[75] In opposite to Dink who saw himself as part of the Armenian *minority* in modern Turkey, Rodney saw himself as part of the black *majority* in African countries like Guyana and Tanzania. In this respect the mode of grounding with the common people in these two 'hypostases' of the intellectuals differs. Although both intellectuals reflected on their societies from the view of the underprivileged in order to improve and strengthen their self-confidence, their concepts and tactics had to differ. (Ethnic) minorities tend to emphasize on the individual and its individuality in order to distance themselves from the others. Dink acted just as a journalist who expressed his private believes and ideas. He felt very sceptical about all kind of wider associations of his activity with any political forces. In opposite, the encouragement of a suppressed majority needs to identify and pursue their common interest. Rodney tried to (re)vitalize the black as *the* majority. In this regard Rodney had to see himself and act as an organic intellectual. Although the GI concept aims at the encouragement of individuals, single persons, the change in and of power predominantly needs the engagement of these individuals, the more the better, to become united and to act as a powerful pressure group.

Therefore, such examples as Dink and Rodney manifest the role of a public intellectual that work in and for the public, but accentuate different concepts and approaches of encouragement. It is important to consider the difference in intention between being and playing part of a minority or a majority, as this decision is the basis for all further tactics and co-operation. Dink stood by himself operating an intellectual professional practice, applying his status and skills to produce different discourse with the help of the printed, the *seed of words*. His main goal was to be the heard voice of the silenced ethnic minority. This role requires thoroughly thought-out individual ethical, ethnical, social position, but lacks engagement into the social network. The tragedy of his death resembles the tradition of individual sacrifice in the conditions when a wider social movement is impossible.

Dink's case shows how difficult it is for an intellectual to act independently in public, at least in repressive societies like modern Turkey. Modern Turkey till today is a *closed society* that understands itself still as the nation of Turks - wherever they live. Turkish is everyone who is a Turk and a Sunni, as all Turks are Sunnis by tradition. It was Dink's concern, his crime and his lasting legacy that he broke with this tradition.

In order to introduce his new paradigm of diversity, Dink could not hide himself behind others, behind a group of people, e.g. the Armenians. He could not insist on being just an Armenian, as he did not wish to be seen as some*thing* different (in comparison with the majority). He wished to be seen first of all as a person, an individual, a citizen. For him it was important to change the paradigm of society building from the principle of homogeneity (*one* state, *one* nation, *one* religion) to the principle of individuality.

Due to the traditions of (modern) Turkey, Turkish people cannot decide to be self-determined. There is always someone who has to be asked as he (she) has the right to decide about you. Dink broke this tradition, as he insisted on his autonomy. He never said '*we* Armenians,' he said '*me* as an Armenian.' In this regard Dink was hated by all traditionalists. Even the Armenian communities were not happy with him, as he criticized their main concern that the Turks have to admit their guilt. Dink, instead, said that the recognition of the genocide will not solve any problem as long as the people (as individuals) on both sides will not learn from the past and behave and act accordingly - as individuals and not as *a* Turk or *an* Armenian, etc.

Dink did not see himself and did not act as an *organic intellectual*. In order to break with the traditional nation building paradigm of modern Turkey he tried to introduce a totally different paradigm based on the principle of the enlightenment. Dink did not act as an *organ* of a social group; he acted as a private person with its own, independent ideas, beliefs and hopes. Nevertheless, he also sought the company of other self-confident individuals who shared his interest in running a bilingual, Armenian-Turkish newspaper.

Dink was recognized by the public most of all as an offender, Dink was stylized by the prosecution as an enemy of Turkishness. Due to the prosecution's beliefs, he as - somehow - Armenian could not be an *organic* part of Turkey. Dink was declared non-*organic*. Dink's murder effected spontaneous solidarity with Dink *as a person*. The protestors against his murder demonstrated against the murder of an individual. Their slogans - 'We are all Armenians,' 'We are all Hrant Dink' - showed that they understood Dink's *existential* approach. For two, three days the demonstrators expressed their belief that it is not important to be a Turk or an Armenian or something else; instead it is important to be a person and to act as a person (and not as someone of this or that group).

Dink acted as an individual, but he also believed in Turkey as an *open society* in which Turks and Armenians, Sunnis and Christians can live in peace. In this regard he can be seen even as an anti-*organic* intellectual. He did not believe in a society built by (antagonistic) social groups like Armenians and Turks, Sunnis and Christians. He could not (and did not) define the function of the society's *organs*. He saw the ambivalence in his actions: he wanted to be seen as a *pigeon*, but he knew that he can influence and maybe change the public opinion only by provoking the public. This dichotomy he could not bridge. The *organs* of the state reacted to Dink's personal attacks respectively hard; and finally he was murdered (with knowledge and acceptance of the state authorities).[76]

Notes

[1] The first biography of Hrant Dink, written by Tuba Çandar, appeared recently (T. Çandar, *Hrant*, Everest Yayınları, Istanbul, 2010).
[2] S. Rosenkranz, 'Sprachrohr der Unsichtbaren', *Stern Online*, 19 January 2007, Viewed on 25 January 2010, <http://www.stern.de/kultur/buecher/henri-nannen-preis-sprachrohr-der-unsichtbaren-560802.html>.
[3] K. Karakaşlı, 'Hrant Dink, der Mensch hinter den Texten', *Von der Saat der Worte*, G. Seufert (ed), Verlag Hans Schiler, Berlin, 2008, p. 18.
[4] His writings for Agos are published by the Hrant Dink Foundation, <http://www.hrantdink.org/yazilar.asp>. The most of these articles are translated into German, but only a few into English.
[5] 'We have defined as intellectuals - that is, people whose work begins and ends with ideas' (T. Sowell, *Intellectuals and Society*, Basic Books, New York, 2009, p. 289).
[6] Article 301 replaced Article 159 of the old penal code which came into effect in 1926 and was amended seven times. (B. Algan, 'The Brand New Version of Article 301 of Turkish Penal Code and the Future of Freedom of Expression Cases in Turkey', *German Law Journal*, Vol. 9(12), 2008, p. 2237).
[7] H. Dink, 'A Pigeon-like Unease of Spirit', *OpenDemocracy*, 22 January 2007, Viewed on 25 January 2010, <http://www.opendemocracy.net/democracy-turkey/pigeon_4271.jsp>; H. Dink, 'The Pigeon-like Unease of My Inner Spirit', *Qantara.de*, Viewed on 25 January 2010, <http://en.qantara.de/webcom/show_article.php/_c-476/_nr-714/i.html>.

[8] Ü. Bilgen-Reinart, 'Hrant Dink: Forging an Armenian Identity in Turkey', *openDemocracy*, 7 February 2006, Viewed on 25 January 2010, <http://www.opendemocracy.net/democracy-turkey/dink_3246.jsp>.
[9] Ibid.
[10] F. Corley, 'Hrant Dink: Armenian Champion in Turkey', *The Independent on Sunday*, 22 January 2007, Viewed on 25 January 2010, <http://www.independent.co.uk/news/obituaries/hrant-dink-433200.html>.
[11] Ibid.
[12] 'in an interview with *Azg,* Dink is quoted as having stated: 'I said during the conference that I am an Armenian, I am no Turk, I am merely a Turkish citizen' (Tall Armenian Tale, 'The Other Side of the Falsified Genocide: An Analysis of Contemporary Armenian Loyalty', *Tall Armenian Tale*, Viewed on 12 November 2010, <http://www.tallarmeniantale.com/Loyalty.htm>).
[13] Sowell, op. cit., p. 285.
[14] Dink, *Von der Saat...*, op. cit., p. 121.
[15] Corley, op. cit.
[16] The Guardian Agencies in Ankara, 'Fury after Police Pictured Posing with Dink Murder Suspect', *GuardianOnline*, 03 February 2007, Viewed on 11 November 2010, <http://www.guardian.co.uk/world/2007/feb/03/turkey.international>.
[17] Ibid.
[18] Günter Seufert is maybe the only expert who focuses on the quasi-familial relationships among Turks, but he restricts this pattern to '*Ağabeyler* und *Hocalar,*' as he works out just the leadership principle (G. Seufert, *Café Istanbul*, Verlag C.H. Beck, München 1997, pp. 31-37).
[19] In line with this conviction, Prime Minister Recep Tayyip Erdoğan called the Turks living in Germany in his speech in Köln on 10 February 2008, 'our citizens' (WeltOnline, 'Das sagte Ministerpräsident Erdogan in Köln', *Welt Online*, 11 February 2008, Viewed on 12 November 2010, <http://www.welt.de/debatte/article1660510/Das_sagte_Ministerpraesident_Erdogan_in_Koeln.html>.
[20] C. Morris, 'Turkey: Angry Man of Europe', *BBC News*, 2 February 2001, viewed on 24 February 2011, <http://news.bbc.co.uk/europe/1150522.stm>.
[21] D. Dumoulin, 'Sunuş',D. Dumoulin (ed), *Atatürk'ten Düşünceler*, Viewed on 24 February 2011, <turkoloji.cu.edu.tr/ATATURK/Atatürk'ten%20Düşünceler.doc>, p. 2.
[22] Welt Online, 'Das sagte Ministerpräsident Erdogan in Köln', op. cit.
[23] A. Durak, 'Ebru. Reflections of Cultural Diversity in Turkey', *Ebru Project*, Viewed on 19 November 2010, <http://www.ebruproject.com/EN/theproject.asp>.
[24] Dink, *Von der Saat...*, op. cit., p. 75.

[25] 'You can play the hero only for yourself' (Ibid., p. 166).
[26] Ibid., p. 171.
[27] Ibid., p. 62.
[28] Ibid., p. 63.
[29] M. Keunen, 'Cartoons Illustrate Lack of Press Freedom in Turkey', *NRCHandelsblad*, 4 February 2009, Viewed on 2 February 2010, <http://www.nrc.nl/international/Features/article2134063./Cartoons_illusae_lack_of_press_freedom_in_Turkey>.
[30] International Freedom of eXchange, 'Two Sentenced for 'Insulting Turkishness' as European Court Rules Against Turkey', *IFEX*, 16 October 2007, Viewed on 25 January 2010, <http://www.ifex.org/turkey/2007/10/16/two_sentenced_for_insulting_turkishness>.
[31] Ibid.
[32] Extramücadele, 'Ne... Eermeniyem diyen', *Extramücadele / Extrastruggle*, Viewed on 24 February 2011, <http://www.extramucadele.com/default.asp?RID=370&sira=0&KID=21>.
[33] J. Szajer, *Unity in Diversity: Proposal for the Representation of National and Ethnic Minorities in the Institutional System of the European Union Committee of National and Ethnic Minorities (CONEM)*, Brussels, 26 February 2003, <http://register.consilium.europa.eu/pdf/en/03/cv00/cv00580.en03.pdf>.
[34] The most famous case is Nâzım Hikmet, one of the most famous Turkish poets. He was imprisoned in Turkey long years, fled to Moscow and was stripped of his nationality in 1951 because of his communist views. Surprisingly he regained his citizenship in January 2009 (A. Flood, 'Turkish Poet Nazim Hikmet Regains Citizenship', *Guardian Online*, 7 January 2009, Viewed on 18 November 2010, <http://www.guardian.co.uk/books/2009/jan/07/turkey-nazim-hikmet>).
[35] R. Lea, 'In Istanbul, a Writer Awaits her Day in Court', *Guardian Online*, 24 July 2006, Viewed on 25 January 2010, <http://www.guardian.co.uk/books/2006/jul/24/fiction.voicesofprotest>.
[36] O. Leonidas, 'Freedom of Expression in Contemporary Turkey: Beyond Article 301', *ELIAMEP Blogs*, 2 September 2009, Viewed on 25 January 2010, <http://blogs.eliamep.gr/en/oikonoleon/freedom-of-expression-in-contemporary-turkey-beyond-article-301/>.
[37] BBC News, 'Top Novelist Acquitted in Turkey', *BBC News*, 21 September 2006, Viewed on 25 January 2010, <http://news.bbc.co.uk/2/hi/europe/5366446.stm>.
[38] S. Rainsford, 'Turkish Novelist Case collapses', *BBC News, Istanbul*, 21 September 2006, Viewed on 25 January 2010, <http://news.bbc.co.uk/2/hi/europe/5366048.stm>.

[39] S. Kleid, 'Elif Safak: The Bastard of Istanbul' (Book Review), *KQED Public Media for Northern CA*, 27 March 2007, Viewed on 25 January 2010, <http://www.kqed.org/arts/literature/article.jsp?essid=14802>.
[40] Fowler, op. cit.; R. Lea, op. cit.
[41] E. Shafak, *Bastard of Istanbul*, Penguin Books, London, 2007, pp. 53-54.
[42] A. Chrisafis, 'Turkey Warns France over Armenian Genocide Bill', *Guardian Online*, Viewed on 25 January 2010, <http://www.guardian.co.uk/world/2006/oct/11/turkey.eu>.
[43] I.N. Grigoriadis, *Upsurge amidst Political Uncertainty: Nationalism in Post-2004 Turkey*, SWP Research Paper, Stiftung Wissenschaft und Politik, German Institute for International and Security Affairs, Berlin, 2006, p. 13, Viewed on 25 January 2010, <http://www.swp-berlin.org/common/get_document.php?asset_id=3380>.
[44] G. Othman, 'Orhan Pamuk, the Armenian Genocide and Turkish Nationalism', *AsiaNews*, 18 May 2009, Viewed on 25 January 2010, <http://www.asianews.it/index.php?l=en&art=15272>.
[45] Hürriyet İnternet Okurları, 'Nobel'e 'Ermeni' Gölgesi düştü', *Hürriyet*, 12 October 2006, Viewed on 25 January 2010, <http://www.hurriyet.com.tr/gundem/5246961.asp?m=1&gid=112&srid=3428&oid=1>.
[46] ISTANBUL Milliyet, 'Türkiye'nin NOBEL Yorumu', *Milliyet Online*, 4 December 2006, Viewed on 25 January 2010, <http://209.85.229.132/searchq=cache:XJ63NI-MvegJ:www.milliyet.com.tr/2006/12/04/guncel/agun.html>.
[47] H. Dink, 'I Have the Right to Die in the Country I Was Born in', *Bilkent University*, 25 January 2007, Viewed on 26 January 2010, <http://www.bilkent.edu.tr/~crs/hrantdink.htm> (the journalist's last interview he granted to Ellen Rudnitsky and Mirko Schwanitz, International Organization of Journalists, two days before he was murdered).
[48] Grigoriadis, op. cit., p. 15.
[49] Today's Zaman Istanbul, 'Ergenekon Coup Planner called Army Friends for Help', *Today's Zaman, E-Gazette*, 30 January 2008, Viewed on 22 January 2010, <http://209.85.229.132/search?q=cache:tWtACF7Cma4J:www.todayszaman.com/tz-web/>.
[50] B. Gürdoğan, 'Turkey's Ergenekon Investigation: A Political Witch-Hunt', *The Comment Factory*, 1 November 2010, Viewed on 17 November 2010, <http://www.thecommentfactory.com/turkey%E2%80%99s-ergenekon-investigation-a-political-witch-hunt-3813>.
[51] Today's Zaman Istanbul, 'Ergenekon Coup Planner called Army Friends for Help', op. cit.
[52] Aydın Satranç İl Temsilciliği, '30 Ağustos Zafer Bayramı Turnuvası', *Aydın Satranç İl Temsilciliği*, 30 August 2009, Viewed on 26 January 2010, <http://www.aydinsatranciltemsilciligi.com>.

[53] Grigoriadis, op. cit., pp. 13-14.
[54] Ibid., p. 14.
[55] E. Shafak, 'There is no Clash of Civilizations', *Qantara.de*, 2005, Viewed on 26 January 2010, <http://www.qantara.de/webcom/show_article.php/_c-476/_nr-459/i.html>.
[56] D. Bering, *Die Intellektuellen. Geschichte eines Schimpfwortes*. Clett-Cotta im Ullstein Taschenbuch, Frankfurt a.M., Berlin & Wien, 1982, p. 36.
[57] Dink, *Von der Saat...*, op. cit., p. 35.
[58] Ibid., p. 173.
[59] Sowell, op. cit., p. 2.
[60] The term 'organic intellectual' dates back to Antonio Gramsci's 'distinction between intellectuals as an organic category of every fundamental social group and intellectuals as a traditional category' (A. Gramsci, 'The Intellectuals', *Selections from the Prison Notebooks*, International Publishers, New York, 2010, p. 15).
[61] The Committee to Protect Journalists lists 20 cases of journalists murdered in direct reprisal for their work since 1992 (Committee to Protect Journalist, '20 Journalists killed in Turkey since 1992/Motive confirmed', *Committee to Protect Journalists*, Viewed on 19 November 2010, <http://www.cpj.org/killed/mideast/turkey>).
[62] A. Gramsci, 'The Intellectuals', and 'State and Civil Society', *Selections...*, op. cit.
[63] Another important case is the murder of the well respected and very influential investigative journalist Uğur Mumcu who died on 24 January 1993 outside his home in Ankara when the C-4 plastic bomb placed in his car exploded. Another journalist, Ahmet Taner Kışlalı, who also worked for the newspaper *Cumhuriyet*, was killed by an explosive device placed on his car on 21 October 1999. (International Press Institute, 'Ahmet Taner Kislali', *The Global Network for a Free Media*, Viewed on 19 November 2010, <http://www.freemedia.at/our-activities/justice-denied/impunity/ahmet-taner-kislali>).
[64] International Press Institute, 'Abdi Ipekci, Turkey: World Press Freedom Hero (honoured in 2000)', *The Global Network for a Free Media*, Viewed on 17 November 2010, <http://www.freemedia.at/awards/abdi-ipekci>.
[65] Ibid.
[66] TRT, 'A Brief Overview', *TRT*, Viewed on 17 November 2010, <http://www.trt.net.tr/generic/sayfatasarimigoster.aspx?taslakkodu=20f7fd62-42d2-4a41-ae30-129a363f6ae0&dil=en>.
[67] K. Krüger, 'Der Vatikan stecke selbst dahinter', *Frankfurter Allgemeine Zeitung Online*, 15 November 2010, Viewed on 17 November 2010, <http://www.faz.net/s/Rub510A2EDA82CA4A8482E6C38BC79C4911/Doc

~ECFD2DE0FB8E74C7F899E34E566812356~ATpl~Ecommon~Scontent.ht ml>.
[68] Ibid.
[69] Dink, *Von der Saat*…, op. cit., p. 180.
[70] M. Zambak, 'Football Diplomacy between Ankara and Yerevan', *Asia News*, 9 May 2008, Viewed on 26 January 2010, <http://www.asianews.it/php?l=en&art=13141>.
[71] Destekleyenler, 'Ermenilerden Özür diliyorum', *özür diliyorum*, December 2008, Viewed on 26 January 2010, <http://www.ozurdiliyoruz.com>.
[72] A. Gakavian, 'A Genocide, a Turkish Apology and an Armenian Thank You', *Garoon Monthly*, Sydney, March 2009, Viewed on 26 January 2010, <http://www.realchange.nareg.com.au/documents/Armenian_TurkishRelations_2009Feb.pdf>.
[73] Auswärtiges Amt, 'A New Chapter in Turkish-Armenian Relations', *Auswärtiges Amt*, 12 October 2009, Viewed on 26 January 2010, <http://www.auswaertiges-amt.de/diplo/en/Laenderinformationen/Armenien/091012-tuerkei-armenien-annaeherung,navCtx=34882.html>.
[74] S. Mahlomaholo and V. Netshandama, 'Post-Apartheid Organic Intellectual and Knowledge Creation', 2011, this volume.
[75] T. Adeleke, 'Walter A. Rodney and the Instrumentalist Construction and Utilization of Knowledge', 2011, this volume.
[76] A. Becerik, 'Wronged by the State, Not by the People', An Interview with H. Sancak, trans. H. Sancak into German and by C. Collins into English, in *Qantara.de*, 11 February 2011, Viewed on 26 February 2011, <http://www.qantara.de/webcom/show_article.php/_c-476/_nr-1467/i.html>.

Bibliography

Aarskog, B.H., 'A Constitution for Europe'. Art. I-8. *Uni Digital*. Viewed on 13 November 2010, <http://gandalf.aksis.uib.no/~brit/EU-CONST-EN-cc/TITLEI-DEFINITIONANDOBJECTIVESOFTHEUNION.html#Topic15>.

Algan, B., 'The Brand New Version of Article 301 of Turkish Penal Code and the Future of Freedom of Expression Cases in Turkey'. *German Law Journal*. Vol. 9(12), 2008, pp. 2237-2251, Viewed on 25 January 2010, <http://www.germanlawjournal.com/pdfs/Vol09No12/PDF_Vol_09_No_12_2237-2252_Developments_Algan.pdf>.

Amnesty International, 'Turkey: Article 301 is a Threat to Freedom of Expression and Must be Repealed Now!'. *Amnestyusa*. 1 December 2005, vViewed on 25 January 2010, <http://www.amnestyusa.org/document.php>.

Auswärtiges Amt, 'A New Chapter in Turkish-Armenian Relations'. *Auswärtiges Amt.* 12 October 2009, Viewed on 26 January 2010, <http://www.auswaertiges-amt.de/diplo/en/Laenderinformationen/Armenien/091012-tuerkei-armenien-annaeherung,navCtx=34882.html>.

Aydın Satranç İl Temsilciliği, '30 Ağustos Zafer Bayramı Turnuvası'. *Aydın Satranç İl Temsilciliği.* 30 August 2009, Viewed on 26 January 2010, <http://www.aydinsatranciltemsilciligi.com>.

BBC News, 'Top Novelist Acquitted in Turkey'. *BBC News.* 21 September 2006, Viewed on 25 January 2010, <http://news.bbc.co.uk/2/hi/europe/5366446.stm>.

Becerik, A., 'Wronged by the State, Not by the People'. An Interview with H Sancak. *Qantara.de.* 11 February 2011, Viewed on 26 February 2011, <http://www.qantara.de/webcom/show_article.php/_c-476/_nr-1467/i.html>.

Bering, D., *Die Intellektuellen. Geschichte eines Schimpfwortes.* Clett-Cotta im Ullstein Taschenbuch, Frankfurt a.M., Berlin & Wien, 1982.

Bilgen-Reinart, Ü., 'Hrant Dink: Forging an Armenian Identity in Turkey'. *openDemocracy,* 7 February 2006, Viewed on 25 January 2010, <http://www.opendemocracy.net/democracy-turkey/dink_3246.jsp>.

Çandar, T., *Hrant.* Everest Yayınları, Istanbul, 2010.

Chrisafis, A., 'Turkey Warns France over Armenian Genocide Bill'. *Guardian Online.* Viewed on 25 January 2010, <http://www.guardian.co.uk/world/2006/oct/11/turkey.eu>.

Committee to Protect Journalists, '20 Journalists Killed in Turkey since 1992/Motive Confirmed'. *Committee to Protect Journalists.* Viewed on 19 November 2010, <http://www.cpj.org/killed/mideast/turkey>.

Corley, F., 'Hrant Dink: Armenian Champion in Turkey'. *The Independent on Sunday.* 22 January 2007, Viewed on 25 January 2010, <http://www.independent.co.uk/news/obituaries/hrant-dink-433200.html>.

Destekleyenler, 'Ermenilerden Özür diliyorum'. *Özür diliyorum.* December 2008, Viewed on 26 January 2010, <http://www.ozurdiliyoruz.com>.

Dink, H., 'A Pigeon-like Unease of Spirit'. *OpenDemocracy*. 22 January 2007, Viewed on 25 January 2010, <http://www.opendemocracy.net/demo cracy-turkey/pigeon_4271.jsp>.

——, 'I Have the Right to Die in the Country I Was Born In'. *Bilkent University*. 25 January 2007, Viewed on 26 January 2010, <http://www.bil kent.edu.tr/~crs/hrantdink.htm>.

——, 'The Pigeon-Like Unease of My Inner Spirit'. *Qantara.de*. Viewed on 25 January 2010, <http://en.qantara.de/webcom/show_article.php/_c-476/_nr-714/i.html>.

——, 'The Water finds its Crack: an Armenian in Turkey'. *OpenDemocracy*. 19 January 2009, Reprint from 13 December 2005, Viewed on 26 January 2010, <http://www.opendemocracy.net/democracy-turkey/europe_turkey_armenia_3118.jsp>.

——, *Von der Saat der Worte*. Verlag Hans Schiler, Berlin, 2008.

——, 'Yazılar'. Uluslararası Hrant Dink Vakfı / International Hrant Dink Foundation (ed), *Uluslararası Hrant Dink Vakfı*. Viewed on 9 November 2010, <http://www.hrantdink.org/yazilar.asp>.

Dumoulin, D., 'Sunuş'. *Atatürk'ten Düşünceler*. Viewed on 24 February 2011, <turkoloji.cu.edu.tr/ATATURK/Atatürk'ten%20Düşünceler.doc>.

Durak, A., 'Ebru: Reflections of Cultural Diversity in Turkey'. *Ebru Project*. Viewed on 19 November 2010, <http://www.ebruproject.com/EN/theproject.asp>.

Extramücadele, 'Ne... Eermeniyem diyen'. *Extramücadele / Extrastruggle*, Viewed on 24 February 2011, <http://www.extramucadele.com/default.asp?RID=370&sira=0&KID=21>.

Flood, A., 'Pamuk Insult to Turkishness Claims Return to Court'. *Guardian Online*. 15 May 2009, Viewed on 26 January 2010, <http://www.guardian.co.uk/books/2009/may/15/pamut-insult-turkishness-court>.

——, 'Turkish Poet Nazim Hikmet regains Citizenship'. *Guardian Online*. 7 January 2009, Viewed on 18 November 2010, <http://www.guardian.co.uk/books/2009/jan/07/turkey-nazim-hikmet>.

Fowler, S., 'Turkey, a Touchy Critic, Plans to Put a Novel on Trial'. *The New York Times*. 15 September 2006, Viewed on 25 January 2010, <http://www.nytimes.com/2006/09/15/world/europe/15turkey.html>.

Gakavian, A., 'A Genocide, a Turkish Apology and an Armenian Thank You'. *Garoon Monthly*. Sydney, March 2009, Viewed on 26 January 2010, <http://www.realchange.nareg.com.au/documents/Armenian_TurkishRelations_2009Feb.pdf>.

Gramsci, A., *Selections from the Prison Notebooks*. International Publishers, New York, 2010.

Grigoriadis, I.N., *Upsurge amidst Political Uncertainty, Nationalism in Post-2004 Turkey*. SWP Research Paper, Stiftung Wissenschaft und Politik, German Institute for International and Security Affairs, Berlin, 2006, Viewed on 25 January 2010, <http://www.swp-berlin.org/common/get_document.php?asset_id=3380>.

The Guardian Agencies in Ankara, 'Fury after Police Pictured Posing with Dink Murder Suspect'. *Guardian Online*. 3 February 2007, Viewed on 11 November 2010, <http://www.guardian.co.uk/world/2007/feb/03/turkey.international>.

Gürdoğan, B., 'Turkey's Ergenekon Investigation: A Political Witch-Hunt'. *The Comment Factory*. 1 November 2010, Viewed on 17 November 2010, <http://www.thecommentfactory.com/turkey%E2%80%99s-ergenekon-investigation-a-political-witch-hunt-3813>.

Hürriyet İnternet Okurları, 'Nobel'e 'Ermeni' Gölgesi düştü'. *Hürriyet*. 12 October 2006, Viewed on 25 January 2010, <http://www.hurriyet.com.tr/gundem/5246961.asp?m=1&gid=112&srid=3428&oid=1>.

International Freedom of eXchange, 'Two Sentenced for 'Insulting Turkishness' as European Court Rules Against Turkey'. *IFEX*. 16 October 2007, Viewed on 25 January 2010, <http://www.ifex.org/turkey/2007/10/16/two_sentenced_for_insulting_turkishness/>.

International Press Institute, 'Abdi Ipekci, Turkey. World Press Freedom Hero (honoured in 2000)'. *The Global Network for a Free Media*. viewed on 17 November 2010, <http://www.freemedia.at/awards/abdi-ipekci>.

——, 'Ahmet Taner Kışlalı'. *The Global Network for a Free Media*. Viewed on 19 November 2010, <http://www.freemedia.at/our-activities/justice-denied/impunity/ahmet-taner-kislali>.

ISTANBUL Milliyet, 'Türkiye'nin NOBEL Yorumu'. *Milliyet Online*. 4 December 2006, Viewed on 25 January 2010, <http://209.85.229.132/search?q=cache:XJ63NI-MvegJ:www.milliyet.com.tr2006/12/04/guncel/agun.html>.

Keunen, M., 'Cartoons illustrate Lack of Press Freedom in Turkey'. *NRC Handelsblad*. 4 February 2009, Viewed on 2 February 2010, <http://www.nrc.nl/international/Features/article2134063.ece/Cartoons_illustrate_lack_of_press_freedom_in_Turkey>.

Kleid, S., 'Elif Şafak: The Bastard of Istanbul' (Book Review). *KQED Public Media for Northern CA*. 27 March 2007, Viewed on 25 January 2010, <http://www.kqed.org/arts/literature/article.jsp?essid=14802>.

Krüger, K., 'Der Vatikan stecke selbst dahinter'. *Frankfurter Allgemeine Zeitung Online*. 15 November 2010, Viewed on 17 November 2010, <http://www.faz.net/s/Rub510A2EDA82CA4A8482E6C38BC79C4911/Doc~ECFD2DE0FB8E74C7F899E34E566812356~ATpl~Ecommon~Scontent.html>.

Lea, R., 'In Istanbul, a Writer Awaits her Day in Court'. *Guardian Online*. 24 July 2006, Viewed on 25 January 2010, <http://www.guardian.co.uk/books/2006/jul/24/fiction.voicesofprotest>.

Leonidas, O., 'Freedom of Expression in Contemporary Turkey: Beyond Article 301'. *ELIAMEP Blogs*. 2 September 2009, Viewed on 25 January 2010,<http://blogs.eliamep.gr/en/oikonoleon/freedom-of-expression-in-contemporary-turkey-beyond-article-301/>.

Milliyet, 'Sezer'den *Çılgın Türkler* Mesajı...'. *Tüm Gazeteler*. 19 March 2006, Viewed on 26 January 2010, <http://www.tumgazeteler.com/?a=140>.

Morris, C., 'Turkey: Angry Man of Europe'. *BBC News*. 2 February 2001, Viewed on 24 February 2011, <http://news.bbc.co.uk/europe/1150522.stm>.
Network of Concerned Historians, 'Campaigns, Hrant Dink'. *Network of Concerned Historians*. 2010, Viewed on 14 November 2010, <http://www.concernedhistorians.org/content_files/file/CA/48f2.pdf>.

Othman, G., 'Orhan Pamuk, the Armenian Genocide and Turkish Nationalism'. *Asia News*. 18 May 2009, Viewed on 25 January 2010, <http://www.asianews.it/index.php?l=en&art=15272>.

Pamuk, O., 'Dankesrede'. *Friedenspreis des Deutschen Buchhandels 2005. O. Pamuk, Ansprachen aus Anlass der Verleihung*. Börsenverein des Deutschen Buchhandels (ed), Börsenverein des Deutschen Buchhandels, Frankfurt am Main, 2005.

——, 'Teşekkür'. *Friedenspreis des Deutschen Buchhandels 2005, O. Pamuk, Ansprachen aus Anlass der Verleihun*. Börsenverein des Deutschen Buchhandels (ed). Börsenverein des Deutschen Buchhandels, Frankfurt am Main, 2005.

PanArmenian.Net, 'Sisli Mayor Accused of Organization of Dink Funeral with Pro-Armenian Slogans'. *Armenian Online News*. 23 February 2007, Viewed on 26 January 2010, <http://www.hamovhotov.com/timeline/401>.

Preis, H.N., 'Nominations 2006, Hrant Dink, Press Freedom'. *Henri Nannen Preis*. Viewed on 25 January 2010, <http://www.henri-nannen-reis.de/award_winners_2006.php?id=55&award=Press+Freedom>.

Rainsford, S., 'Killing of Dink Shocks Turkey'. *BBC News*. 22 January 2007, Viewed on 26 January 2010, <http://news.bbc.co.uk/2/hi/europe/419.stm>.

——, 'Turkish Novelist Case Collapses'. *BBC News. Istanbul*, 21 September 2006, Viewed on 25 January 2010, <http://news.bbc.co.uk/2/hi/europe/5366048.stm>.

Rosenkranz, S., 'Sprachrohr der Unsichtbaren'. *Stern Online*. 19 January 2007, Viewed on 25 January 2010, <http://www.stern.de/kultur/buecher/henri-nannen-preis-sprachrohr-der-unsichtbaren-560802.html>.

Szajer, J., *Unity in Diversity: Proposal for the Representation of National and Ethnic Minorities in the Institutional System of the European Union Committee of National and Ethnic Minorities (CONEM)*. Brussels, 26 February 2003, <http://register.consilium.europa.eu/pdf/en/03/cv00/cv00580.en03.pdf>.

Shafak, E., *Bastard of Istanbul*. Penguin Books, London, 2007.

——, 'In Istanbul, a Crack in the Wall of Denial, We're trying to Debate the Armenian Issue'. *The Washington Post*. 25 September 2005, Viewed on 25 January 2010, <http://www.washingtonpost.com/wp-dyn/content/article/2005/09/23/AR2005092302365.html?referrer=emailarticle>.

——, 'There Is No Clash of Civilizations'. *Qantara.de*. 2005, Viewed on 26 January 2010, <http://www.qantara.de/webcom/show_article.php/_c-476/_nr-459/i.html>.

Seufert, G., *Café Istanbul. Alltag, Religion und Politik in der modernen Türkei*. Verlag C. H. Beck, München, 1997.

Sowell, T., *Intellectuals and Society*. Basic Books, New York, 2009.

Spiegel Online International, 'Turkey Drops Orhan Pamuk Trial, Avoiding EU Condemnation'. *Spiegel Online*. 23 January 2006, Viewed on 26 January 2010, <http://www.spiegel.de/international/0,1518,396786,00.html>.

Today's Zaman Istanbul, 'Ergenekon Coup Planner Called Army Friends for Help'. *Today's Zaman, E-Gazette*. 30 January 2008, Viewed on 22 January 2010, <http://209.85.229.132/search?q=cache:tWtACFtodayszaman.com/tz-web/>.

TRT, 'A brief Overview'. *TRT*. Viewed on 17 November 2010, <http://www.trt.net.tr/generic/sayfatasarimigoster.aspx?taslakkodu=20f7fd62-42d2-4a41-ae30-129a363f6ae0&dil=en>.

Welt Online, 'Das sagte Ministerpräsident Erdogan in Köln'. *Welt Online*. 11 February 2008, Viewed on 12 November 2010, <http://www.welt.de/debatte/article1660510/Das_sagte_Ministerpraesident_Erdogan_in_Koeln.html>.

Zambak, M., 'Football Diplomacy between Ankara and Yerevan'. *Asia News*. 9 May 2008, Viewed on 26 January 2010, <http://www.asianews.it/index.php?l=en&art=13141>.

Zaptçioğlu, D., 'Der verlorene Sohn, Pamuk und die Türken'. *Spiegel Online*. 13 October 2006, Viewed on 26 January 2010, <http://www.spiegel.de/ultur/literatur/0,1518,442333,00.html>.

Not a Sin, but a Side Effect: Collaboration and Knowledge Creation by the Organic Intellectuals

Olga Procevska

Abstract
Collaboration between intellectuals and power is usually discussed in the contexts of authoritarian and totalitarian regimes. In most cases it is defined in diplomatic or moralistic terms (either as a technique for survival or a sin). I propose a slightly different look at the problem of collaboration that reaches beyond both contexts of repressive regimes and the interpretational dichotomy of diplomacy or morality. I believe that collaboration of intellectuals should be regarded specifically because they are engaged in essentially ideological (power-related) work - creating and disseminating knowledge. My aim in this paper is to investigate a broader set of factors surrounding the notion of collaboration, attachment, engagement and detachment, and autonomy. By considering the generally and currently important conditions of intellectual work, a new type of organic intellectual can be distinguished: one that finds itself and, to employ Mannheim's terminology, floats freely between the identity of a politically affiliated player in the life of the community and of a detached thinker and critic of the latter at the same time.

Key Words: Intellectuals, collaboration, autonomy, knowledge, community, organic intellectual.

*****

1. Introduction

Long ago Julien Benda wrote his famous manifesto on the independency of intellectuals and claimed that their distance from politics is a measuring stick of their fairness. Since then, the most important bricks in the edifice called 'the intellectual' - like truth, the nation, the public sphere, universality, objectivity - have been deconstructed, abandoned or simply have gone out of fashion. But still academic and popular discourses show a significant desire to define and self-identify intellectuals in terms of the binary opposition of autonomy, distance and counter-power (as moral obligations of the intellectual) on the one side, and collaboration and engagement (as a selfish, sinful or at least a problematic choice) on the other.[1] Thus a dissident, living and working against power is regarded as the only *right* public role of the intellectual. It is a particularly acute issue in post-socialist societies where tolerance of power or of the *status quo* is the most serious reproach for an intellectual. Inna Kochetkova, who has written on Russian intellectuals, explains it by their experience with totalitarian and authoritarian Soviet regimes, while sociologists Georg Konrád and Ivan Szelényi highlight the roots of this 'ethical-normative' approach in defining the public roles of intellectuals in theoretical Marxism.[2]

The term 'organic intellectual,' introduced by Antonio Gramsci, has been widely used to describe intellectuals, who are affiliated with a political movement or a particular social class, who do not claim the position of standing above (or aside) all society to represent the universal values, but who acknowledge their ties with the community they came from.[3]

It has been used by some to testify to their commitment to the development of their community while others have avoided it as a byword, demonstrating the complexity and vagueness of the term 'organic intellectual' and also the importance of this aspect in the identity of the intellectual. The authors of the articles in this part of the book also highlight the important portion of contradiction between 'power' and 'intellectual,' which the concept of the organic intellectual contains. Sechaba Mahlomaholo and Vhonani Netshandama define organic intellectual as a symbolic space, where 'the privileges as well as the power of bourgeois academic position on the one hand and the gaping wounds of powerlessness and poverty of the underclass on the other, meet.'[4] Tunde Adeleke replaces the 'organic intellectual' with the more specific 'Guerrilla intellectual:' 'embedded within an oppressive system and working to undermine or destroy it from within.'[5]

I have no intention of describing the history of collaboration between intellectuals and power, or resistance against it; this has been well done before.[6] I believe that the notion of collaboration has to be reinterpreted, released from the trap of the abovementioned opposition as well as from the context of authoritarianism/totalitarianism, to which it is usually applied. The issue of collaboration of intellectuals has to be reconsidered in terms of (1) the formation of the intellectual as a social construct, (2) the functions of the intellectual and (3) recent tendencies of intellectual work.

2.   **Autonomy as Ideology**

Guyanese intellectual Walter Rodney declares: the intellectual is by default an enemy of the masses until he or she proves otherwise.[7] Political philosopher Michael Walzer observed that since ancient times intellectuals (he uses the term 'social critics') developed the identity of outcast heroes. They deliberately distanced themselves from home, wandered to gain objectivity and upon their return did not regard their community as cognate. They were embarrassing strangers for these communities and therefore were hated both by the power holders and the common people. The risk of social repulsion is what constituted the heroic identity of the social critic.[8] Political scientist Stefan Auer considers that the history of ancient Greece provided a justification for distancing from politics for every generation of intellectuals ever since.[9]

However, the discourse of the autonomy of intellectuals (I would even call it a paradigm or, as Bourdieu puts it, 'in a sense the professional ideology of intellectuals') acquired its normative status in the 20th century.[10] Sociologist Raewyn Connell summarizes it as follows:

> One of the most enduring beliefs about intellectuals is that they stand in opposition to the bourgeois world. The writer starving in a garret, the prophet speaking truth to power, the laboratory scientist shut away from the world, are among our most cherished images of intellectual life. This literary idea became formative in the 20th-century sociology of intellectuals.[11]

Konrád and Szelényi point out that the development of this paradigm happened to a great extend due to the conceptualization of intellectuals *from outside*: for so long sociologists and philosophers characterized intellectuals as 'bearers of transcendence in society' that the latter gradually started to regard themselves as 'the most universal, generic type of humanity.'[12]

However, both external and self-definitions of the intellectuals as dissidents most frequently contain references not to ancient times but to the so-called Dreyfus affair.[13] It was the first well-known case when intellectuals united in a conscious political (in the broad sense of the word) action. What I consider the most important aspect of the Dreyfus affair is that intellectuals then claimed to represent universal values, and by that they also claimed a universal status for themselves - of figures standing above particular financial, political, national or social obstacles, always oppositionists of the power, guards of the truth.

Although not the only carrier of the autonomy paradigm, Julien Benda can surely be called one of its most influential representatives; therefore his beliefs deserve special attention. His book *La trahison des clercs* first appeared in the 1920s and was later re-published many times and translated into English with the title *The Betrayal of the Intellectuals* or *The Treason of the Intellectuals*. In his book Benda uses imperious statements and an exalted style to define intellectuals (whom he calls 'clerks') as people opposed to material values:

> [...] all those whose activity essentially is not a pursuit of practical aims, all those who seek their joy in the practice of an art or a science or metaphysical speculation, in short in the possession of non material advantages.[14]

According to Benda, clerks can choose between two positions in relation to political power: disinterest (Benda gives Leonardo da Vinci as an example) or criticism (like Emile Zola).[15] Benda argues that the ideal type of intellectual became extinct at the end of the 19th century when intellectuals started to relate to politics in a different way: they 'began to play the game of political passions.'[16] By 'passion' Benda means a truly deep involvement:

> [...] the clerks now exercise political passions with all the characteristics of passion - the tendency to action, the thirst for immediate results, the exclusive preoccupation with the desired end, the scorn for argument, the excess, the hatred, the fixed ideas.[17]

Political commitment has become a source of pride for intellectuals, Benda concludes: 'the modern clerk is determined to have the soul of a citizen and to make vigorous use of it; he is proud of that soul.'[18] Benda's judgment on this is categorical: political games are in no way compatible with the status of the intellectual, because when involved in politics, truth ceases to be a higher value than patriotism.[19] Benda opposes emotionality and truthful knowledge, thus the concept of 'emotional knowledge' for him has no sense. However, there are alternatives to the Bendian approach that are elaborated in *Part III* of this volume.

Russian philosopher Nikolay Berdyayev has views similar to those of Benda: he states that the preoccupation with politics, so typical of the Russian intelligentsia in 19th century, has led to a distorted attitude towards the truth (and subsequently to the failure of the intelligentsia during the Revolution of 1905):

> [...] love for equalizing justice, for the social good, for the well-being of the people has paralyzed the love for truth, almost destroyed the interest in truth. [...] The intelligentsia could not have a disinterested attitude towards philosophy, because it was selfish towards the truth itself, it demanded truth to be a weapon to change society, for social well-being and the happiness of the people.[20]

In this chapter there are several examples of an intellectual consciously choosing patriotism and political struggle.[21] In the views of Benda and Berdyayev, they betrayed the truth; in the self-conceptions of these intellectuals, using knowledge to achieve political aims is the only way not to betray the functions of the intellectual.

Benda points out that for politically engaged intellectuals, the collective identity of a particular political or social group suppresses their individualism; they regard their work not as an expression of individual concerns, dreams, aspirations and talents, but as 'a manifestation of a collective mind.'[22] Benda argues that only community intellectuals are allowed to belong to 'a corporation whose sole cult is that of justice and of truth,' because the duty of the intellectual is to be an advocate only of universal, not social group- or community-tied, values.[23]

Similarly, the founder of the sociology of knowledge, Karl Mannheim, when writing on intellectuals, also regards the attachment to the community as a defect. In his *Ideology and Utopia* he argues that the way to overcome omnipresent relativism and create all-embracing, total knowledge is synthesis: an ultimate aim of the sociology of knowledge and at the same time a sophisticated and dynamic operation that, according to Mannheim, is not suitable for every person or social group. It is a special function of the intellectuals - an 'unanchored, *relatively* (original emphasis) classless stratum.'[24] According to Mannheim, intellectuals acquire the ability to reach beyond the world-views of different social groups, perform synthesis and create totality of knowledge in the process of education when they are gradually *uprooted*, detached from their social origins.[25]

The assumption that the status of the intellectual requires a deliberate alienation from his or her origins, distancing from what the intellectual criticizes, a kind of exile (exile as an indication of the *quality* of the intellectual) was further developed by literary and social theorist Edward Said. He also builds his understanding of intellectuals on values of universalism and disassociation of their work when he defines the intellectual as someone,

> [...] whose place is to publicly raise embarrassing questions, to confront orthodoxy and dogma (rather than produce them), to be someone who cannot easily be co-opted by governments or corporations, and whose raison d'être is to represent all those people and issues that are routinely forgotten or swept under the rug. The intellectual does so on the basis of universal principles: that all human beings are entitled to expect decent standards of behavior concerning freedom and justice from worldly powers or nations, and that deliberate or inadvertent violations of these standards need to be testified and fought against courageously.[26]

This definition is already ambivalent. First, Said seems to ignore that although 'universal values' are widespread, that does not make them natural and unquestionable; they are socially constructed, contextualized and mutable over time. Second, according to Said, the independence of the intellectual is mandatory when one is talking about governments, but in relation to social movements and the like, commitment is preferable. Later Said personalizes this argument, saying that he never accepted offers to become a consultant for governments or the media, but always was glad to help social movements.[27] This brings about a discussion: if the engagement with power-holders is risky to the fairness of intellectual's judgment, then why should engagement with social movements be regarded as different?

The answer of the *opposition-as-professional-ideology-of-intellectuals* is simple: because the truth always lies outside the government. Therefore using knowledge in the political struggle is acceptable only when it is used against the ruling class and in favor of the oppressed; otherwise the intellectual commits the sin of collaboration with the power. The positions of Walter Rodney and Hrant Dink, described in the papers by Tunde Adeleke and Georg Simet respectively, are insightful examples of this ideology.

I have here consciously interconnected Benda, Mannheim and Said to show the development of the argument on the autonomy of the intellectuals from the form of imperatives and uncompromising manifestations to uncertainties, concealment and ambivalence. It is not difficult to explain: if Benda and Mannheim were writing in the context of relative stability of concepts and ideologies, then Said was already operating under postmodern conditions with the dismantling of objectivity and the triumph of diversity, uncertainty and ambiguity.

3. The Intellectual of Postmodernity

These conditions also demand a different identity and public role for the intellectual. In Zygmunt Bauman's terms, this would be the intellectual-interpreter as opposed to the intellectual-legislator.

The theory of intellectuals by sociologist Zygmunt Bauman makes a distinction between two modes of social existence and also describes two corresponding types of intellectuals: modernity and the intellectual-legislator, postmodernity and intellectual-interpreter. Modernity is characterized by order, control, rationality, hierarchy and totality.[28] The intellectual of modernity, the legislator, expresses authoritative statements that legitimate certain knowledge - defines which ones among the myriad of possible opinions are the right ones. The validity of the declarations of intellectuals is supported by their better access to knowledge than the rest of the society possesses.

Status claims based on having special knowledge are too important to the understanding of the intellectual to leave this issue without at least a short inquiry. First, it has to be remarked that, according to sociologist Pierre Bourdieu, knowledge produced by intellectuals is an essentially political matter:

> [k]nowledge of the social world and, more precisely, the categories that make it possible, are the stakes, par excellence, of political struggle, the inextricably theoretical and practical struggle for the power to conserve or transform the social world by conserving or transforming the categories through which it is perceived.[29]

Bourdieu emphasizes that intellectuals are participants in a 'symbolic struggle over the production of common sense.'[30] He explains that in this battle there are two strategies: (1) 'an *idios logos* with which an individual tries to impose his point of view while taking the risk of reciprocity' and (2) '*official nomination*, an act of symbolic imposition that has behind it all the strength of the collective, the consensus, the common sense.'[31] Bourdieu emphasizes that intellectuals are typically closer to the second than to the first extreme, because they are educated by an official system, they operate within state-maintained institutions or conventional communication channels (be they the columns in a newspaper or speeches at a demonstration), they use collectively approved qualifications and titles to underpin their status.[32] The statement of Bourdieu does not imply that discourses of intellectuals are always in consensus with the position of the power-holders; it just means that the ability of the intellectuals to speak out and be heard is potentiated collectively under the existing system of social relations.

Besides, not only intellectuals are dependent on systemic requirements, but also those who have the most power in the system are reliant on the intellectuals. As sociologist Jerome Karabel puts it, 'whatever the underlying antagonisms, the relations among economic, political, and cultural elites are under ordinary circumstances cooperative,' because

> [f]rom the perspective of those who wield political and economic power, intellectuals possess crucial specialized knowledge as well as the important ideological capacity to legitimate (or, in some cases, delegitimate) the prevailing order. And from the viewpoint of intellectuals, political and economic elites for their part control resources without which it would be difficult, if not impossible, for them to carry out their role as producers of culture.[33]

In spite of the abovementioned conditions, intellectuals like to think of themselves as living in the 'universe of pure disinterestedness, free 'commitment,'' as Bourdieu points out.[34] He contradicts this statement by saying that intellectuals are always implicitly representing somebody/something in the public sphere:

> [...] one has to take seriously the fact that intellectuals are the object of a de facto delegation, a comprehensive, tacit delegation [...] and one has to analyze the social conditions in which this delegation is received and used.[35]

Delegation, he continues, often occurs by the mechanism of identifying not with the particular discourse of the intellectual, with the content of his or her communication, but rather with the "style,' the accent, the manner, the relation to language' and other subtle characteristics of the intellectual.[36] Although the delegation is almost always unofficial and very often unconscious, intellectuals still enter the public sphere as the delegates of common worries and aspirations.

Elena Gapova, a theorist of post-communist societies, asserts, that by usurpation of the role of 'the voice of the people' and by claiming the exclusivity and importance of their knowledge, intellectuals develop the hegemony of expertise, thus creating a demand for their knowledge in policy-creating, educational and other institutions.[37] Bourdieu offers a similar notion:

> [...] intellectuals take upon themselves the usurped right to legislate in all matters in the name of a social competence that is often quite independent of the technical competence that it seems to guarantee.[38]

In turn, philosopher Michel Foucault (in a conversation with another philosopher, Gilles Deleuze) states that being a part of the power implementation system, intellectuals smother the voices of the people, prevent them from directly expressing their views by labeling their knowledge as inferior to the knowledge of experts.[39]

Elena Gapova admits that the process of usurpation is especially characteristic of post-soviet societies. To claim their status as possessors and creators of exclusive knowledge, intellectuals use their 'historical legacies, local networks, ethnic identities or social capitals of the families' - resources that come from the Soviet past but are meaningful in post-Soviet contexts, too.[40] Sociologist Michael Kennedy explains that there are two sources of the influence of intellectuals in Eastern Europe: first, the 'control over a special form of teleological knowledge,' and second, the 'historic role as leaders of East European nations.'[41] In turn Konrád and Szelényi believe that intellectuals not only in socialist countries, but always tend to masquerade their own interests as the interests of the whole society, hence maintaining their power.[42]

Sociologist Jeffrey C. Alexander presumes that the usurpation of the role of the truth teller, the guardian of the universal and absolute, is a necessary condition for an intellectual to enter the public sphere with his or her judgments. He believes that the intellectual has to 'embody the myth of universalism,' use 'the great narrative myths of our time, to sing about the possible triumph of progress, to strike the chords of national, regional and ideological myths about equality and democracy.'[43]

Bauman argues that postmodern intellectuals use their access to knowledge in a different way, adopt a different identity and thus - another public role. Postmodernity for Bauman means living within fragmented truths that are assigned to various models or praxes of living, where relativity of knowledge is not something that the intellectual should strive to overcome as in Mannheim's theory, but something that has to be accepted (and even respected) as inevitable.[44] The intellectual then becomes an interpreter who connects different models, traditions and truths. His or her function is not to be the preacher of one single truth, but the communication facilitator who can enhance understanding.[45]

The philosopher Rory J. Conces proposes a substantially similar concept of the hyperintellectual - engaged, but not partisan: 'a social critic, a political educator, and a man of action bundled in a way that is indicative of non-partisanship.'[46] According to Conces, an intellectual should be an insider as much as is needed for empathy and compassion, 'insofar as he or she cares about the society in question, a caring that is predicated on the possession of the moral virtues of courage, compassion, and a good eye.'[47]

So the concepts of disinterest and distance, autonomy and alienation are fully applicable only to the intellectual-legislator, but not to the intellectual-interpreter, to whom understanding and identification are more important. Bauman emphasizes that both modes of being an intellectual do not exclude each other; one person can assume the role of a legislator in one context and of an interpreter in another.[48]

4. **Autonomy Now**

The intellectual-interpreter can also be called a new type of organic intellectual. Political and social theorist Antonio Gramsci, the inventor of the famous concept, understood organic intellectuals as those who are aware of their embedment in the political struggle as opposed to the identity of detachment inherent to traditional intellectuals. Organic intellectuals do not claim impartiality, but acknowledge having sympathies.[49] Henceforth I will not try to interpret the theoretical position of Gramsci, but simply describe organic intellectuals as those, whose identity is based on their interconnectedness with a particular institution, community or society. I believe the concept of organic intellectual can be used beyond a Marxist perspective in a wider set of contexts than Gramsci could ever imagine, because I consider an organic intellectual as a new type, the only really possible type of intellectual today. And I will try to explain why.

First, because of the political nature of knowledge and demands of postmodernity already discussed. But also for several less global reasons. For example, theoreticians of intellectuals often tend to neglect a simple (even primitive) aspect: intellectuals have to earn a living for themselves and their families or else be supported. So the intellectual is either dependent on financial sources for her or his work or on patrons who compensate her or his detachment from financial sources. Thus, autonomous intellectuals, as philosopher Virginia Held calls them, 'Robinson Crusoe-like men accumulating possessions on intellectual islands without strong social ties' are hardly possible.[50] Held argues against Benda's idea of non-materialism of intellectuals, stating that intellectual work implies that a set of social and financial arrangements have made it possible.[51]

Intellectuals also engage in the collaboration with power in ways that are much more mundane and also subtle, and therefore much less often condemned than the passionate political commitment described by Benda. These collaborative relations are even rarely classified as 'collaboration,' allowing intellectuals to ignore their incompatibility with the ideology of autonomy and dissidence. For example, many intellectuals are employed in institutions that are established to match the specific, not universal needs: to create knowledge that can be applied in the community / the power holders. Intellectuals typically produce that knowledge in the process of continued communication between the community and intellectuals: in universities, think-tanks, advisory councils, etc. 'The state' even in liberal capitalist systems is one of the most influential determinants in funding knowledge creation, which means that decisions are regularly made on the political level. Under conditions of economic slowdown and following budget cuts, priority is usually given to those projects or institutions that are regarded as useful for the community. Sociologist E. Stina Lyon remarks that it is a common tendency in the knowledge society to strengthen the control over intellectuals, to demand 'more immediate political and economic returns for money invested in the development and dissemination of 'social knowledge.''[52] She concludes that this indicates the lack of trust in intellectuals and lessens their ability to be autonomous, free-floating.

The most obvious form of interconnectedness between the knowledge of intellectuals and the community is so-called policy-driven research, where questions are stated by policy-makers, and the researcher's task is to create knowledge (in the form of data, but more importantly - conclusions, statements and theories) for making political choices. Alternatively, as in the situation described by Sechaba Mahlomaholo and Vhonani Netshandama, research questions are dictated by the observed needs of the community and research targets the improvement of the lives of community members (specifically, it can be called community-driven research or subaltern research as Mahlomaholo and Netshandama do). Albeit to avoid the temptation to label knowledge created this way as nonobjective and thus *not real* intellectual knowledge and not to fall into the trap of simplistic and unfounded structuralist categorization, one has to acknowledge that it also carries several important risks.

These risks emerge in both the question-asking and the answer-giving stages. The essence of policy/community-driven research is that researchers are looking for the things that interest others, but not the ones that researchers themselves may find important. Usually these research questions already carry some predisposition about the state of things that emerge from prior policies. But if the answers researchers find contradict these predispositions and suggest politically difficult or disadvantageous choices for politicians, they may well be ignored. Since researchers may be aware of this risk, they may become biased, because they have to choose between providing politically acceptable knowledge and producing useless information that would be left on the shelf.[53]

Besides, the professional autonomy of intellectuals is also declining because the process of knowledge creation itself currently is becoming more collaborative. It applies both to the academic and public knowledge of intellectuals. For example, Nikita Basov provides a detailed insight into networks of intellectual collaboration.[54] The historian and researcher of intellectual movements Clive E. Hill applies the same idea to the political (public) appearances of intellectuals, saying that the 'collaboration between intellectuals through joint authorship of texts (notably manifestos), through translations and editorial work for periodical publications is a recurring feature of the modern world.'[55]

5. Rethinking the Organic Intellectual

Finally, what distinguishes intellectuals in the public sphere from ordinary hooligans and provocateurs is that they explore, criticize and manifest their positions for a reason. This reason (which at the same time is the main function and raison d'être of the public intellectual) is some kind of improvement in the institution/community/society he or she speaks about. The destination where the knowledge of the intellectual and his/her interventions into the public sphere lead is betterment. To achieve this goal he or she has to be concerned, to see and feel the consequences of his or her action. The sociologist James Petras even claims that the work of intellectuals (for example, the findings of their research) is relevant (can be trusted) only if intellectuals are embedded in the society they research, so that their work creates consequences for themselves as well.[56] Thus, being an organic intellectual does not mean being irresponsible; the accountability of the organic intellectual is even more demanding than that of the traditional, autonomous intellectual.

Being an organic intellectual is also not a retreat for safety or comfort as when collaboration is regarded in authoritarian or totalitarian contexts. Identifying with a social group or ideology, which the intellectual defends or criticizes, often is uncomfortable and risky. Examples range from non-violent social antipathy toward intellectuals to the disturbance of their careers to threats on their lives. Both Walzer and Sartre argue that identifying with what the intellectual defends or criticizes requires more courage than distancing and choosing exile. Walzer notes that by admitting 'loyalty and acknowledging the kinship' the social critic has to be daring and that the more specific and less absolute his or her criticisms are, the more they are effective.[57] Sartre, in turn, criticizes intellectuals who 'produce works that serve no end' and says that they act like pure consumers in relation to society because of their fears:

> [t]he truth is that unsure of his social position, too fearful to stand up to the bourgeoisie from whom he draws his pay, and too lucid to accept it without reservations, he has chosen to pass judgment on his century and has thereby convinced himself that he remains outside it, just as an experimenter remains outside the system of his experiment.[58]

The cases studies in this chapter present several peculiarities of the role and identity of the organic intellectual. Adeleke writes about Rodney as a 'Guerrilla intellectual,' Simet writes about an organic intellectual who doesn't identify himself as an organic intellectual. Mahlomaholo and Netshandama tell a personal story about intellectuals, who identify with their community but are aware of their inevitable distance from it and at the same time don't oppose power.

The example of Rodney demonstrates how an intellectual can solve the antagonism of being a part of the power system and being a dissident. The identity of the 'Guerrilla intellectual' allows an intellectual to present (to him/herself and to the public) the collaboration with power as an eventually revolutionary activity: first by obeying the rules of the system to gain status and influence, then by using them to destroy the system. If the privileges of knowledge and status are used in favor of the powerless, then the intellectual's collaboration with the power is not regarded as a sin. Rather it is just a side effect on the road for achieving the ultimate goal - the liberation of the oppressed; the condition for becoming a truly organic intellectual. Hrant Dink, in turn, does not present himself as an organic intellectual; however, he is obviously acting in favor of his ethnic community and is perceived as representing the collective interests of it in the public sphere. Not recognizing oneself as an organic intellectual does not mean one is unconscious or hypocritical about one's status; rather it is an approach of not choosing a readymade identity. The article of Mahlomaholo and Netshandama shows that the identity question may indeed be difficult for the intellectual because when the lines between the elite and the powerless are clearly drawn, the intellectual stays in the obscure space between the two.

These aspects disorganize the integrity of the concept of the 'organic intellectual' in the Gramscian sense. They also characterize the ambiguous status of the *new organic intellectual*, which I tried to describe here. The new organic intellectuals are devoted to their community (they are no hooligans; they wish the best for their community and see the improvement of it as an ultimate goal of their work). At the same time, they acknowledge the distance from it by the power of their knowledge, status, or the will and the ability to criticize. Thus, their identity is built simultaneously on two seemingly contradictory approaches to intellectual work: the independent scholar/critic and the engaged missionary. The contradiction also emerges when one is trying to define the intellectual's relation to power and its implementation system: the intellectual cannot be detached from power, but he/she also cannot be a servant of it. As I have argued, this ambiguousness arises from the simultaneous influence of several aspects: (1) the dissolution of structuralist-approach categories, such as truth vs. treason; (2) the fragile balance between disassociation and engagement that always characterizes an intellectual; and (3) the economic, technological and sociological conditions of knowledge creation that currently characterize intellectual work.

These factors impose an uncertain, fragmented (one may say post-modern) and difficult-to-describe identity upon an intellectual. The major difficulty is the inability to arrange it around the opposition of universal truth on the one side and the sin of collaboration on the other. The new organic intellectual emerges when these formations are deconstructed, but not just to build another structuralist opposition on their ruins; they are abandoned in favor of the vague, situational, contextual role of *the new organic intellectual*. Mannheim was talking about the intelligentsia that is floating free from social classes. *The new organic intellectual* rather flows freely between the classes and different identities, acknowledging the belonging to the elite and at the same time advocating for the interests of the oppressed and collaborating with the power holders when finds it necessary. The notion of collaboration as treason and a sin and the *liquid identity* of the new organic intellectual are not compatible, because they belong to different frames of reference: one to the era of the intellectual-legislator (which most probably has ended) and the other to the postmodern condition (which we are probably now experiencing).

Notes

[1] See S. Collini, *Absent Minds: Intellectuals in Britain*, Oxford University Press, Oxford, New York, 2006, p. 64; on structuralism as a prevailing approach towards defining intellectuals see J. Li, 'Intellectuals' Political Orientations: Toward an Analytical Sociology', *Asian Social Science*, Vol. 6(12), 2010, pp. 10-11.

[2] I. Kochetkova, *The Myth of the Russian Intelligentsia: Old Intellectuals in the New Russia*, Routledge, London, New York, 2010, pp. 13-14; G. Konrád & I. Szelényi, *The Intellectuals on the Road to Class Power*, Harvester Press, Brighton, 1979, p. 8.

[3] А. Грамши, *Тюремные тетради,* Политиздат, Москва, 1991, с. 327-328.

[4] S. Mahlomaholo and V. Netshandama, 'Post-Apartheid Organic Intellectual and Knowledge Creation', 2011, this volume.

[5] T. Adeleke, 'Walter A. Rodney and the Instrumentalist Construction and Utilization of Knowledge', 2011, this volume.

[6] See, e.g., T. Judt, *Postwar: A History of Europe Since 1945*, Penguin Books, London, 2005.

[7] Adeleke, op. cit.

[8] M. Walzer, *The Company of Critics: Social Criticism and Political Commitment in the Twentieth Century*, Basic Books, New York, 2002, pp. 15-20.

[9] S. Auer, 'Public Intellectuals, East and West: Jan Patocka and Vaclav Havel in Contention with Maurice Merleau-Ponty and Slavoj Zizek', *Intellectuals and Their Publics: Perspectives from the Social Sciences*, C. Fleck, A. Hess and E.S. Lyon (eds), Ashgate Publishing, Burlington, 2009, p. 89.

[10] P. Bourdieu, *Sociology in Question*, Sage Publications, London, Thousand Oaks, New Delhi, 1994, p. 43.

[11] R. Conell, 'Building the Neoliberal World: Managers as Intellectuals in a Peripheral Economy', *Critical Sociology*, Vol. 36(6), 2010, p. 777.

[12] Konrád and Szelényi, op. cit., p. 13.

[13] P. Bourdieu, *Sociology in Question*, op. cit., p. 43.

[14] J. Benda, *The Betrayal of the Intellectuals*, Beacon Press, Boston, 1959, p. 30.

[15] Ibid.

[16] Ibid., p. 31.

[17] Ibid., p. 32.

[18] Ibid.

[19] Ibid., pp. 37-38.

[20] Н. Бердяев, 'Философская истина и интеллигентская правда'. *Вехи: сборники статей 1909-1910. Интеллигенция в России*. Н. Казакова (ред.), Молодая гвардия, Москва, 1991, p. 30.

[21] See Adeleke, op. cit.; Mahlomaholo and Netshandama, op. cit.; G.F. Simet, 'Possibilities and Risks of Influencing Public Knowledge: The Case of Hrant Dink', 2011, this volume.
[22] Ibid., p. 46.
[23] Ibid., p. 41.
[24] K. Mannheim, *Ideology and Utopia*, Routledge, New York, 1991, pp. 135-140.
[25] Ibid.
[26] E. Said, *Representations of the Intellectual*, Vintage Books, New York, 1996, p. 11.
[27] Ibid., pp. 86-87.
[28] Z. Bauman, *Legislators and Interpreters: On Modernity, Post-modernity, and Intellectuals*, Polity Press, Cambridge, 1989, pp. 3-4, 111, 116-117.
[29] P. Bourdieu, 'The Social Space and the Genesis of Groups', *Theory and Society*, Vol. 14, 1985, p. 729.
[30] Ibid., p. 731.
[31] Ibid., p. 732.
[32] Ibid., p. 733.
[33] J. Karabel, 'Towards a Theory of Intellectuals and Politics', *Theory and Society*, Vol. 25, April 1996, pp. 210.
[34] Bourdieu, *Sociology in Question*, op. cit., pp. 36-37.
[35] Ibid.
[36] Ibid.
[37] E. Gapova, 'Post-Soviet Academia and Class Power: Belarusian Controversy over Symbolic Markets', *Studies in East European Thought*, Vol. 61, 2009, p. 286.
[38] Ibid., p. 45.
[39] М. Фуко, *Интеллектуалы и власть: избранные политические статьи, выступления и интервью*, Праксис, Москва, 2002, pp. 68-69.
[40] Gapova, op. cit., p. 286.
[41] M.D. Kennedy, 'The Intelligentsia in the Constitution of Civil Societies and Post-Communist Regimes in Hungary and Poland', *Theory and Society*, Vol. 21(1), 1992, p. 29.
[42] G. Konrád and I. Szelényi, op. cit., p. 14.
[43] J.C. Alexander, 'Public Intellectuals and Civil Society', *Intellectuals and Their Publics...*, op. cit., pp. 21-22.
[44] Bauman, op. cit., pp. 4, 118-119, 127.
[45] Ibid., pp. 5, 143.
[46] R. Conces, 'The Role of the Hyperintellectual in Civil Society Building and Democratization in the Balkans', *Studies in East European Thought*, Vol. 59, 2007, p. 203.

[47] Ibid., p. 206.
[48] Bauman, op. cit., pp. 145-146.
[49] A. Грамши, *Тюремные тетради*, op. cit., pp. 327-330.
[50] V. Held, 'The Independence of Intellectuals', *The Journal of Philosophy*, Vol. 80, October 1983, p. 572.
[51] Ibid., p. 573.
[52] E.S. Lyon, 'What Influence? Public Intellectuals, the State and Civil Society', *Intellectuals and Their Publics...*, op. cit., p. 82.
[53] K. Calavita, 'Engaged Research, Goose Bumps, and the Role of the Public Intellectual', *Law & Society Review*, Vol. 36, 2002, p. 8.
[54] Н.В. Басов, 'Коллективное создание знания в современном обществе: интеллектуальная коммуникация в сетевых ансамблях'. *Общество знания: от идеи к практике. Коллективная монография в 3-х частях. Часть 3. Когнитивные аспекты становления общества знания*, В.В. Василькова и Л.А. Вербицкая (ред.), Скифия-принт, Санкт-Петербург, 2011 (в печати).
[55] C. Hill, 'Do Intellectuals Make a Difference?', *Intellectuals, Identities and Popular Movements*, C. Hill (ed), Middlesex University Press, London, 2000, p. 2.
[56] J. Petras, 'The Metamorphosis of Latin America's Intellectuals', *Latin American Perspectives*, Vol. 17, 1990, pp. 102-112.
[57] Walzer, op. cit., p. 20, pp. 235-236.
[58] J.P. Sartre, 'Introducing *Les Temps Modernes*', *What is Literature? And Other Essays*, Harvard University Press, Harvard, 1988, p. 249.

Bibliography

Bauman, Z., *Legislators and Interpreters: On Modernity, Post-Modernity, and Intellectuals*. Polity Press, Cambridge, 1989.

Benda, J., *The Betrayal of the Intellectuals*. Beacon Press, Boston, 1959.

Bourdieu, P., 'The Social Space and the Genesis of Groups'. *Theory and Society*. Vol. 14, 1985, pp. 723-744.

Bourdieu, P., *Sociology in Question*. Sage Publications, London, Thousand Oaks, New Delhi, 1994.

Calavita, K., 'Engaged Research, Goose Bumps, and the Role of the Public Intellectual'. *Law & Society Review*. Vol. 36, 2002, pp. 5-20.

Collini, S., *Absent Minds: Intellectuals in Britain*. Oxford University Press, Oxford, New York, 2006.

Conces, R., 'The Role of the Hyperintellectual in Civil Society Building and Democratization in the Balkans'. *Studies in East European Thought*. Vol. 59, 2007, pp. 195-214.

Fleck, C., Hess, A. and Lyon, E.S. (eds), *Intellectuals and Their Publics: Perspectives from the Social Sciences*. Ashgate Publishing, Burlington, 2009.

Gapova, E., 'Post-Soviet Academia and Class Power: Belarusian Controversy over Symbolic Markets'. *Studies in East European Thought*. Vol. 61, 2009, pp. 271-290.

Held, V., 'The Independence of Intellectuals'. *The Journal of Philosophy*. Vol. 80, October 1983, pp. 572-582.

Hill, C. (ed), *Intellectuals, Identities and Popular Movements*. Middlesex University Press, London, 2000.

Judt, T., *Postwar: A History of Europe since 1945*. Penguin Books, London, 2005.

Karabel, J., 'Towards a Theory of Intellectuals and Politics'. *Theory and Society*. Vol. 25, April 1996, pp. 205-233.

Kochetkova, I., *The Myth of the Russian Intelligentsia: Old Intellectuals in the New Russia*. Routledge, London, New York, 2010.

Konrád, G. and Szelényi, I., *The Intellectuals on the Road to Class Power*. Harvester Press, Brighton, 1979.

Mannheim, K., *Ideology and Utopia*. Routledge, New York, 1991.

Petras, J., 'The Metamorphosis of Latin America's Intellectuals'. *Latin American Perspectives*. Vol. 17, 1990, pp. 102-112.

Said, E., *Representations of the Intellectual*. Vintage Books, New York, 1996.

Sartre, J.P., *What is Literature? And Other Essays.* Harvard University Press, Harvard, 1988.

Walzer, M., *The Company of Critics: Social Criticism and Political Commitment in the Twentieth Century.* Basic Books, New York, 2002.

Басов, Н.В., 'Коллективное создание знания в современном обществе: интеллектуальная коммуникация в сетевых ансамблях'. *Общество знания: от идеи к практике. коллективная монография в 3-х частях. Часть 3. Когнитивные аспекты становления общества знания.* В. В. Василькова и Л. А. Вербицкая (ред.), Скифия-принт, Санкт-Петербург, 2011 (в печати).

Грамши, А., *Тюремные тетради.* Политиздат, Москва, 1991.

Казакова, Н. (ред.), *Вехи: сборник статей 1909-1910. Интеллигенция в России.* Молодая гвардия, Москва, 1991.

Фуко, М., *Интеллектуалы и власть: избранные политические статьи, выступления и интервью.* Праксис, Москва, 2002.

Part III

Intellectuals in the Arts: Emotional Knowledge Creation

Art and the Passion of Intellect

Carlos David García Mancilla

Abstract
The peculiarities of cognizing through art have always been a highly intriguing issue. Struggling through the restrictions of the Cartesian thought modern intellectuals dwelt on the role of passions in knowledge creation which takes place during the creation of artwork. Though Cartesian tradition stipulated a distance and difference between passions and thought, the concern about the mysterious nature of the emotions made the intellectuals of Modernity consider art as a means to grasp the essences and phenomena which the rational mind is unable to conceive. By painting a picture of these considerations we affirm that the boundary between emotions and thought is artificially constructed, and there are intellectual preconditions to conceptualize fundamental unity between them. We also stress that purely rational forms of discourse are inefficient to understand this unity, while thinking artistic knowledge and experience gives us a chance to go into the depth of it and then to extend our understanding of intellectual and cognitive activity.

Key Words: Art, knowledge, intellectual, philosophy, passion.

*****

'I think therefore I am' is the statement of an intellectual who underestimates toothaches. 'I feel, therefore I am' is a truth much more universally valid, and it applies to everything that's alive. My self does not differ substantially from yours in terms of its thought. Many people, few ideas: we all think more or less the same, and we exchange, borrow, steal thoughts from one another. However, when someone steps on my foot, only I feel the pain. The basis of the self is not thought but suffering, which is the most fundamental of all feelings. - *Milan Kundera*

This chapter, based on the implications of the modern philosophy, will show how emotions elicited by art play a role in cognition and speak of philosophers of modern era as intellectuals who, though restricted by the Cartesian paradigm, made this explicit in their works. Thus we pursue two goals. The first is to reveal the drawbacks of restricting cognition only to rational thought and the ways of overcoming these by thinking of the sphere of art and emotional knowledge received there. The second is to expose that the intellectual should be considered not only a thinker but also the one who can get his/her intellectual insights through art, which the philosophers of the modern era have so clearly displayed and which is similarly justified by contemporary intellectuals (see chapter by Heaney).[1]

Nowadays it is rather fashionable to state that separation of art and emotions lead to liberation of art and the increase of artistic self-consciousness. As an example we can recall the avant-garde art that tended to rationalize its enterprise. Here, nevertheless, we are focusing on the views of modern philosophers who argued that emotions and art are inseparable. We consider these views important for elaborating the problematic areas of art, emotions and cognition, integral for this part of the book. First, because we have inherited much of the modern paradigms of taste, in other words, we expect from art the epiphany that was expected, for example, in romanticism. As a result, we often misunderstand the voice of new art, we disdain its creations, or we renounce passionate enjoyment of it in order to engage with it as mere data. Second, the consideration of the modern era allows us to understand the reasons and arguments of intellectuals that renounce the passions; it helps in analyzing the discourse of division between understanding and feelings, which led to many simplifications and machinations. Being aware of this discourse we appreciate why art is sometimes regarded as suspicious in its connection with feelings and passions.

Further we will try to describe the modern discourse of division between ratio and the passions and the place of art in this relation. Modern philosophers treated art as if it had a *double nature*. Art appeared to them as knowledge which encroaches upon the mysterious land of the passions. It should be also emphasized that writing on the modern point of view on art we shed light only on particular aspects of the subject, while overlooking a certain heritage in conceptualizing art and the passions. Thus, we exclude the ideas of analytic philosophy although they contain deep and interesting statements about the passions. However, a focused point of view undoubtedly makes explicit provoking thoughts of many intellectuals that constituted the *spirit* of Modernity, the spirit of division we still *suffer*.[2]

There is a deep abyss between thought, the world and life. But it is a cliff forged by thought itself, as a presupposition of its own activity. There are some bonds where thought and the world forcedly approach each other and separate due to their contrary natures. Many words have been spent attacking and protecting the tendentious division between subject and object. What we will consider in detail is a different relation-separation, the one between the subject and the individual, a division catalyzed by the passions.

Passion, the *pathos*, has been established by Modernity as something indeterminate, obscure, out of reach of power and thought. Is passion itself really obscure? Descartes considers it to be most proximate and intimate to us.[3] This obscurity ascribed to passion is the first symptom of separation, of what we call the *ontological distance*. When thought unweaves and distances from life and watches it as the spectator of a big drama, when 'life is a dream' and the world is an enormous theater, this distance opens and the thought, without knowing or willing it, bears the division and suffers.[4] This is the nature of the passion of Modernity. And we might ask, are there passions in thought? For it is precisely the *a-patheia* of thought that forges its separation.

Very few things can be as common and abysmally unequal as the passions. Every being that belongs to the human gender, in all its history, is always a passionate being. We could even say that life itself is the result and container of these passions. They are, doubtlessly, important. In contrast, no human being, taken as an individual, can feel what others feel in the same form he feels it.[5] We might know that someone is sorrowful, ireful or glad, but we cannot feel or live his sadness or cheer as ours.

One of the main issues of postmodern philosophy is an attempt to dissolve the idea of what is traditionally called essence and the power of predeterminism and ideology that this supposes. To propose that there is something proper or characteristic of all humanity is to fall into the trap of essence. Nevertheless, we will treat the passions *as if* they were uniform across all our gender, *as if* the only mutable thing was the manner in which they are understood, esteemed and discursively represented. We will suppose that the lived passions of others - now and hundreds years ago - are similar to what we in our individual prisons live. As Descartes stated, passions are 'so near that it is difficult to argue that they are something different from what is felt.'[6] It is surely a prejudgment to argue that every other should feel the same way as oneself, but is just a fixed point to depart from not only in quest of knowledge but also in search of life itself.

For centuries the only discourse of intellectuals concerning passions reduced them to the maxim of controlling their wild flow. Even the ideas of good and evil were established as the possibility of ruling or being ruled by passions. The complexity of passions was kept in oblivion because of this reductive approach; passions were seen as something that should be denied. Modernity is *consciously* preoccupied with the apparent negativity of passions and of sentiments.[7] This means that it turns its sight towards the shadow of passions without ignoring them as happened before. This is the reason why passions become numbered among the sentiments, which is an even more diffuse concept. What are sentiments? They are irrational and obscure, inhabiting places that reason cannot comprehend or face boundaries of its influence. Thus, sentiments include the passions, intuition, outbursts of genius and mysticism. It is, as Schopenhauer mentions, a *trash* concept where all the irrational or unknowable is thrown. Passions are also irrational, but not because they possess a lack of order. It is enough to look at contemporary psychology to be aware of the most probable patterns ascribed to an emotion, a will or an impulse.[8] They are classified as irrational because they are beyond the dominion of the intellect and the consciousness. They fall on us without being wished, chosen or predicted. They are passions because we are in a passive state relative to them: not because they are passive themselves, but because they fetter with their own dynamics our freewill.[9] The mastery over passions, formerly considered as morally positive, is merely an indirect and simulated trick. Modernity is suspicious of the irrationality of passions because in most instances a lonely reason would not act as a passionate being acts.

Similar discourses of sentiments and passions clearly appear in the explanations of art that modern intellectuals espouse. It was tacitly admitted by them that the enigma of passions preconceived as shadowy could be revealed, or even rationally seized in works of art.[10] Therefore intellectual discourse concerning the arts in Modernity is rather demonstrative of the place and role of emotions.

The revision of the conceptualization of the passions through art in Modernity reveals a great deal of interesting and important details and brings to light new perspectives about the passions. One of the purposes of this brief text is to argue the importance of turning back and looking at Modernity in order to understand the passions not only through their ideal conceptualization, but also their mistakes. Modernity is an era where intellectuals, the *owners* of reason and the new science, of method and objectivity, had to invent a fable - a world where reason was prior. This fable lacked life; being individuals, intellectuals couldn't have pure intellects and thus witnessed the mystery of passions, prompting them to search for the key to them - in arts.

From the classical age and the epoch of Romanticism we inherit the idea that something is revealed in art; that art says more than what is represented in it, that art is a kind of knowledge.[11] Nevertheless, knowledge has its own demarcated paths that it uses to achieve certainty. For Descartes, who made personal comprehension of knowledge a cornerstone of cognition, knowledge is obtained only by deduction or intuition.

Within this perspective on knowledge, the ability and nature of reason are essentially simple. From two known and related propositions a third unknown one could be concluded in a syllogism. Of course, the rising sciences of the modern age and the systems of knowledge were a lot more complex and immensely more intricate. Large chains of syllogistic relations made up their constitutive parts and basic structure, but the problem of indicating the beginning of such knowledge chains remained; in other words only an un-deduced assertion could give birth to deductive knowledge. This state of affairs is clear and evident in itself, known by intuition.[12]

It was not this contradiction alone that made the conception of knowledge as deduction weak. Works of art didn't allow intellectuals to understand them through a chain of deductions. How could one assume that a work of art communicates in the same way as positive science as a result of predictable and invariable sequences of facts? Deductive paradigms of knowledge are not necessarily applicable to artistic phenomena.

Nevertheless there is something intriguing in the modern era that protects art from being excluded from the domain of knowledge and forces us to consider something extra that is revealed in art. If art does not proceed by deduction, there is only one possibility for its activity: it must be knowledge gained by intuition. Art is generally considered to be intuitive, which means immediate knowledge. Any other deductive knowledge although it may be intricate or complex, and no matter how fast an individual ratio passes from one link of the deductive chain to the other - can be reproduced with clarity and understood by any other rational being. But art is different. The work of art gives its content and revelation, its past and elaboration, simultaneously without unweaving the whole process behind its sole presence. The work of art appears in its completeness; whereas the truth gained by deductive knowledge needs the support of synthesis.[13] If we try to analyze and unweave the work of art as if it was a deductive process, we will find out that it clearly inhibits such an attempt. Any rational being can grab a complicated and long deduction, and understand what science concludes and why it concludes this or that. Compared to this the process and the originality of art is obscure, in spite of its presence which is completely and immediately known. The obscurity of the origin of art and its elusive nature of *veiled revelation* needs a character that goes beyond 'rational knowledge' and discovers a message that deductive reasoning alone cannot discover. The intellectuals propose a way of going beyond reason in order to understand the deep and mysterious essence. This character is, as Schopenhauer declares, like an archer who manages to hit a target that no one else can see. This is the genius. Someone who can reveal a deep truth which lies under other truths as primary; such truth was thought to be expressed in art. Infinity, considers Schelling, never appears as infinity.[14] The foundation of all things, unreachable for reason, can only *appear* as knowledge if it is limited; but beyond any limits it is the work of art and the far sight of genius.

Some intellectuals, modern and contemporary, view this perspective on art as eccentric for more or less obvious reasons. According to them art is a copy or imitation of reality and, as Plato argued, the copy has a lower degree of being comparing to the original; it lacks a real basis in reality. In art, it was thought, not truth but only verisimilitude dwells.[15] The so-called truth in art is so obscure that it is difficult to explain what it consists of: what exactly gets disclosed in it or what the work of art indicates. As Fontanelle thought about music: *sonate, que me veux tu?* What is it that art expresses beyond empirical reality, that can't be explained by reason because of its limited tools? What kind of truth does it say without saying, in interplay of light and shade?

Intellectuals, philosophers or artists, in thinking about their own activity, have made an immense effort to bring to the light of deductive reason exactly what it is that happens in art. The Enlightenment and Romanticism gave birth to an enormous number of written and theoretical works dedicated to art. Since then art and thought keep company with each other like two trees that stand side by side. According to the specific intellectual system of every philosopher, art has a specific and important role. Whatever truth art reveals through *intuition* in these systems, it is a transcendent one, unreachable via deductive knowledge or *adequate* experiential truth. Art's truth appears to be original, related to the fundament of existence and to the essence of mankind; in other words, it is ontological truth.

Imitation is no longer considered a mere copy constantly failing to identify with what is copied.[16] Artistic imitation for the moderns is one that is more perfect than what it represents. As Diderot and Schopenhauer assume, *mimesis* shows not what the things are, but what they should be; for nature gives birth to countless beings without hitting upon the perfection that the genius moulds in the unique work of art.[17] Art says even more to the moderns. It points to what is unreachable by any other means. At least for two of the most important intellectuals of Modernity - Schelling and Schopenhauer - art reveals fundamental truth. The essence of all things cannot be understood or explained by finite reason; there is no cause before it to which reason could appeal in order to cognize it.[18] Such a fundament can only be defined through the metaphors of the artistic image. Beyond the veil of idealism, which is one of the effects of the mentioned ontological distance, these two intellectuals show an obscure situation where the world and the thought of this world are only reachable and known in the light and shade of art.

It can occur that art and passions escaping from reason relate in a negative manner. In other words, both coincide in that they can't be precisely explained by reason and can be correlated with one another only in relation to this negative condition. To our mind this sort of thinking is false, because passions and art are brought together by their own interconnections. Art emerges from passions; it is frequently directed towards them. Some of the intellectuals of the idealistic tradition emphasized that sight is needed to explain the world.[19] The intellectuals of Enlightenment, Rousseau and Diderot in particular, considered that finite human nature contained the stigma of its finiteness precisely in its passions.[20] The imitation of nature, art, is only possible by seeding nature with humanity. The world becomes understandable to us when it transforms from nature into something proximate to us, when it is humanized and reflected in human handiwork, when it awakens a vestige of humanity.[21] The so-called objectivity of positive sciences builds its views on prejudgments which imply the ontological distance; art dissolves this distance.

In art we recognize our finiteness and our passions without living them through. Its pedagogical impulse is notorious. Art, especially lyrical one, in particular poetry, reveals to us the passions that normally enslave us. Certain music, for example, appears and its sound is mournful. I feel sadness which is not mine. We do not suffer the passion of sadness in its stream; we contemplate it and understand it. When we see the passions occurring in others we do not feel or understand their emotional state. At most we can compare it with what ourselves have felt earlier in life. Strong passions can blind us. We cannot be observers and the observed at the same time. The moderns propose that art shows passion in itself; not an individual love or sadness, but the universal passion of love and sadness.

It was considered that nothing could show us the 'reason of the heart' more clearly than its staging. We argue that the difficulty of acquiring virtue, of methodically discovering a clear idea of good and evil and of finding a correct path to follow in life depends mostly on the passions. Art is thus a guide for our actions *par excellence*. As the text by Nenko will later propose, art allows for a sort of intersubjectivity which makes transgression from lonely self-centered passion to a universal feeling of being and connectedness possible. It could be said that we *understand* our passions in an intuitive manner because we immediately know when we have them; they are as near to us as anything else could be, but we somehow do not 'know' them because they can't be put in tangible terms. When we read 'Othello' we *know* what jealousy in oneself and in others is. We can call this *emotionally driven knowledge*, where what is known is not a statement or a proposition.[22] It is as immediate as our own passions without being ours. Using this same example, if we try to explain what jealousy is, thousands of psychological, sociological or philosophical sentences would be imprecise, but the sole character of Othello in the drama of Shakespeare would express it holistically and saliently.

Concluding from the ideas of *The Great Theater of the World* by Calderón de la Barca to the *Paradox of the Comedian* by Diderot, the intellectuals in Modernity incline constantly to the concept of the scission. There is a deep difference between those who live on the stage and those who are spectators: the direction of the sight is decisive for what we are. Those living life do not understand it, they just do it. The *urgency* of action and passion blind us and blunt contemplation.[23] The hero and the saint, in Schopenhauer's philosophy, are the only ones capable of breaking free from themselves and denying the individual, his/her passions or will, in order to achieve a far sight that is barely distinguished from totality. In his philosophy, sanctity and heroism are expressed in art and barely anywhere else. How could it be possible to understand, from individuality, an experience that denies the individual, language and experience itself? Thereby, the hero dwells mostly in the tragedy or the drama but not in life. The hidden foundation, the unity of the will, becomes *visible* only through art. Schelling regards the way in which the hero defeats necessity, his/her own destiny in a similar manner; both, freedom and necessity, conquerors and conquered manifest in the tragedy what happens secretly in the world.[24]

Theories of the passions are numerous in Modernity; whether passions are taken as the essence of the world - as will or anxiety - or as the essence of humanity, only the poetical word is able to grab and approximate them to us.[25] To speak about something which we cannot speak about, it is necessary to ply a language that goes beyond rational language - the language of art.

L'abbé Batteux said that it is impossible to achieve happiness until the passions are in accordance with reason.

> A heart which contradicts the lights of the spirit or a spirit which condemns the movements of the heart can only produce an internal war that poisons every moment of life.[26]

It was argued that the ontological distance is necessary to understand life, because it is important for an intellect to be estranged from real actions and, with them, from passions. Descartes makes a fable of his philosophy; he thinks *as if* the *cogito* was a lonely and simple source of truth. The absolute truth of the phrase *I think,* therefore *I am* depends on the impossibility of denying existence as soon as there is consciousness, an immediate and intuitive knowledge of oneself. Nevertheless, the *I* is not a particular or individual *I*: it is the *I* of reason and consciousness which, aiming to reach an absolute certainty for the sake of science, has to deny the *I* which is every one of us, the individual *I*. World and life alike become a fable with the pure subject of knowledge. Modernity drowns between these two phantoms, and the tabooing of passions is a very important reason for this. The proclaimed irrationality of passions and their sublime dulls the work of thought, and the immense importance of passions for action leads thought to abandon life. The intellectuals of Modernity, in their quest for truth, broke humanity apart. One of the strongest criticisms by Nietzsche against the modern age was his condemnation of this resignation and denial of life.

Art in Modernity sought to return thought to life by understanding and mastering the passions. The explanations of passions by contemporary neurology, for example, reveal on-going chemical processes in the brain; but can this explication really demonstrate what is actually lived as a passion? Biological descriptions of the passions are not sufficient in themselves: as mentioned before, to live passion is not the same as to understand it. Only art can show what life is, and it does so without the necessity of actually having to live its story through. Art opens the world to this special knowledge that is not based on grounded arguments or cause-effect analysis. Art is immediately understood because it is the knowledge of emotions or passions which are immediate to oneself. A longer reconsideration of the philosophy of the modern era opens up the possibility of interpreting the phenomenon of passions as an actual problem by paying it the attention it deserves. Even if the postmodern period has endeavored to explode the antique idols of the *substance* and the *subject*, it lacks reflection on the separation between life and thought inherited from Modernity. The modern era sees in art a response to its anxiety and to the plea for life it was loosing. Although the criticism of modern knowledge has reconsidered many prejudgments of it, we will always be inheritors of the world proposed by Modernity. We still live the passions of Modernity and have not turned our sights from it to recreate ourselves in the light of the responses this age has given to its own tragedy. Let's go back to the arts and listen to what they tell us about the world and ourselves.

Notes

[1] C. Heaney, 'Emotional Intelligence: Literature, Ethics and Affective Cognition in J.M. Coetzee's *Disgrace*', 2011, this volume.

[2] The *spirit* should not be considered in a Hegelian perspective. It is more like *ideology* which we consider as a structure of unsaid ideas that lie under every discourse and thought. We regard this deep unsaid statement as a part of the already mentioned separation.

[3] See: R. Descartes, *Passions de l'âme*, Levrault, Paris, 1823, VIII, p. 14.

[4] *The Life is Dream* and *The Great Theater of the Word* are both works of the Spanish writer Calderón de la Barca, who lived in the middle of the modern era.

[5] The word 'feel' in English is not quite precise due to the extension of its meaning. It could be taken as mere experience, an empirical sensation, or as signifying a certain passion. In Spanish the meaning of the word 'padecer' has the sense of 'passion:' something that even without being chosen is carried. They both derive from the Greek word 'pathos.' Such a meaning is intended for every use of the word 'feel.'

[6] See: R. Descartes, Ibid., p. 15.

[7] In this text we assimilate 'passions' and 'emotions' into the former. In fact, 'passion' indicates passivity, for we are passive to it, while 'emotion' denotes

how the same phenomenon leads us to action being its *motor*. In contrast, the 'sentiment' is in modernity a confusing concept that includes passions and emotions - and many other things.

[8] Nevertheless the specific views of psychology and psychoanalysis are rooted in the same *spirit of the distance* that we have mentioned. Distance, for example, is one of the principal psychological tools that enables a researcher to be an objective spectator.

[9] Freedom is, of course, another immense problem; a mystery, as Montaigne used to say. Whether it exists or not it causes contradictions for the modern thinker. We are not considering freedom in particular, but its relation with passions and art.

[10] As was already mentioned, certain forms of contemporary art no longer pursue the imperative of 'revealing emotions' for they have critically abandoned this principle in order to achieve freedom and autonomy.

[11] It should be emphasized that art in the classical perspective is mostly seen as imitation. The avant-garde challenged the idea of imitation. Nevertheless conclusions on art in this text should be critically applied to postmodern art, which deserves a separate study.

[12] The fact that every intellectual system in modernity begins from a different starting point or is built in a different manner gives evidence for the presence of immanent errors in this way of thinking. Descartes himself mentioned this difficulty, though his solution (*I think, therefore I am* gives an immediate truth through which every other possible truth can be reached) was reinterpreted by other philosophers in a different way. It is an interesting irony, which won't be analyzed here because of lack of space.

[13] Under 'synthesis' we mean the union of the nexuses into the aforementioned chain of knowledge.

[14] See F.W. Schelling, *Filosofía del arte*, Tecnos, Madrid, 1999, p. 126.

[15] See D. Diderot, *Oeuvres Esthetiques*, Bordas, Paris, 1988, VII, p. 332.

[16] Nenko (O. Nenko, 'From Eye Irritation to Emotional Knowledge', 2011, this volume) outlines a contrasting perspective, pointing out that the imitation of art cannot be considered as a mere copy.

[17] A. Schopenhauer, *El Mundo como Voluntad y Representación II*, FCE, Barcelona, 2003, p. 356.

[18] It is a commonplace in modern epistemology to consider reason as a structure which works through certain simple and basic procedures, in a predominantly cause-effect chain. We can only understand those things that are experienced through this structure. We can see this idea mainly in the principle of sufficient reason of Leibniz (see G. Leibniz, *Opera Philosophica*, Aalen, 1974, pp. 245-250 and Schopenhauer's version (see A. Schopenhauer, *La cuádruple raíz del principio de razón suficiente*, Gredos, Madrid, 1981).

The whole work is dedicated to this principle. Also in the Analogies of Experience from Kant (see I. Kant, *Crítica de la Razón Pura*, Alfaguara, Madrid, 2000, pp. 211-245).

[19] The postulates of idealistic tradition can be rapidly understood with de Quincy's explanation: if we had to wear yellow glasses, we would see the world in this color. Of course, there is a world outside the yellow glasses but we are unable to see it in its real colors because our sight is yellow; we can only perceive what is available to us through the structure of reason. Thus we *see* what we can *see*, which is not necessarily what the things actually are (see T. de Quiencey, *Los últimos días de Emmanuel Kant*, Valdemar, Madrid, 2000, p. 112).

[20] *Emile* by Rousseau, besides its pedagogical inquiries, is a treatise of human finiteness of which the passions are the sign (see J. Rousseau, *Emilio*, Edaf, Madrid, 2000, pp. 323-353).

[21] Rousseau rejects art as another manifestation of the institutions and the culture that have set humanity apart from its natural path, but his thinking on the arts as an institution is valuable. The accordance between passions and thought that Rousseau focuses on is also peculiar to the modern arts theory perspective considered here.

[22] The concept of *emotionally-driven knowledge* is considered in every text of *Part III* though it is understood in different ways.

[23] See R. Descartes, op. cit., p. 187. For Descartes thought is barely capable of ruling action because it needs time and meditation while action cannot wait. Even more important is that if reason pretends to rule life, it should be capable of taking every step of action with precision. Thus, according to Descartes, there should be infinite science to rule life with method.

[24] See Schelling, Ibid., p. 436.

[25] Both theories of Will and Anxiety of Schopenhauer and Schelling respectively are very similar in their last foundations, even though they distance one from the other in the development of their intellectual systems. They both consider that at the bottom of all things is a sort of original hunger - a simple and infinite desire, which rules the world and consciousness.

[26] C. Batteux, *Les beaux arts réduits à un même principe*, Durand, Paris, 1743, p. 124.

Bibliography

Batteux, C., *Les beaux arts réduits à un même princip*. Durand, Paris, 1743.

Descartes, R., *Oeuvres de Descartes*. Levrault, Paris, 1823.

Diderot, D., *Oeuvres Esthetiques*. Bordas, Paris, 1988.

Kant, I., *Crítica de la Razón Pura*. Alfaguara, Madrid, 2000.

Leibniz, G., *Opera Philosophica*. Scientia, Aalen, 1974.

Quiencey, T., *Los últimos días de Emmanuel Kant*. Valdemar, Madrid, 2000.

Rousseau, J., *Emilio*. Edaf, Madrid, 2000.

Schelling, F., *Filosofía del arte*. Tecnos, Madrid, 1999.

Schopenhauer, A. *La cuádruple raíz del principio de razón suficiente*. Gredos, Madrid, 1981.

Schopenhauer, A., *El Mundo como Voluntad y Representación II*. FCE, Barcelona, 2003.

Emotional Intelligence: Literature, Ethics and Affective Cognition in J.M. Coetzee's *Disgrace*

Claire Heaney

Abstract
This chapter aims to complicate the emerging picture of art as a possible source of emotional knowledge creation by investigating the complex relationship between ethics and aesthetics. J.M. Coetzee's *Disgrace*, through a sustained engagement with the aesthetic ideology of the Romantic tradition, challenges the moral authority of literary inheritance, forcing the reader to confront the uncomfortable possibility that, rather than enlightening us, aesthetic engagement might instead provide a justifying framework for unethical attitudes and behaviour. I trace the cognitive path traversed by the novel's central character, the intellectual David Lurie, as he is forced by a series of extreme personal experiences to reconsider the relationship of art to wider social structures. Initially an admirer of Romantic art, Lurie comes to recognize that its conceptual schema conceals a worldview that is ethically questionable. Paradoxically, however, the power of art is retained when Lurie uses it to uncover and express his newfound knowledge of the world and the self. I argue that Lurie's story is a complex and ambiguous development from aesthetic 'not-knowing' and even ignorance towards a deeper emotional involvement with the surrounding world, one in which sympathy, emotion, and the imagination are viewed as valuable components of knowledge.

Key Words: Knowledge, emotion, aesthetics, Romanticism, intellectualism, J.M. Coetzee, *Disgrace*.

*****

The question of the relationship of art to knowledge has been a longstanding source of anxiety for philosophers. Plato's condemnation of art as twice-removed from reality exemplifies a certain scepticism about the truth value of artistic expression that characterized much of Western philosophy until the eighteenth century. With the emergence of the 'aesthetic turn' in German idealist philosophy art was awarded a newly respectable cognitive status, one that was grounded in emotion and individual experience. The aesthetic turn embodied an emerging sensitivity to subjective modes of knowing and a move away from purely rational, 'objective' forms of cognition. But the question of what, if any, kind of knowledge we gain through art, and the relationship of artistic knowledge to scientific knowledge, is far from exhausted.

This paper examines the collision of the aesthetic turn with the ethical turn, on-going since the 1990s, in literature and philosophy. Through reference to J.M. Coetzee's 1999 novel, *Disgrace*, a work which is centrally preoccupied with the relationship between aesthetics and ethics, I aim to question how far literature can be understood as providing a source of enlightenment, what role our emotions play in the construction of ethical knowledge, and how this knowledge relates to more traditional models of rational cognition.

Disgrace's plot is structured around two instances of sexual abuse: the first committed by David Lurie, the novel's central protagonist, when he aggressively coerces a young student, Melanie Isaacs, into a brief sexual relationship; while the second sees Lurie's role reversed as he becomes the victim of a violent robbery that culminates in the brutal gang rape of his daughter Lucy. The novel's narrative reveals how art significantly and ambiguously impacts both Lurie's evolving consciousness and the quality of his knowledge as he makes this transition from perpetrator to victim.

Through its characterization of David Lurie, *Disgrace* queries a strong divide between art and other social pursuits, responding to the ancient Platonic debate between ethics and aesthetics by staging an immanent critique of aesthetic tradition, a critique which in turn raises wider questions about reason and the possibility of self-knowledge. I will look firstly at how Lurie's engagement with aesthetic tradition is presented in the early part of the novel, before going on to consider Lurie's evolving relationship with Romanticism in the aftermath of Lucy's rape. Finally, I conclude with a consideration of how far Lurie's newly critical engagement with literary tradition in the later part of the novel, as evinced through the construction of his opera, signals a viable opportunity for literature to transcend the potentially abusive power of aesthetic tradition and provide a positive stimulus toward ethical responsibility.

Both teacher and scholar of Romanticism, Lurie is characterized at the beginning of *Disgrace* as the aficionado of a cultural tradition which is shown to be increasingly under fire in contemporary South Africa. Professor at Cape Technical University (formerly 'the Cape Town University College'), Lurie's role has metamorphosed during 'the great rationalization' of the South African higher education system after apartheid: once professor of modern languages, he is now, following the closure of the University's Classics and Modern Languages department, 'adjunct professor of communications.'[1]

Unsurprisingly, Lurie finds that he has little to offer as a teacher in this newly 'emasculated institution of learning.'[2] Having 'no respect for the material he teaches,' the 'dinosaur' Lurie senses only 'blank incomprehension' from his students, whom he regards (with no little condescension) as blind to the sophisticated rhetoric and sensibilities of Romantic art - 'Post-Christian, post-historical, post-literate, they might as well have been hatched from eggs yesterday.'³ A central concern of *Disgrace*, then, is to what extent Lurie's Romantic ideals (or indeed Lurie himself) can have meaning or purpose in modern South Africa. As Gareth Cornwell notes, Lurie is 'painfully aware of the inappropriateness of his education' for 'the world he inhabits;' and the novel's trajectory 'functions to develop this incipient critique of the relevance of the Western Romantic heritage in contemporary South Africa.'⁴

In the early part of the novel, Lurie's behaviour is motivated by his identification with an ethical/aesthetic attitude that is predicated upon four basic tenets:

(1) A neo-Platonic faith in Beauty as a real property.
(2) A Byronic defence of the 'rights of desire.'
(3) A belief in the priority of subjective imaginative response over objective engagement with the other (the Wordsworthian ethic of blindness).
(4) The autonomy of aesthetics from wider social norms.

1. **The Rights of Desire**

As befits a teacher of Romanticism, the framework for Lurie's aesthetic philosophy is largely drawn from the Romantic tradition. Before his students, Lurie draws implicit parallels between himself and Byron, characterizing the latter as unjustly dogged by notoriety and scandal, a 'man who found himself conflated with his own poetic creations.'⁵ The comparison ingeniously both invites and rejects readings of Byron as a symbol for Lurie (and indeed for Coetzee himself), allowing Lurie to situate himself as a libertine defender of desire against the mechanized forces of conventional society.

From Byron, Lurie inherits a possessive attitude towards women, as well as the idea that, as he informs Melanie, female beauty is a consumable commodity: 'a woman's beauty does not belong to her alone. It is part of the bounty she brings to the world. She has a duty to share it.'⁶ As lines go, this one is smoother than most: but what would it mean to actually believe such a statement? *Disgrace* subjects Lurie's aesthetic credo to functionalist interrogation, investigating what the consequences might be of a sincere identification with this rhetoric. The novel reads on one level as a damning indictment of the falsifying nature of Lurie's aesthetic outlook and an exposure of its misogynist and objectifying logic.

The immediate consequence of Lurie's espousal of his Byronic rights of desire in *Disgrace* is his 'not quite' rape of Melanie. Repeatedly, Lurie ransacks an exhausted aesthetic and emotional vocabulary in his descriptions of Melanie, characterizing her in objectifying animalistic terms as variously 'my little dove,' 'poor little bird,' and a beauty who 'does not own herself.'[7] Alone for the first time together in Lurie's home, we see Melanie consistently frustrate Lurie's attempts to draw her into his cultural universe - she is 'not so crazy about Wordsworth,' lacks the time to write poetry, and remains unmoved by Lurie's recording of a Norman McLaren dance (most probably *Pas de Deux*, 1968).[8] Against Lurie's literary idols, Byron and Wordsworth, Melanie posits modern feminist writers: Toni Morrison, Alice Walker, and Adrienne Rich; carefully distancing herself from Lurie's emotional vocabulary: 'I wouldn't call it a passion exactly.'[9] Their encounter is cut short when Lurie quotes Shakespeare's first love sonnet, the rarefied language serving only to alienate Melanie further: '[t]he pentameter, whose cadence once served so well to oil the serpent's words, now only estranges.'[10] That Melanie's resistance to Lurie takes the form of ideological opposition to his cultural rhetoric is significant, for it serves to highlight the potentially abusive power of Lurie's identification with Romanticism (a point which is further wryly alluded to by Lurie's naming of his daughter after the unfortunate heroine of Wordsworth's Lucy poems).[11]

2. Blindness

Along with Byron, Wordsworth provides a key archetype for Lurie's aesthetic philosophy.[12] In class, Lurie elucidates a Wordsworthian conception of love as a form of wilful misreading:

> 'like being in love,' he says. 'If you were blind you would hardly have fallen in love in the first place. But now, do you truly wish to see the beloved in the cold clarity of the visual apparatus? It may be in your better interest to throw a veil over the gaze, so as to keep her alive in her archetypal, goddesslike form.'[13]

That Lurie's conception of love is expressly based upon the upholding of Platonic archetypes, rather than engagement with the concrete particularity of the loved one, suggests a model of behaviour which actively privileges blindness as a legitimate ethical and aesthetic response, and proves key to understanding Lurie's relationship with Melanie (as well as his estrangement from the other women in his life: Soraya, Dawn, Rosalind and Lucy). Following on from a discussion of the 'Cambridge and the Alps' section of the sixth book of *The Prelude*, in which Wordsworth expresses his grief upon encountering the 'soulless image' of the real Mont Blanc, which 'usurped upon' the 'living thought' of the scene in the poet's imagination, Lurie's conception of love is expressly egoistic, privileging the (male) artist's imaginative experience at the expense of the (objectified female) other.

Using a standard trope, familiar from *Dusklands* (1974) and *In the Heart of the Country* (1977), Coetzee shows this logic in action, juxtaposing Lurie's idealized version of events with an altogether more sordid narrative in a move which explicitly foregrounds the falsifying power of Lurie's aesthetic discourse.[14] In Lurie's first version of events, he 'makes love' to Melanie on a rainy night, praising her clear, simple, perfect form, and stumbles from climax into 'blank oblivion.'[15] The next paragraph presents a contrastingly prosaic account: the rain has stopped, Lurie lies slumped atop a frowning Melanie, his trousers around his ankles and his hands groping her breasts, surrounded by discarded items of underwear. Significantly, however, Lurie immediately supplants his apprehension of the absurd and rather sordid nature of this encounter with yet another cultural mask: '*[a]fter the storm*, he thinks: straight out of George Grosz.'[16] A similar narrative dislocation occurs later when Lurie forces himself on Melanie: Melanie's 'absurd' gopher slippers suggesting reality's stubborn resistance to Lurie's self-justifying insistence that he is driven by 'Aphrodite, goddess of the foaming waves.'[17] Lurie's identification with the Romantic imagination thus allows him to privilege his own selfish impulses at the expense of the concrete particularity of the other, and ultimately to sublimate his own uneasy apprehension that his actions are 'undesired' by Melanie.

3. Aesthetic Autonomy

Lurie's reluctance to fully engage with the ethical implications of his aesthetic attitude is further demonstrated by his quixotic refusal to conform to the moralizing demands of the University's inquiry into his relationship with Melanie. During the hearing into his conduct, chaired by Manas Mathabane, Professor of Religious Studies, Lurie puts forward 'reservations of a philosophical kind' against the terms of the inquiry, pleading guilty to the charges against him but refusing to entertain the inquiry's wider request for a statement of contrition.[18] Lurie's resistance to the procedural norms of the inquiry signals not only his resistance to institutionalized standards of justice (an aspect of the novel that has been thoroughly explored in relation to the inquiry's obvious resemblances to the South African Truth and Reconciliation Commission), but also his wider refusal to recognize that his affair with Melanie has public as well as private ramifications. Rejecting Farodia Rasool's claim that the 'wider community' has a legitimate entitlement to interrogate his behaviour, Lurie once again falls back on an aesthetic justification of his actions: 'Eros entered [...] I became a servant of Eros.'[19] Lurie's aesthetic outlook thus provides a way for him to dodge the threat of moral opprobrium by claiming that his actions took place in an aesthetic realm which is autonomous from the sphere of ethics.

4. After the Storm - Educating the Eye

Initially a would-be libertine defender of masculine 'rights of desire,' Lurie is forced, following his daughter's rape, to confront the catastrophic personal and social implications of his earlier attitudes. Part of this process entails the discovery of a new ethical perspective on the aesthetic legacy of Lurie's literary masters. Contemplating a painting of *The Rape of the Sabine Women*, Lurie asks himself '[w]hat had all this attitudinizing to do with what he suspected rape to be: the man lying on top of the woman and pushing himself into her?' before going on to reconsider Byron's rights of desire:

> among the legions of countesses and kitchen maids Byron pushed himself into there were no doubt those who called it rape. But none surely had cause to fear that the session would end with her throat being slit. From where he stands, from where Lucy stands, Byron looks very old-fashioned indeed.[20]

Critics have tended to read this statement in terms that are critical of Romantic discourse, viewing it as evidence of Lurie's evolving ethical consciousness at this point in the novel. Lucy Valerie Graham, for example, reads this moment as 'a critique of the Romantic/humanist posturing that obscures, even justifies, forsaking ethical responsibility in the realm of life.'[21] Peter McDonald agrees that Lurie gradually comes to appreciate 'the extent to which his male Romantic literary heroes might have legitimated patriarchal exploitation.'[22] Melinda Harvey goes even further, arguing that, insofar as the Romantic tradition provides a legitimating framework for Lurie's abusive behaviour in the novel, Wordsworth himself 'becomes embroiled in David's disgrace.'[23]

However, despite the novel's emphasis on the role that aesthetic tradition plays in perpetuating Lurie's abusive attitudes, *Disgrace*'s relation towards its Romantic predecessors remains more determinedly dialogic and less straightforwardly rejectionist than these readings suggest. In many ways the novel reads as a faithful re-enactment of Byronic tradition. Lurie, with his literary passions, his rebellious arrogance, his disrespect for social institutions, self-destructive behaviour and eventual exile is in fact a rather apt Byronic hero. Other features of Byron's thought, in particular the ironic self-reflexivity of his writing and his championing of animals (and dogs in particular) register in *Disgrace* in a wholly unironic fashion.[24] Indeed, Byron himself was one of the earliest critics of Romanticism, and Coetzee's use of this figure to criticize Romantic thought is thus entirely consistent with that tradition.

Romance scholar Margot Beard argues that critics may well be reading the novel's intertextuality one-sidedly by foregrounding Coetzee's criticisms of the Romantic tradition without paying due attention to the ways in which *Disgrace* operates from within, not outside, that tradition. Pointing out that Lurie frequently 'misuses' Byron and Wordsworth, Beard argues that Lurie's biggest problem is that he consistently *fails* to learn the lessons offered by his supposed 'masters.'[25] Characterizing Lurie's 'shockingly instrumental' use of Wordsworth to convey 'covert intimacies' to Melanie as 'both disrespectful of the poem and blind to the deeper implications of the lines,' Beard argues that, despite pontificating before his class, Lurie 'shows no sign of internalizing that vital Romantic concept, the empathetic imagination.'[26]

Beard's contention that Lurie has failed to internalize the true lessons of Byron and Wordsworth finds support in a range of narrative dissonances within the text. We learn, for example, that Lurie, a 'disgraced disciple' of the Romantics, 'has never had much of an eye for rural life. Despite all his reading in Wordsworth. Not much of an eye for anything, except pretty girls; and where has that got him?'[27] Confronted with the devastating consequences of his own aesthetic outlook, however, Lurie's reaction against his literary heroes is tempered by an acknowledgement that it might actually be his own skewed interpretation of their message which is at fault: 'so much for the dead masters. Who have not, he must say, guided him well. Aliter, to whom he has not listened well.'[28] This raises a question which is nowhere conclusively answered in the novel: is Lurie capable of developing a more sensitive relation to his literary ancestors and his female contemporaries, can this old dog learn new tricks, or '[i]s it too late to educate the eye?'[29]

5. **Abstraction vs. Affection**

Disgrace pursues a deliberately ambiguous relation to Romantic tradition that allows Coetzee to pose difficult ethical questions without prematurely answering them. The issue of rape becomes a means through which Lurie is forced to confront his own past behaviour, to question (along with the reader) whether we can equate the rape in the artwork with Lucy's contemporary experience of rape (an uncertain comparison given that 'rape' in the historical context actually referred to kidnapping) and more pressingly whether Lurie's 'not rape' of Melanie (as well as his purchase of Soraya) can be similarly equated with Lucy's ordeal. Perhaps most importantly, Lucy's rape challenges Lurie to try for the first time to emotionally identify with the victims of violence, and discover whether 'he has it in him to be the woman.'[30]

Coetzee's relation to Romantic tradition in *Disgrace* is thus dialogic rather than simply rejectionist. In the novel, Romanticism operates both as a self-justifying prejudice which motivates Lurie's unethical behaviour, and as a legitimate model for learning to rectify that behaviour. This is because, as Beard's critique suggests, the Romantic tradition grounds the cognitive function of narrative not upon abstract rational argument, but instead in the dialogic practice of reading (and writing), a process which in turn relies upon the activation of positive prejudices, namely sympathy, emotion and the imagination. Lurie's crucial failure in *Disgrace* is his wilful refusal to engage precisely these critical faculties. His complacent attachment to attitudes that he senses are unjustifiable is shown to be a product not only of his idealization of the Wordsworthian ethic of blindness, but also of his wider reluctance to engage emotionally (rather than intellectually) with the people and situations he faces. Like Byron's Lucifer, Lurie's 'madness [is] not of the head, but heart.'[31]

In addition to his role as a disciple of Romanticism, Lurie figures in *Disgrace* in a more general way as an icon of rational discourse. In fact, despite his strenuous defence of the 'rights of desire,' Lurie is avowedly not a creature of passion. Just as he describes sex with Soraya as 'abstract, rather dry, even at its hottest,' he finds fatherhood 'a rather abstract business.'[32] Immediately after the attack on the farm, Lurie seeks to comfort himself by trying to rationalize the incident in light of what he knows of the political context of South Africa: '[t]hat is the theory; hold to the theory and to the comforts of theory.'[33] His initially dismissive attitude towards Lucy's friend Bev Shaw is similarly predicated upon his resistance to her emotional engagement with the animals she treats. By contrast, Lurie urges Lucy not to 'lose perspective,' confidently asserting his rational faith that humans 'are of a different order of creation from the animals,' and thus that the ethical treatment of animals is a matter of 'simple generosity' rather than of fear of retribution.[34]

From the outset, however, Lucy resists her father's rationalizing influence, a resistance that only becomes more pronounced following the rape. Repeatedly Lucy dismisses her father's attempts to persuade her to leave the farm, insisting that she is 'not going back for the sake of an idea. I'm just going back.'[35] Later, she accuses Lurie of 'misreading' her, reminding him that 'Guilt and salvation are abstractions. I don't act in terms of abstractions. Until you make an effort to see that, I can't help you.'[36]

In the aftermath of Lucy's rape, Lurie's detached philosophical posturing is reversed, and he becomes instead a vigorous advocate of legal authority, pressurizing Lucy to report her attackers to the police. Now identified as victim, rather than perpetrator, Lurie finds himself replaying Melanie's father's earlier role, demanding (unsuccessfully) that Petrus recognize the 'violation' that has been inflicted upon his daughter: *'If it had been your wife instead of my daughter*, he would like to say to Petrus, *you would not be tapping your pipe and weighing your words so judiciously.*'[37] For Lurie, himself a notorious weigher of words, the irony is acute. For the first time, he has been brought into a position which engages his emotions, an affect that enlarges the narrow rationalism of his earlier outlook and painfully reveals the inadequacy of his former attitudes.

Michael Inwood's Hegel dictionary defines the sixteenth century meaning of '*abstrhieren*' (to abstract) as a derivation from the Latin '*abstrahere*,' literally, 'to draw away, remove (something from something else).'[38] To make something abstract is then, quite literally, to remove it from its context. *Disgrace* opposes abstract (or disembodied) modes of thought with the pragmatic, affective change in circumstance that Lurie is forced to undergo, grounding cognitive knowledge in the concrete circumstances of the individual life. Only from this emotionally engaged perspective can grace be achieved. As Elleke Boehmer argues, 'In both this novel and *The Lives of Animals,* intellectual distance is the first safeguard of a self-regarding vanity; it must be sacrificed for true abnegation to be experienced.'[39]

Lurie's newly engaged perspective is reflected in the novel through his changing attitude towards animals. He finds himself inexplicably sympathizing with Petrus' two mangy sheep, who, destined for slaughter, have been tethered in a barren field which affords no pasture for grazing. Unconsciously, Lurie draws parallels between the sheep and Melanie: 'Sheep do not own themselves, do not own their lives. They exist to be used, every last ounce of them, their flesh to be eaten, their bones to be crushed and fed to poultry.'[40] This affinity between the objectified status of animals and Lurie's attitude towards women is further referenced through Melanie's sacrificial surname. Whereas earlier Lurie had characterized Melanie in animalistic, poetic language, the terms of his discourse are now reversed as he comes to reconsider the practical implications of his earlier ethical and aesthetic judgments. Lurie's obscure concern for the fate of the animals is the outpouring of a nascent sense of humility, the beginnings of an acknowledgement of his morally disgraced state.

6. The Sympathetic Imagination

In this emerging spirit of self-denial, Lurie takes up a role that he had earlier considered beneath him. His work at the animal shelter, assisting Bev Shaw euthanize vagrant dogs, brings him into a newly sympathetic relation with the radically marginalized perspective of animals, a relation which Lurie himself is at a loss to explain: 'He does not understand what is happening to him. Until now, he has been more or less indifferent to animals. Although in an abstract way he disapproves of cruelty, he cannot tell whether by nature he is cruel or kind.'[41] The novel tentatively suggests a model of ethics that is based not on abstract laws or reasoned arguments, but rather on pragmatic, sympathetic engagement. Lurie takes upon himself the duty of disposing of the dead bodies of the euthanized dogs, despite and because of the fact that his reasons for doing so remain inexplicable to him. Although the practical import of this act of memorializing remains dubious, the respect that Lurie pays to the animals' dead bodies operates as a kind of penance for his earlier egocentric behaviour, providing a model of ethical sympathy that transcends rational justification. Lurie 'saves the honour of corpses because there is no one else stupid enough to do it. That is what he is becoming: stupid, daft, wrongheaded.'[42]

Disgrace's staging of a sympathetic imaginative mode of ethical engagement is taken up again in Coetzee's next novel, *Elizabeth Costello* (2003). In a critique that bears an obvious resemblance to David Lurie's initial refusal to engage sympathetically with the perspectives of women and animals in *Disgrace*, Costello argues that the horror of the Nazi death camps was made possible only because of a certain 'willed ignorance' on the part of ordinary Germans, a refusal to see that amounted to an abdication of humanity.[43] For Costello, the true horror of the holocaust lies in this wilful refusal to empathize with fellow beings, the deliberate failure of the killers 'to think themselves into the place of their victims.'[44]

Citing Thomas Nagel's famous question 'What Is It Like to Be a Bat?' (1974), Costello refutes Nagel's conclusion that we can only imagine what it would be like to *behave* as a bat, since the essence of bat-being remains fundamentally inaccessible to the human mind. For Costello, Nagel's denial of the power of imagination is 'tragically restrictive, restrictive and restricted.'[45] Instead, Costello argues that human knowledge is not 'abstract,' but 'embodied:' '[t]o be a living bat is to be full of being: being fully a bat is like being fully human, which is also to be full of being.'[46] Humans and animals alike are for Costello embodied souls whose consciousness is predicated upon 'the sensation - a heavily affective sensation - of being a body with limbs that have extension in space, of being alive to the world.'[47] Costello takes seriously the possibility that humans can empathize with nonhuman modes of being, arguing that 'the sympathetic imagination' knows no bounds:

> [t]he heart is the seat of a faculty, *sympathy*, that allows for us to share at times the being of another. Sympathy has everything to do with the subject and little to do with the object, the 'another,' as we see at once when we think of the object not as a bat [...] but as another human being.[48]

For Costello, philosophy's reluctance to engage imaginatively and sympathetically with the lives of animals is a testament to the dangers of instrumental reason. Rejecting traditional philosophical modes of discourse, Costello argues that

> both reason and seven decades of life experience tell me that reason is neither the being of the universe nor the being

> of God. On the contrary, reason looks to me suspiciously like the being of human thought; worse than that, like the being of one tendency in human thought. Reason is the being of a certain spectrum of human thinking. And if this is so, if that is what I believe, then why should I bow to reason this afternoon and content myself with embroidering on the discourse of the old philosophers?[49]

Literature provides Costello (and Coetzee) with a form of speaking that is not as tightly bound by the standards of abstract reason as traditional critical or analytical discourse. In a speech to the Weekly Mail Book Week in Cape Town in 1988, Coetzee famously defended storytelling as 'an other' mode of discourse, defined against history and 'historical disciplines' (a phrase which appears to operate as a catch-all term for any nonfictional critical or analytic discourse). Against history, Coetzee argued for an autonomous literature, one that 'operates in terms of its own procedures and issues in its own conclusions,' and thereby resists forming a subsidiary of historical discourse and thus becoming 'checkable' by history 'as a child's schoolwork is checked by a schoolmistress.'[50]

7. Self-Deceiving Animals

As Garcia notes in this volume, modern philosophy has increasingly questioned a strong divide between reason and emotion, and viewed art as being more responsive to the basic unity between reason and emotion than purely rational forms of discourse.[51] Coetzee's championing of the sympathetic imagination, and the literary means by which he expresses this argument, can thus be seen to participate in a wider philosophical process of questioning the limitations of traditional rational discourses. We should be wary, however, of reading Coetzee's privileging of literary discourse in straightforwardly utopian terms. On the contrary, *Disgrace* explicitly acknowledges the limitations of the sympathetic imagination, systematically enacting the necessary limits of any historically-contingent attempt at reading (or writing). These limits are foregrounded in the novel through Lurie's references to Flaubert's *Madame Bovary* (1857). Returning from his regular Thursday afternoon rendezvous with Soraya,

> [Lurie] thinks of Emma Bovary, coming home sated, glazen-eyed, from an afternoon of reckless fucking. *So this is bliss!*, says Emma, marvelling at herself in the mirror. *So this is the bliss the poets speak of!* Well, if poor ghostly Emma were ever to find her way to Cape Town, he would bring her along one Thursday afternoon to show her what bliss can be: a moderate bliss, a moderated bliss.[52]

The irony of this allusion is profound given what we know of Lurie's later behaviour in the novel. He is of course just as guilty as Emma Bovary of disastrously playing out the paradigms of Romantic literature - with the key difference being that, unlike Emma, Lurie has read *Madame Bovary*. Coetzee thus shows Lurie falling prey to the perils of Romantic discourse *in spite of* his reflexive awareness of the potential dangers of such discourses. Despite his self-justifying attempts to define himself as a libertine disciple of Eros, Lurie's actual motivations are shown to be rather more nebulous. Lurie, like Byron's Lucifer, 'doesn't act on principle but on impulse, and the source of his impulses is dark to him.'[53]

Lurie's own critical oeuvre further sharpens the irony: he has written three books, each of which proves paradigmatic for his own later behaviour. The first, on Boito and the Faust legend, deals with the story of an aging academic whose first act after signing a contract with the devil is the rape of a teenage girl. The second, on Richard of St Victor, investigates vision as Eros (the patron of male love, as opposed to Aphrodite, who governs love between men and women); while the third deals with Wordsworth and 'the Burden of the Past.'[54] The implications of this critique of reflexivity for Coetzee's own literature are stark: as well as calling into question the possibility of any meaningful distinction between Romantic and post-Romantic thought, Coetzee questions literature's ethical utility, suggesting that artistic education is inadequate as a tool of ethical enlightenment.

Lurie's status as teacher is in this respect significant, for despite his complacent observation that 'the one who comes to teach learns the keenest of lessons, while those who come to learn nothing,' Lurie in fact fails to learn anything until he has renounced his claim to authority and begun instead to embrace his disgraced state.[55] Like Byron's *Don Juan,* Lurie's education, rather than developing his ethical maturity, in fact provides a stimulus toward and legitimation for his unethical behaviour.[56] This dichotomy between education and ethics is further highlighted by Melanie's father, Mr Isaacs, a figure of natural justice in the novel, who chastises Lurie: 'you may be very educated and all that, but what you have done is not right.'[57]

Rather than privileging an autonomous literature, then, *Disgrace* systematically enacts the necessary limits of any historically-contingent attempt at understanding. Coetzee acknowledges the situatedness of art in the world, the fact that art exists in a kind of privileged social space and may ultimately promote a rather conservative form of knowledge, one that does not significantly challenge and in fact might actively reinforce existing social hierarchies. Through its characterization of David Lurie, *Disgrace* stages a confrontation with the educated, self-conscious reader, foregrounding the limitations of reflexivity in a move which raises serious questions about both Coetzee's moral status as educated writer, and our role as educated readers.

This critique raises an uncomfortable question: If even sensitive, reflective readers are subject to mystifying false consciousness, what then remains of literature's ethical value? It is possible to read the novel in the most pessimistic of terms, as an enactment of the inevitable failure of art to provide ethical enlightenment. But such a reading prematurely forecloses the possibility of discovering a form of writing which is sensitive to these concerns and evolves a mature response to them, a possibility to which Coetzee remains deeply committed. Instead, what *Disgrace* demonstrates is that literature *alone* is inadequate as a source of ethical instruction. In order for art to create emotional forms of knowledge that are at the same time ethical, in order for it to edify as well as to inform, *Disgrace* suggests that it is necessary for the reader to recognize what Coetzee has called the '[overwhelming] fact of suffering in the world,' to begin to feel (rather than merely think) the pain of others.[58]

The novel suggests that, if artistic forms of knowledge creation are to have a positive ethical impact, it is necessary to recognize the intersubjective basis of emotional experience, to combine intellectual perspectives with an emotional posture of concern, a being-towards-the-other that involves making a leap of imagination from one's own experiences to caring for the experiences of others. As Nenko notes in this volume, aesthetic emotions do have the capacity to elevate us spiritually and morally, but they are not attained through 'in-depth speculation, but in feeling [oneself] interconnected with the other.'[59]

8. The Music Itself

In this sense David Lurie's development from critic to artist is important, because it suggests that it may well be through the processes of creating art, rather than by merely consuming it, that the emotional and ethical faculties (sympathy, imagination, and love) are best developed. With this in mind, I conclude with a consideration of how far Lurie's newly critical engagement with literary tradition in the later part of the novel, as evinced through the construction of his opera, signals a viable opportunity for literature to transcend the potentially abusive power of aesthetic tradition and provide a positive stimulus toward ethical responsibility.

Lurie's gradual recognition of the limitations of his aesthetic outlook takes him on a voyage of discovery as he seeks to uncover an order of discourse that is responsive to alternative modes of being, a quest that is embodied in *Disgrace* through the evolution of Lurie's opera. Originally intended as a chamber opera celebrating Byron's last great love affair in Italy, the form and content of Lurie's work undergo a drastic transformation as he is ineluctably confronted with the range of voices whose perspectives he has hitherto been deaf to.

As the opera develops, Lurie moves strategically away from traditional modes of representation, the 'lush arias' he had envisioned at the start of his project gradually falling away layer after layer, until finally what remains of the music is strummed on a tuneless banjo to the accompaniment of a howling dog. The opera's studied bathos operates both as a reproach to the hubris of Lurie's earlier Romantic posturing, and as an ironic commentary upon *Disgrace* itself: '*Out of the poets I learned to love*' chants Byron in a 'cracked monotone,' '*but life, I found* (descending chromatically into F) *is another story.*'[60] Marvelling at 'what the little banjo is teaching him,' Lurie observes that

> six months ago he had thought his own ghostly place in *Byron in Italy* would be somewhere between Teresa's and Byron's: between a yearning to prolong the summer of the passionate body and a reluctant recall from the long sleep of oblivion. But he was wrong. It is not the erotic that is calling to him after all, nor the elegiac, but the comic. He is in the opera not as Teresa nor as Byron nor even as some blending of the two: he is held in the music itself, in the flat, tinny slap of the banjo strings, the voice that strains to soar away from the ludicrous instrument but is continually reined back, like a fish on a line.[61]

Coetzee here hints at his own position within the work of art, which resides neither in a straightforward identification with Lurie, nor in a moralistic defence of Lucy, but rather in 'the music itself,' the hauntingly discordant narrative voice which so frequently disrupts from within the surface of Lurie's narration. 'So this is art,' Lurie thinks, 'and this is how it does its work! How strange! How fascinating!'[62]

Lurie's opera thus enacts *Disgrace*'s own fragile status as a site of engagement with literary tradition. Returning then to my earlier question, is it possible to view Lurie's opera as signalling an opportunity for art to transcend the coercive force of aesthetic tradition and provide a viable stimulus toward ethical responsibility? My answer, tentatively, is yes. But this fragile potential is lost utterly as soon as we begin to neglect literature's historically situated status, its relationship to concrete power structures in the real world, as well as our position as readers (and writers) within such structures.

9. Conclusion

Disgrace posits a learned individual, David Lurie, who is brought by the twin forces of extreme emotional experience and artistic practice to confront the limitations of his abstract intellectual worldview. Initially, David's faith in the Romantic ideals of his literary masters, Byron and

Wordsworth, leads him to blindly follow his own desires and to privilege his own egoistic wishes above the needs of others. Following his disastrous affair with Melanie, his public disgrace, and his daughter's rape, however, Lurie develops a newly critical relationship to his Romantic forerunners, becoming more sensitive to the ways in which literary tradition has tended historically to exclude the voices and perspectives of women.

But, in spite of its critical bent, *Disgrace* does not represent an outright rejection of Romantic ideology so much as demonstrate its continued relevance to modern life. Lurie's experience of emotional trauma prompts him to realize just how badly he has misunderstood his masters, and to seek for the first time to engage emotionally, sympathetically and imaginatively with the perspectives of others, notably women and animals. This newfound ethical perspective is in turn embodied in the novel through David's opera, an artwork which puts into practice the lessons that David has begun, finally, to learn from the Romantics.

David's journey towards greater ethical maturity is not represented as complete or even certain in *Disgrace*; he remains a flawed, egocentric character even at the novel's close. In much the same way, the novel refuses to pass final judgment on the question of the relationship of art to ethics. The idea that the practice of writing might provide one way to expand our emotional horizons is hinted at, gestured towards, hoped for, but nowhere finally affirmed. Through its form as well as its content then, *Disgrace* embodies a model of artistic knowledge creation which is concrete, dialogic, and reflexive, that reaches beyond the abstraction of theory towards a sympathetic, imaginative engagement with others, and that, crucially, is honest about the fragile indeterminacy of its own ethical status.

Notes

[1] This 'rationalization' of the education system is of course not unique to South Africa - Coetzee's own lengthy involvement with the American academy may well provide further context for Lurie's exasperation here. See J.M. Coetzee, *Disgrace*, Penguin, London, 2000, p. 3. For a critical account of this trend in academia see J. van Andel, 'The Rationalization of Academia: From *Bildung* to Production', 2011, this volume.

[2] Coetzee, *Disgrace*, op. cit., p. 4. Lurie's dissatisfaction with the increasing capitalistic mechanization of the South African higher education system mimics Coetzee's own frustrations with current trends in academia. Having worked as an academic for over 40 years in America, South Africa, and now Australia, Coetzee has commented that '[what has] happened to universities, in my view, had little to do with creating higher standards and everything to

do with imposing a business model on them;' and that as a result 'Universities seem to me to be fairly miserable places nowadays.' In part then, Lurie's nostalgia for a time when his scholastic talents were socially valued can be seen as an altogether unironic reflection of Coetzee's own discomfort with modern utilitarian teaching trends. See J.M. Coetzee and J. Poyner, 'J.M. Coetzee in Conversation with Jane Poyner.' *J.M. Coetzee and the Idea of the Public Intellectual*, J. Poyner (ed), Ohio University Press, Ohio, 2006, pp. 23-24.

[3] Ibid., p. 32.

[4] G. Cornwell, 'Disgraceland: History and the Humanities in Frontier Country', *English in Africa*, Vol. 30(2), 2003, p. 58.

[5] Coetzee, *Disgrace*, op. cit., p. 31.

[6] Ibid., p. 16.

[7] Ibid., pp. 18, 32, 34.

[8] Ibid., pp. 13-14. The title of this dance subtly reinforces the egoistic nature of Lurie's interaction with Melanie at this point, translating as 'not both.'

[9] Ibid., p.13.

[10] Ibid., p. 16.

[11] Wordsworth's series of five short poems ('A Slumber Did My Spirit Seal,' 'She Dwelt Among the Untrodden Ways,' 'Strange Fits of Passion I Have Known,' 'Three Years She Grew in Sun and Shower,' and 'I Travelled Among Unknown Men') composed between 1770 and 1850, are emblematic of the latent hostility of the Romantic tradition's aestheticisation of women. These enigmatic love poems, narrated by a male hero, take a kind of perverse delight in the inevitable demise of the love object, Lucy: 'What fond and wayward thoughts will slide / Into a lover's head! / 'O mercy!' to myself I cried, / 'If Lucy should be dead!'.' W Wordsworth, 'Strange Fits of Passion I Have Known'. *The Collected Poems of William Wordsworth*, Wordsworth Editions, London, 1994, p. 125.

[12] Coetzee, *Disgrace*, op. cit., p. 13.

[13] Ibid., p. 22.

[14] For a detailed investigation of Coetzee's use of this technique, see D. Attridge, 'Modernist Form and the Ethics of Otherness'. *J.M. Coetzee and the Ethics of Reading*, University of Chicago Press, London, 2004, pp. 1-31.

[15] Coetzee, *Disgrace*, op. cit., p. 19.

[16] Ibid.

[17] Ibid., p. 25.

[18] Ibid., p. 47.

[19] Ibid., p. 52.

[20] Ibid., p. 160.

[21] Graham's sweeping evocation of a 'Romantic/humanist' tradition is here perhaps too vague to carry much critical weight, but this reading also fails on a wider level to recognize the way in which Lurie's critical re-evaluation of his earlier aesthetic credo here is less straightforwardly rejectionist than might at first appear. The passage upon closer reading appears deeply ambiguous: what Lurie actually criticizes is less Byron's particular deployment of rape than the violent brutality of modern forms of rape. Rather than demonstrating Lurie's eschewal of literary tradition, we here see the determinedly dialogic nature of Coetzee's intertextual approach. See L.V. Graham, 'Reading the Unspeakable: Rape in J.M. Coetzee's *Disgrace*', *Body, Sexuality, and Gender: Versions and Subversions in African Literatures 1*, F. Veit-Wild and D. Naguschewski (eds), Rodopi, London, 2005, p. 263.

[22] P. McDonald, 'Disgrace Effects', *Interventions*, Vol. 4(3), 2002, p. 328.

[23] M. Harvey, 'Re-educating the Romantic: Sex and the Nature-Poet in J.M. Coetzee's *Disgrace*', *Sydney Studies in English*, Vol. 31, 2005, p. 97.

[24] Byron's affection for animals is well-documented. Unusually for his time, he followed a largely vegetarian diet (although he did occasionally binge upon meat). Upon the death of his favoured pet, Boatswain, in 1808, Byron went so far as to have a monument constructed in memorial of the animal, installing it at Newstead Abbey and inscribing it with the poem, 'Inscription on the Monument of a Newfoundland Dog:' 'the poor dog, / in life the firmest friend, / The first to welcome, foremost to defend, / Whose honest heart is still his master's own, / Who labours, fights, lives, breathes for him alone, / Unhonour'd falls, unnoticed all his worth, / Denied in heaven the soul he held on earth: / While man, vain insect! hopes to be forgiven, / And claims himself a sole exclusive heaven.' G.G. Byron, 'Inscription on the Monument of a Newfoundland Dog', *Byron: Complete Poetical Works*, F. Page (ed), Oxford University Press, Oxford, 1970, p. 54.

[25] M. Beard, 'Lessons from the Dead Masters: Wordsworth and Byron in J.M. Coetzee's *Disgrace*', *English in Africa*, Vol. 34(1), 2007, p. 61.

[26] Ibid., p. 64.

[27] Coetzee, *Disgrace*, op. cit., pp. 46, 218.

[28] Ibid., p. 179.

[29] Ibid., p. 218.

[30] Ibid., p. 160.

[31] Ibid., p. 33.

[32] Ibid., pp. 3, 63.

[33] Ibid., p. 98.

[34] Ibid., p. 74.

[35] Ibid., p. 105.

[36] Ibid., p. 112.
[37] Ibid., p. 119 (original italics).
[38] M.J. Inwood, *A Hegel Dictionary*, Blackwell, London, 1992, p. 29.
[39] E. Boehmer, 'Not Saying Sorry, Not Speaking Pain: Gender Implications in *Disgrace*', *Interventions*, Vol. 4(3), 2002, pp. 342-351, p. 348.
[40] Coetzee, *Disgrace*, op. cit., p. 123.
[41] Ibid., p. 143.
[42] Ibid., p. 146.
[43] J.M. Coetzee, *Elizabeth Costello*, Vintage, London, 2004, p. 64. In *Dusklands*, Eugene Dawn similarly characterizes American conduct in Vietnam as the consequence of a failure of sympathy: '[for] a while we were prepared to pity them, though we pitied more our tragic reach for transcendence. Then we ran out of pity.' J.M. Coetzee, *Dusklands* (1974), Vintage, London, 2004, p. 18.
[44] Coetzee, *Elizabeth Costello*, op. cit., p. 79.
[45] Ibid., p. 76.
[46] Ibid., p. 77.
[47] Ibid., p. 78.
[48] Ibid., p. 79.
[49] Ibid., p. 67.
[50] Ibid.
[51] See C.D.G. Mancilla, 'Art and the Passion of Intellect', 2011, this volume.
[52] Coetzee, *Disgrace*, op. cit., pp. 5-6.
[53] Ibid., p. 33.
[54] Ibid., p. 4.
[55] Ibid., p. 5.
[56] Byron's ironic account of Don Juan's ethical education proves instructive for an understanding of *Disgrace*'s critique of literature's ability to function as a source of ethical knowledge creation: 'Sermons he read, and lectures he endured, / And homilies, and lives of all the saints; / To Jerome and to Chrysostom inured, / He did not take such studies for restraints; / But how faith is acquired, and then ensured, / So well not one of the aforesaid paints / As Saint Augustine in his fine Confessions, / Which make the reader envy his transgressions.' Byron, 'Don Juan' (1821) Canto the First, XLVII (1821). *Byron: Complete Poetical Works*, op. cit., p. 642.
[57] Coetzee, *Disgrace*, op. cit., p. 38.
[58] J.M. Coetzee, *Doubling the Point: Essays and Interviews*, D. Atwell (ed), Harvard University Press, Cambridge, MA, 1992, p. 248.
[59] O. Nenko, 'Aesthetic Emotional Experience: From Eye Irritation to Knowledge', 2011, this volume.

[60] Coetzee, *Disgrace*, op. cit., p. 185.
[61] Ibid., pp. 184-185.
[62] Ibid., p. 185.

Bibliography

Attridge, D., *J.M. Coetzee and the Ethics of Reading*. University of Chicago Press, London, 2004.

——, 'J.M. Coetzee's *Disgrace*: Introduction.' *Interventions*. Vol. 4(3), 2002, pp. 315-320.

Beard, M., 'Lessons from the Dead Masters: Wordsworth and Byron in J.M. Coetzee's *Disgrace*'. *English in Africa*. Vol. 34(1), 2007, pp. 59-77.

Boehmer, E., 'Not Saying Sorry, Not Speaking Pain: Gender Implications in *Disgrace*'. *Interventions*. Vol. 4(3), 2002, pp. 342-351.

Byron, G.G., 'Don Juan'. *Byron: Complete Poetical Works*. Page, F. (ed), OUP, Oxford, 1970.

——, 'Inscription on the Monument of a Newfoundland Dog'. *Byron: Complete Poetical Works*. Page, F. (ed), OUP, Oxford, 1970.

Coetzee, J.M., 'The Novel Today'. *Upstream*, Summer 1988, pp. 3-5.

——, 'Into the Dark Chamber: The Novelist and South Africa'. *New York Times*. Sunday, January 12, 1986, Late City Final Edition, Section 7, p. 13, Column 1.

——, 'André Brink and the Censor'. *Research in African Literatures*. Vol. 21(3), Autumn 1990, pp. 59-74.

——, *Doubling the Point: Essays and Interviews*. Atwell, D. (ed), Harvard University Press, Cambridge MA, 1992.

——, *Dusklands*. Vintage, London, 2004.

——, *In the Heart of the Country*. Vintage, London, 2004.

——, *Disgrace*. Penguin, London, 2000.

——, *Elizabeth Costello*. Vintage, London, 2004.

Cornwell, G., 'Disgraceland: History and the Humanities in Frontier Country'. *English in Africa*. Vol. 30(2), 2003, pp. 43-68.

Graham, L.V., 'Reading the Unspeakable: Rape in J.M. Coetzee's *Disgrace*'. *Sexuality, and Gender: Versions and Subversions in African Literatures 1*. Veit-Wild, F. and Naguschewski, D. (eds), Rodopi, London, 2005.

Harvey, M., 'Re-Educating the Romantic: Sex and The Nature-Poet in J.M. Coetzee's *Disgrace*'. *Sydney Studies in English*. Vol. 31, 2005, pp. 94-109.

Head, D., *The Cambridge Introduction to J.M. Coetzee*. CUP, Cambridge, 2009.

Inwood, M.J., *A Hegel Dictionary*. Blackwell, London, 1992.

Marais, M., 'Little Enough, Less than Little: Ethics, Engagement and Change in the Fiction of J.M. Coetzee'. *Modern Fiction Studies*. Vol. 46(1), 2000, pp. 159-182.

McDonald, P., 'Disgrace Effects'. *Interventions*. Vol. 4(3), 2002, pp. 321-330.

McLeod, L., 'Do We of Necessity Become Puppets in a Story?' Of Narrating the World: On Speech, Silence and Discourse in J.M. Coetzee's *Foe*'. *Modern Fiction Studies*. Vol. 52(1), 2006, pp. 1-18.

Poyner, J., 'J.M. Coetzee in Conversation with Jane Poyner'. *J.M. Coetzee and the Idea of the Public Intellectual,* Poyner, J. (ed), Ohio University Press, Ohio, 2006.

Wordsworth, W., 'Strange Fits of Passion I Have Known'. *The Collected Poems of William Wordsworth*. Wordsworth Editions, London, 1994.

——, 'The Prelude'. *The Collected Poems of William Wordsworth*. Wordsworth Editions, London, 1994, pp. 801-893.

Watson, S., 'The Writer and the Devil: J.M. Coetzee's *The Master of Petersburg*'. *New Contrast.* Vol. 22(4), 1994, pp. 47-61.

Aesthetic Emotional Experience: From Eye Irritation to Knowledge

Oleksandra Nenko

Abstract
In this chapter we aim to reveal the cognitive essence of aesthetic emotional experience gained by individuals in the realm full of *evidence* - the visual arts. Though stressing on the sensual and emotional side of cognition, we underline the complexity of the conceptualizations needed *ultima analysi* for understanding knowledge creation. In our opinion, description and analysis of the emotional experience gained through visual arts can be carried out profoundly in the frames of *phenomenological* paradigm, for it considers experience as a complex enterprise of habitation in the world, paying much attention to its emotional aspects. We regard artwork as a multilayer formation having material and symbolic dimensions, as well as interactive dimension that contains subjective positions of the author and the spectator. The latter are presented as 'intellectuals' that involve into a cognitive practice, constitute a corresponding interactive order and create transpersonal aesthetic emotional knowledge. Emotions aroused by the artwork include corporeal sensations and cognitive-evaluative feelings of emotional aesthetic experience that is intentional and intersubjective. Knowledge arises from these multiple sources as a super-subjective phenomenon and constitutes a mode of apprehending the world, an algorithm of sensual transgression from primary physical feeling of oneself to the symbolic complex intersubjective emotional realm of concentrated *life*.

Key Words: Visual arts, emotions, aesthetic emotional experience, phenomenology, emotional knowledge.

*****

1. Aesthetic Experience in the Frames of a Phenomenological Paradigm

Understanding that emotions are important to the human ontology was deeply elaborated in phenomenological paradigm; the 'emotional a priori' (M. Scheler) noted that emotions are the basic structures of human existence. The phenomenologists of wide range paid much attention to emotions, except the founding father of phenomenology Edmund Husserl who wasn't interested that much: M. Heidegger (who also was indebted to S. Kierkegaard and F. Nieztsche), M. Scheler, E. Levinas, J.-P. Sartre, M. Merleau-Ponty, and P. Ricoeur. It was proven that emotional experience goes along with any kind of human relationships, even preceding our conscious realization and reasoning about situations we appear in. The phenomenologists have shown that conventional understanding of cognition, conscience and knowledge is witnessing drawbacks of the Cartesian methodology, i.e. the separation and contrast of the subject and object. In the first chapter of this part of the book Mancilla reveals how Cartesian duality led to the ontological distance between spirit and soul, senses, passions and ratio.[1] Cartesian considerations exclude the before-objective relation to the world possible within the practices of cognition, taking place beyond the discursive limits of 'legitimate' knowledge creation. Below we will consider an area where emotions take a leading role in perception, understanding and identification - art, the visual arts in particular.

Art and its relation to passions, emotions, and sentiments was examined from the antique intellectuals to the postmodern ones. Modern philosophers found in art a bolt-hole to escape from immanent errors of rational thinking; Descartes tried to resolve the mystery of art and its influence on our consciousness through suppressing the dominance of deduction and showing an alternative way of cognition - intuition. As Heaney has shown in the previous chapter, Romanticism and its ideals remaining in some of the contemporary intellectuals extolled the openness to dark and absorbing passions as a way to find one's true self.[2] Phenomenology of art and emotions tries to overcome the drawbacks of modern philosophy, mainly primacy of rationality and reasonable 'normalization,' in building the understanding of the world; and deepen understanding of passions not just as dark forces coming from nowhere, but as kind of relationship to the world. If asked, we wouldn't hesitate to answer, that creation and appreciation of visual arts are closely related to emotions. It is what we witness with our own body, what we live through - our *emotional aesthetic experience* that can be grasped in frames of phenomenological discourse.

Aesthetic experience is one of the most important phenomenological concepts strongly connected with emotions. For John Dewey, who is often referred to as a follower of the phenomenological tradition and a pillar of 'experience research,' art brings aesthetic experience: experience of a unique and fantastical world, of a game played (or being played) upon the senses which results in an emotional state.[3] According to Gadamer, 'Artwork can be defined as its ability to become an aesthetic experience.'[4] Actually, aesthetic experience is a term provoking tough epistemological debates around the nature of knowledge. First to be mentioned is that Dewey saw aesthetic experience rising from everyday experience.[5] Thus, it is not knowledge resulting from intellectual reasoning and rational thought that is aimed to 'purify' knowledge from the everyday common senses and non-objective feelings. Secondly, it is that kind of experience which eliminates cognitive distinctions between objectivism and subjectivism. As Gardner explains it, objectivism in philosophy comes from the idea that the world is given and independent of how we represent it, hence our real knowledge of the world comes from our experiences, which correlate with the world as it really is. However, this is not relevant for aesthetic experience, since in aesthetic experience one does not gain knowledge in the first place. It is rather a kind of personal relationship to the world than a way to gain knowledge. Gardner argues that '[t]he cognitive demand that mind should fit the world does not apply to aesthetic interest, which is in this respect closer to desire than belief - what we want is for the world to fit *us.*'[6] A distinctive emphasis has been put recently that aesthetic experience is a dynamic *two-way* interaction between consciousness and environment in the process of active co-engagement.[7] Hence, the third epistemological challenge: the ecology of (cognitive) existence is enabled by aesthetic experience, a thesis which was also to a large extent elaborated by Dewey. He treats art broadly as any effort taken in any sphere of life to make desired changes in the environment that increase our sense of unity with it. This dynamic rhythmical interaction of the organism and its environment gives grounding to the knowledge about the world and oneself.[8] The sterling process of intellectual inquiry itself should have an aesthetic nature.[9] The variety of the components of aesthetic experience spreads from psycho-motoric skills to emotional encounters and emotional evaluative attitudes, which become part of new identifications and relationships in a world newly sensed. A quintessence of this is *knowledge* of pre-objective *emotional aesthetic background,* which is a province of non-separated, non-alienated, non-pragmatic, non-egoistic meanings belonging to the world image of above-human harmonious structuration.

Taking into the consideration the complexity of the aesthetic experience and its emotional fundament in terms of knowledge as awareness of things and something we implicate into further developments of our thought or action, let us try to look on its ontological story. Tentative speculation on the emotional aesthetic experience allows defining two different levels of individual consciousness where it takes place. One is the spontaneous 'primary' emotion of satisfaction or disgust elicited by the artwork; the other is the reflective emotional judgment or evaluation of the work as beautiful, exciting, ugly or other. Psychologist L. Vigotsky criticized theory of mood differential (or sensual impression) and theory of Einfühlung that referred to these levels respectively theorizing the connection of arts and emotions, but both theories failed to look on their tie in complex.[10] Vigotsky proposed his own conception of the psychology of art as invocation of strong and real affections which are eased into fantasy. Underlining the result of art as an explosion of this affective nervous energy Vigotsky continues the 'catharsis' tradition of discussing art.[11]

Relying on the phenomenological views we see the possibility to go further in consideration of art and emotions: the emotional aspect of the aesthetic experience might be exceptionally intense and transcend ordinary emotional states. Art as a sensual enterprise leads cognition through a series of emotional transformations: from bodily visual perceptions, like form, shape and colour; through basic emotions, e.g., pleasure and disgust; to complex aesthetic emotional states, like empathy, harmonious and lofty co-feeling. In general, art gives one a chance to feel existential exceeding of the bounds and at the same time - intensify one's embeddedness in the world, being-in-the-world (Heidegger). Aesthetic emotional experience enables leaping into 'authentic,' non-fragmented naturalness and withal provokes feeling possibility for multiple presences, having a transpersonal nature. Emotions pierce through the work of art while perceived and the image evokes feeling of a world of the 'Unreal,' so aesthetic emotional experience elevates cognition to investigate life as a whole.

2. Where Everything Begins: The Aesthetic Sensual Perception

Husserl treats painting as possessing its own materiality: space and time, colours, canvas, etc. While looking at the picture, the observer enters its picturesqueness: the picture acts by its colour, light, size, shape, material.[12] The colours possess a certain power of words, so in order to reach the sense of the image it is necessary to set one's eyes into motion.

This game of motion and material provokes feelings within the human body.[13] The image in its neutrality is able to be a thing that speaks to the observer: *here I am and you feel me*. This is happening in spite of the constraints of sociocultural contexts, rules of thinking and feeling, and even lack of names for a sensation in one's emotional vocabulary. Since Aristotle these bodily phenomena are recognized as physiological part of the phenomenology of emotions.[14] Sometimes phenomenologists lost sight of these 'simple' bodily feelings, concentrating on the pure transcendent emotions in cognition (e.g., pure speculation was Husserl's aim). M. Merleau-Ponty, among the others, returned the 'materiality' of the subject to the field by underlining motility or bodily engagement of the subject into the process of cognition.[15] Merleau-Ponty emphasized that only visual art draws on the 'fabric of brute feelings.'[16] The sensible and unsealed world such as it is for our life and our body (not always for our intelligence) makes the ground of art. The perception of the existing world and creation of the inner homothetic image of it do not go on in a human as 'informational machine', but in his/her actual body and other bodies that are related to it. 'Quality, light, colour, depth, which are there before us, are there only because they awaken an echo in our body and because our body welcomes them.'[17] In particular, Merleau-Ponty brought up James' earlier considerations of the embodiment of emotions and their functional warmness in the cognition of the world opposite to the coldness of the intellectual representations.[18] Both the artist and the viewer can proceed to deeper emotions only when colour and light irritate their eye.

The materiality of an artwork appeals to emotions of the first order consciousness or non-reflective consciousness, which is about the mere experience of what an event is like.[19] First-order emotional experience is the outcome of the 'natural attitude' towards objects of perception.[20] It directly represents what 'it feels like' to see an image as it is.[21] But the material space of the picture is not identical to the one we perceive in the picture; the invisible part of the space belonging to the picture is in contrast to the part of space which can be grasped by experience.[22] In 'Phantasie und Bildliche Vorstellung' (1898) Husserl distinguishes between a picture and a thing; it is possible to speak about (a) a picture as a physical thing (a thing that can be hung on a wall or destroyed) and about (b) a picture as an object which appears by means of certain paints and shapes.[23] The entire picture is only a 'window' into the world behind the artistic surface - the fantasy world. The world of the picture through its perspective is oriented towards the observer, who is the centre of orientation of the world of the picture. The picture can be analysed intentionally - constitutively as a 'window.' A window is a noematic correlate of the medial act of 'picture awareness,' i.e. nothing but the pure phenomenon of the picture.[24] It opens a visible path to the world of *Phantasie*.

Husserl's successor and most influential critic, M. Heidegger, also postulates that a work of art is not an ordinary object, an utensil, but above all the ground upon which real qualities are transformed into imaginary ones by the artist's will.[25] This is also the ground where subjective truth appears. Intentionally objectivized experiences are born in mind: experiences artist has at the moment he/she is creating an artwork or experiences of an observer at the moment he/she recognizes and shapes an aesthetic object; inner seeing as opposed to 'external' observation plays the main role here.

What is the *Lebenswelt* of an image, what is it needed for, what does it bring to the soul and mind of their author and observer? Analysing Dürer's engraving *Knight, Death and the Devil* Husserl states, that an observable image is an invitation to an imaginary world given in new sensual frames of perception which contents exceed the deliverances of the ordinary perceptual experience. Depiction and imagination through the physical lines of the engraving make it possible to leap into a quasi-existential world. For Husserl, fantasy worlds are completely free worlds, each object of fantasy abiding in the fantasy world as a quasi-world. The peculiarity of fantasy lies in its arbitrariness, i.e. in arbitrary self-will.[26] The representatives of the Munich phenomenological group, e.g., M. Beck, stressed that the value of art is in the value of irrational - 'the pure that of being [...] as contrast to the sphere of species as the sphere of rational.'[27]

In contrast to the world of 'given,' a picture opens a window to the world of 'make believe.' Husserl sees fantasizing as a step taken by an observer towards the world of an image, after the materiality of the image is perceived. From artist's perspective the world of art is created by transferring fantasy into reality; the artist plays with the real on the other side of the actual. What comes to the foreground is the thing itself, the work of art, and artists introduce their creation - a new thing - into actuality.[28] The road artist takes - from her/his world situatedness to fantasy and back to actuality - is quite similar to the observer's: he/she goes from perception bound up with the present to fantasy world and back to the reality, but in a new emotional state.

Through this tense emotional figurative 'window' opened by the subjectivity of the author or the viewer, they can immerse in observation of the fantastic but probable image of reality and with that, due to a strong emotional impulse, accomplish removal from practical objectivity to reality seen from an illusionary perspective - more concentrated, radiated and suggestive. A work of art transcends the postulated dichotomy between subject and object because it is experienced with a significant existential density. Overcoming this dichotomy, the transcendence, is a mystical feeling, occurring as if in front of the higher 'observer,' whether it is named God or nature, a spiritual essence or inter-personal network, which is transparently present in the process of artistic creation or perception.

3. Who Are We: The Subjectivity of Aesthetic Emotional Experience

In the midst of the *subjectivity* of the author and the observer (being in the world in some emotional state), the experience and the (self-) consciousness means also the awareness of one's past experiences and current emotions a piece of art arises. When we come across an art image - especially when it is new for us, complicated, or even wild - our tacit background knowledge, which is backed up by an emotional pre-reflective mode, is stressed. We start to appraise our emotions, start to be aware of them. We engage active apperception: the observer feels the content of the image and of himself as two distinct facts of consciousness. What constantly occurs as a problem is the boundary which must be crossed in order to reach the art world from the real world. What is valuable is that awareness of the emotion of something 'weird' helps us to cognize them. This state of awareness is attributed to the reflective or second-order consciousness.[29] Some of the authors attribute the awareness (at least in a non-focal, pre-reflective way) to all conscious emotions, whenever they occur.[30]

In relation to the subjectivity and awareness emotions are often regarded as cognitive-evaluative judgments or as preceded by some cognitive or evaluative concepts. Nevertheless, the on-going critique states that 'cognitive models of emotion representation reduce emotions to categories something like categories of furniture.'[31] Robert C. Solomon in his later works argues that emotions are not merely judgments of the world, but are 'engagements with the world.' Regardless, 'emotions are structured and thoroughly permeated by judgments and concepts.'[32] According to Collingwood, art is an *expression* of the artist's emotions in the sense that it is the elucidation and articulation of the artist's emotional state. Expression is an imaginative activity, production of an 'imaginative vision.'[33] It is the expression of emotion in this imaginative vision that marks the true work of art, not skill and technique alone. So the subjectivity in the domain of visual arts can be seen in: (a) visual perception which causes 'bodily' emotions; (b) emotional cognitive-evaluative judgments and dispositions due to the aesthetic experience; and (c) personal way of seeing, which results from *engagement* in the world, embeddedness-in-the-world.

Intuition and imagination lead to the 'life world' and make the spectator forget the practical reason (transcend it) and become a *pure subject*. Phenomenological aesthetic reflection neutralizes the original attitude of experience and practical action.[34] The concentrated passions, imagination and intuition are far more valuable than the ability to analyse, compare and conclude, which are often enlisted as the most important creative skills of 'intellectuals.' K. Higgins distinguishes aesthetic emotions which are: (1) pure or unadulterated; (2) more subtle than the coarse emotions; 3) raised to a higher or a more spiritual state; (4) more appropriate; (5) more cultured and (6) associated with greater maturity. Aesthetic emotions can elevate us spiritually and morally and lead to a better understanding of ourselves and others through awareness of the on-going processes of creation, performance and appreciation.[35] Still, the author or the spectator gains this purification not in in-depth speculation, but in feeling her/himself interconnected to the *other*.

To give an example of artistic aesthetic experience we would like to quote Mark Rothko, a well-known modern artist whose famous large paintings in colour provoked so much discussion. When proclaimed an abstractionist because of the use of pure colour as a material, tool and idea, he disagreed with this, writing that the essence of his paintings was

> only in expressing basic human emotions - tragedy, ecstasy, doom, and so on. And the fact that a lot of people break down and cry when confronted with my pictures shows that I can communicate those basic human emotions [...]. The people who weep before my pictures are having the same religious experience I had when I painted them. And if you, as you say, are moved only by their colour relationship, then you miss the point.[36]

4. What Do We Feel: The Intentionality of Aesthetic Emotional Experience

The emotions a subject has about the aesthetic world of a work of art are directed towards something in it or are intentional. Intentionality is not the mere cognition of some separated 'object.' *Intentionality* - the central concept of the phenomenology of emotions - signifies that emotions arouse towards an image or something in this image, something undefined ('the Unknown') and something 'we care about.'[37] These emotions are reflected, they are second-order consciousness. Intentionality allows one to find a new layer in the perceived materiality of a work of art (e.g., surface, colors, etc.) - the discourse dimension, i.e. embodied possibility of perceiving the world presented by the work; in fact such layers are large in number - multiple - and they should not be separated, for they form a complex work of art. The intentional aspect at a glance seems quite ordinary, focusing on the work of art with a passive and disinterested attitude, but further phenomenological studies reveal an extraordinary relationship between spectator and work of art.[38] Moreover nowadays 'intentionality' in research is also regarded as a 'mental representation.'[39] Thus, it is possible to consider emotional experiences additionally as representational mental states that present objects to the subject in a particular way.

Visual perception of a painting gives more than visual perception of a painted fence. 'The visual aspect of an aesthetic experience with a painting is emphasized by complete unity, lucidity, eminence and originality.'[40] The emotional aspects of aesthetic experience are much more important than its cognitive aspects, which by some authors are regarded as relatively ordinary since promoting spontaneous recognition of the subject matter.[41] The realm of visual art can form multidimensional and novel 'province of meanings.' If we try to reveal where creativity is explicated in artistic 'province of meanings,' the first possible answer will be in the continuum of the *content* - semantic side (i.e. the work of art can visualize and make salient previously unnoticed elements of existence) and in the continuum of the *surface* - formative side (i.e. new configurations of applied materials, techniques and styles). The different surfaces that works of art show us are: (1) the fragments of reality that are made salient, in spite of their marginalization, sublimation, or unjust simplification; (2) the abstract concepts that are grasped visually in their concreteness; (3) the discursive and thus limited formative principles, which are second-orderly recombined to allow new knowledge.

The figurative language of the visual arts from ancient Greek philosophers until now has been connected with the mimesis: imitation and artful representation of the 'nature' object. Imitation generated feelings crucial for cognitive proceeding: *trust* (the image is trusted because we find correspondences with our sensual experience), (aesthetical) *delight* received due to discovery of artistic 'adroitness' in concrete piece of art. However, the aesthetic emotional experience gained through art is not the only one. The art of avant garde in the 20th century made it apparent that the representation of the object is not what the work of art really shows. Avant garde art became a large enterprise of *resistance*. It transformed the mode of imitation; there was no more mere representation of the 'Nature' in it. Authors and audiences took a huge step to the complicated emotions needed to create as well as to perceive the world expressed in abstract or distinct from reality symbols. The resistance in any trend of visual arts aims to transcend the experience-based (and thus incomplete) feelings of reality, the natural and technical restrictions of what can be visibly sensed, and the ideological directions of what can be emotionally experienced into new imaginary world of abstract intuitive make-believe. Different avant garde art objects made it evident, that tense emotional experience can cumulate not only as a result of spotting virtuosic imitations but also from emotional suggestion that relies upon experiencing ties between different realms. Creation of complex cultural objects, which are spaces for creation of new senses and understanding, according to A. Schutz, rests upon the interconnection of different worlds of experience through 'appresentation' in one horizon.[42] We can feel and sense the 'Obscure', the 'Unknown', and such emotions can result into concentrated 'sense' of the possible world even before the concepts or interpretations are made. The emotions here are the indicators of the possible world presence even if we do not understand it.

Painting is not a mere imitation also because it is not the object itself, for the existing object can't be wholly recreated. As mentioned earlier, the painting is made with oil and brushes on material canvas, which nature is the given fact the artist can't change. What he *has* added is the arrangement of colour and light, but not in the form of an order of spots on the tablecloth, but as an arranged variety - a *life*.[43] It is this life of construction and destruction that is created through the figurative surface, which we perceive in its visible virtuality. The spectator's aesthetic experience emerging from different works of art is different not only because of varying visual perception and recognition, but because of emotions that differ according to the painting's subject matter. Susanne Langer, showing the symbolism of the artwork, stresses that its variable symbolic forms stand for different emotions that we want to express and that we are eager to feel. Our interest in some kind of art 'arises from an intimate relation to the all-important life of being;' art is not simulating feelings - it is expressing them symbolically in a form of sentience.[44] These symbols do not speak of what the artist feels, but of what he/she imagines of feelings, of the 'inner life' and this exceeds his/her personal case.[45]

The arousal of aesthetic emotions and step into the *Lebenswelt* of the artwork needs some embodied, material (in a wide sense of this word) formations. What are these certain features of the appearance that bring together 'sophisticated' spots for bodily senses and impulses for profound emotions? To our mind, the most considerable (though not the only ones) mechanisms of creative visualization significant for creation of emotions are *visual metaphor* and *visual paradox*. Metaphor is considered to be a basic element of the process of cognition, though it is discussed mainly on the material of verbal or written language.[46] It has been often analysed as a resource for the creative cognitive experience, because it is a space of inter-conceptual, inter-realm and intersectoral connections within the structures of meanings.

The mechanism that should be considered as unique for arts is the possibility that newly created metaphors open: to perceive and sense the novel 'strangeness' created by the artist, that is not yet a matter of conceptual experience. Many authors have emphasized the *apprehensibility* that is emerging with the help of the metaphors; the combination of several different realms via intuition that can be perceived and cognized only with emotion because the rationality doesn't allow for non-logical combinations. Creating the visual metaphor is a way to combine several visual contexts, the tie between which is not genetic or organic, but aesthetically can be perceived as having a resemblance. Play with perspective (Magritte), play with form, unexpected colours for the everyday life objects, unexpected combination of colours as feeling of the world sui generis (not through recognized objects) make up several examples.

Visual paradoxes stand for disruption of habitual seeing and interpreting, for example, the destruction of human body in cubism allows us to see the purity of forms behind the rules of forms. Some of the paradoxes require establishment of the visual traps. For example, the art of transition shows us numerous manifestations of these mechanisms. Visual becomes fugitive in impressionism, cubism reverses the point of view from a single eye perspective to a totality of possible views taken from all points around the object (person) being depicted.[47]

Considering metaphors and paradoxes one should take into consideration that emotionally they enable the flow of *visual suggestion* as sensual/emotional condensation and *visual purification* as the process of total accomplishment of an aesthetical emotion and its release.

5. Where all is One: The Intersubjectivity of Aesthetic Emotional Experience

We allowed ourselves this little retreat to language-related conceptual analysis of creativity in the realm of works of art to show the possibilities it opens. However, attention to these details can't give us the understanding of the visual arts as a unity initiating aesthetic emotional experience as a platform for knowledge. To go into the deep of it we should remember what we previously said of subjectivity, intentionality, alternative world and perception, as well as to mind, that the paths of the artist and the viewer are developing and meeting in interplay with one another, while the creation itself lies in-between. Analysis of this interactivity leads to the most important concept: the concept of *intersubjectivity* of aesthetic emotional experience, which helps to attain the multiplicity and inter-correlations of views required for creative vision.

For the first time indications of intersubjectivity were described above through the fact that non-ordinary artistic experience incorporates reciprocal influence of different modes of perception and action between the artist and the object.[48] Moving forward, intersubjectivity is found arising in communication between the author and the audience from an overlap of intentionalities and subjective moduses required to achieve highly affective feelings and senses. Thus emotional aesthetic experience rests on the possibility to achieve the vision and existential feeling of bonds within everyone and everything in the environment, the artist and spectator and an aesthetic object in particular. This interconnectedness constitutes the phenomenological depth of the visual art.

Creation lies in-between the closed systems of minds and bodies - in the ties binding them. The emotional aesthetic knowledge is a dynamic connection which links aesthetic representation of an object and engagements of the artist and the spectator with it and with the world.

M. Dufrenne in 'Phenomenology of Aesthetic Experience' considers the spectator as a 'subject who, instead of making him a consciousness in general so as to think an objective world, responds to the subjectivity of the work through his own subjectivity.'[49] Dufrenne emphasizes a depth of feeling that rejoins the depth of aesthetic object in a special bond of 'reciprocity.'[50] The world of the work is the life world (Husserl's Lebenswelt) that cannot be reduced to the objective world. Dufrenne links the affectivity of feeling to the 'affective a priori' that belongs to the subject and object alike: 'feeling itself affective knows the affective [quality] as a primary sign of the object.'[51] Between aesthetic object and appreciative subject there is a sensing-feeling 'communion.'[52] The aesthetic object the creator manifests, the spectator inhabits and immerses in the imaginary world that is affective and expressive. Their subjectivities rejoin in deep emotional bond, and there is room enough for their unique feeling and expressing in the aesthetic world.

Aesthetic experience for Dufrenne, on the contrary to Heidegger, who defined the concept in terms of passive reception of the representational spectator, is an active access into the world of the art-work in its full nuance and annunciatory truth.[53] This active engagement requires specific emotional states based on intersubjectivity. For example, feeling of *empathy* can be regarded as such for it is defined as emotion that is aroused from identification with someone else's representations, values and even plans.[54] Still there is criticism of the empathy and co-feeling as the basis of art experience, e.g., Vigotsky notes that empathy doesn't cover the wholeness of aesthetic and emotional experience.[55]

The aesthetic object is a medium for the intersubjective knowledge which the artist and the spectator get of themselves and of something more. The artist performs his artistic transcendence as if he felt himself in front of an 'Ideal spectator' or 'Superspectator,' and makes the world of the artwork a place which can cultivate certain emotions within certain people and to achieve aesthetic resonance.

The notion of the roots of such intersubjective experience is considerable here; several authors try to find them through psychological mechanisms. Psychoanalysts G. Rose (1992), J. Oremland (1997) elaborate creativity as a meta-ego function resulting into a higher level of human experience.[56] G. Hagman, who writes on aesthetic experience in a renewed and enriched with phenomenological concepts psychoanalytic manner, makes a highly distinguished accent on the intersubjectivity. Intersubjectivity of aesthetic experience is tightly connected with the interaction between mother and child, their relatedness and attachment to each other.[57] In aesthetic experience people recognize this mother-infant tight bond, and the aesthetic object is some kind of its recollection. This relationship is a locus for development of the idealizations of '(M)other' in close tie with 'me' and is an initium of experience of connectedness through love.

Taking these primary relationships as an example to show that the artist's mind is not a closed self-regulating psychological system, we can talk of other aspects which mark the enrootedness of a person in the experience of many kinds of relationships (which can be defined as social, cultural, political, etc.). The main feature of an aesthetic experience, then, is its high emotionality and ability to include such odd elements into one coherent *Erlebnis*, attentive to 'la vie' (A. Bergson). The aesthetic experience leads to aesthetic resonance which finds its way in the conjunction of the vision of the artist in 'which internal aspects of subjectivity and its external aspects - both concretized in the artwork - are conjunctive. The life itself, the *being* or how it feels to be the living person is captured in the aesthetic object.'[58] To feel the life in its essence is the most significant moment in aesthetic experience as well as the most significant feature of cognizing through art is to approach such emotional state, what Mancilla demonstrates vividly in his chapter.[59] According to Hagman

> [t]he core of aesthetic experience contains an intensely interactive component in which the mutual engagement of artist with both artwork and audience results in the emergence of an archaic state of self-experience, associated with the early bond with the mother.[60]

In aesthetic experience the subjectivity should be externalized; not only does the subjective creative action alter an object in some way, but also an artist and his audience enter the intersubjective relationships within themselves and with the world through idealizations.

> [i]dealization is fundamental to our valuation of self, our relationships and our experience in the world. Its source lies in the early affective connection between the infant and the caregiver, during which the communication of mutual idealization arises and is elaborated. [...] Specifically, it is the idealization of the formal organization of the interaction that grants high value to the gestures, shapes, sounds, colours, and rhythms that characterize the interaction of parent and child.[61]

Thus, what was once internal self-experience is externalized in the aesthetic object: the experience of perceiving the work of art becomes experience of other which was once artist's self 'mine' (or can be found in 'me' in the case of an audience). Awareness of the world intersubjectivity, in other words, emotional knowledge of dialectics of one and multitude gained in the result of aesthetic experience resembles spiritual transformations in the process of transpersonal experiences, which are explored by the transpersonal psychologists.[62]

6. Conclusion

In this chapter we have drawn a line connecting different layers of emotions' emergence and existence inherent to cognition through visual art. Approaching art through the prism of cognition and aiming to conceptualize it as a source of emotionally-driven knowledge, one can dwell on the following issues: (a) the emotions elicited by the artwork itself; (b) the emotional ties between artist and significant 'Other' (nature, God, or coarse manifestations of civilization); (c) the emotional relationship between artist and spectator mediated by the artwork. Grounding on the tradition of phenomenological thinking we placed all these components in the continuum of aesthetic emotional experience and made a sketch of its dynamics from the basics - bodily sensations - to its most complex form - emotionally-driven knowledge. We started regarding artwork as a multilayer space, with its materiality and its complex meaning-generating structures. Artwork is a window for transcendence from sensing materiality to experiencing spiritual belonging and attachment. Overcoming stereotype perception and surprise leads to activation of attention and arousal of intense, blended emotions. Reflection and meditation over blended emotions elicited by the artwork lead to awareness of social phenomena - collective representations - hidden in the aesthetic body. This reflection also includes feeling of attachment between the artist and the spectator that allows them to 'see' each other. Thus these alternative 'intellectuals' enter emotional cognitive states with outcomes never possible through pure intellectual speculation. Together all these emotionally-driven reflections give way to recognizing the mutuality and connectedness of the world. We described development of the emotive structures in the following order: bodily sensations are aroused by visual materiality of the artwork; afterwards we experience arousal of more complex emotions as intentional cognitive-evaluative states, oriented towards certain discourse layer of the art-work; the final stage is the envelopment by deep and lofted aesthetic experiences of a fantasy world which shows life intersubjectivity and interobjectivity. The genesis of the emotionally-driven knowledge is possible due to these multiple emotive sources. Thus we define emotionally-driven knowledge as a mode of sensual development from separating and defining primary sensations in one's separate body to complex intersubjective emotional awareness of the transcendent truth of life.

Notes

[1] C.D.G. Mancilla, 'Art and the Passion of Intellect', 2011, this volume.
[2] C. Heaney, 'Emotional Intelligence: Literature, Ethics and Affective Cognition in J.M. Coetzee's *Disgrace*', 2011, this volume.
[3] J. Dewey, *Art as Experience*, Minton, Balch, 1934.
[4] Х.-Г. Гадамер, *Истина и метод*, Москва, Прогресс, 1988, с. 114.
[5] Dewey, op. cit., p. 19.
[6] S. Gardner, 'Aesthetics', *The Blackwell Companion to Philosophy*, N. Bunnin & E.P. Tsui-James (eds), Blackwell, Oxford, 1996, pp. 229-256.
[7] A. Berleant, *Art and Engagement*, Tempel University Press, Philadelphia, 1991.
[8] Such coupling of the organism with its environment, according to Maturana and Varela, is one of the conditions of the life progress, which goes on with complication of cognitive processes. See: H.R. Maturana and F.J. Varela, *The Tree of Knowledge: The Biological Roots of Human Understanding*, Shambala, Boston, 1987.
[9] Dewey, op. cit., p. 38.
[10] Л. Выготский, *Психология искусства*, Москва, Искусство, 1986, с. 256-258.
[11] Ibid., pp. 270-271.
[12] M. Uzelac, 'Art and Phenomenology in Edmund Husserl', *Axiomathes*, 1998, p. 9.

[13] J. Turner, 'The Sociology of Emotions', *Emotion Review*, Vol. 1(4), 2009, p. 341.
[14] R.C. Solomon, 'Emotions in Phenomenology and Existentialism', *A Companion to Phenomenology and Existentialism*, H.L. Dreyfus and M.A. Wrathall (eds), Blackwell Publishing Ltd, Oxford, 2009, p. 292.
[15] M. Merleau-Ponty, 'Eye and Mind', *Twentieth Century Theories of Art*, J.M. Thompson (ed), Carleton University Press Inc., Carleton, 1999.
[16] Ibid., p. 416.
[17] Ibid., p. 419.
[18] W. James, *Principles of Psychology*, Dover, New York, 1950, (original work published 1890), p. 451.
[19] J.A. Lambie and A. Marcel, 'Consciousness and the Varieties of Emotion Experience: A Theoretical Framework', *Psychological Review*, 109, 2002, pp. 219-259; H. Frijda, *The Emotions*, Cambridge University Press, Cambridge, 1986; J.P. Sartre, *Esquisse d'une Théorie Phénomenologique des Emotions*, Hermann, Paris, 1939.
[20] E. Husserl, *Cartesian Meditations: An Introduction to Phenomenology*, Springer, New York, 1991.
[21] T. Nagel, 'What Is It Like to Be a Bat?' *Philosophical Review*, Vol. 83(4), 1974, pp. 435-450.
[22] E. Husserl, 'Phantasie, Bildbewustsein, Erinnerung', *Husserliana XXIII*, Den Haag, Nijhoff, 1980, p. XXIII/519.
[23] Ibid., p. XXUI/109-110.
[24] Uzelac, op. cit., p. 8.
[25] M. Heidegger, 'The Origin of the Work of Art', *Martin Heidegger: The Basic Writings*, Harper Collins, New York, 2008.
[26] E. Husserl, 'Phantasie, Bildbewustsein, Erinnerung', op. cit., p. XXIII/535.
[27] H.S. Sepp and L. Embree, 'Introduction', *Handbook of Phenomenological Aesthetics*, H.R. Sepp and L. Embree (eds), Springer, London, New York, 2010, p. xix.
[28] Uzelac, op. cit., p. 7.
[29] N. Frijda, 'Emotion Experience and its Varieties'. *Emotion Review*, Vol. 1(3), 2009, p. 267.
[30] F. Brentano, *Psychologie vom Empirischen Standpunkt*, Vol. 1, Meiner, Hamburg, 1955 (original work published 1874).
[31] P.M .Niedenthal, M. Maringer, 'Embodied Emotion Considered', *Emotion Review*, Vol. 1(2), 2009, p. 122.
[32] Solomon, op. cit., p. 300.
[33] R.G. Collingwood, *The Principles of Art*, Clarendon, Oxford, 1963, p. 27.

[34] Sepp & Embree, op. cit., p. xv.
[35] K. Higgins, 'Refined Emotion in Aesthetic Experience: A Cross-Cultural Comparison', *Aesthetic Experience*, R. Shusterman and A. Tomlin (eds), Routledge, New York, 2008, pp. 106-126.
[36] J.E.B. Breslin, *Mark Rothko: A Biography*, University of Chicago Press, Chicago, 1993, p. 309.
[37] Solomon, op. cit., pp. 293-294.
[38] B.S. Funch, 'A Psychological Theory of the Aesthetic Experience', *Aesthetics and Innovation*, L. Dorfman, C. Martindale and V. Petrov (eds), Cambridge Scholars Publishing, UK, 2007, p. 4.
[39] R. Reisenzein and S. Doring, 'Ten Perspectives on Emotional Experience: Introduction to the Special Issue', *Emotion Review*, Vol. 1(3), 2009, p. 196.
[40] Funch, op. cit., p. 5.
[41] Ibid., p. 4.
[42] A. Schutz, 'Symbol, Reality, and Society', *Collected Papers, Vol. 1*, Martinus Nijhoff, The Hague, 1962.
[43] S. Langer, 'Feeling and Form', *Art and Its Significance: An Anthology of Aesthetic Theory*, S.D. Ross (ed), State University of New York Press, New York, 1984, pp. 230-231.
[44] Ibid., p. 226.
[45] Ibid., p. 227.
[46] See, e.g., G. Lakoff and M. Johnson, *Metaphors We Live By*, University of Chicago Press, Chicago, 2003.
[47] J. Berger, *Ways of Seeing*, British Broadcasting Corporation and Penguin Books, London, 1972, p. 18.
[48] P. Crowther, *Phenomenology of the Visual Arts (Even the Frame)*, Stanford University Press, Stanford California, 2009, p. 3.
[49] M. Dufrenne, *The Phenomenology of Aesthetic Experience*, Northwestern University Press, Evanston, 1973, p. 198.
[50] Ibid., p. 483.
[51] Ibid., p. 441.
[52] Ibid., pp. 50, 63.
[53] E.S. Casey, 'Aesthetic Experience', *Handbook of Phenomenological Aesthetics*, H.R. Sepp and L. Embree (eds), Springer, London, New York, 2010, p. 5
[54] For example, see: K. Oatley, 'An Emotion's Emergence, Unfolding, and Potential for Empathy: A Study of Resentment by the 'Psychologist of Avon', *Emotion Review*, Vol. 1(1), pp. 24-30.
[55] Vigotsky, op. cit., p. 258.

[56] G. Rose, *The Power of Form (Expanded Edition)*, International Universities Press, New York, 1992; J. Oremland, *The Origins and Dynamics of Creativity*, International Universities Press, Madison, CT, 1997.
[57] G. Hagman, *Aesthetic Experience. Beauty, Creativity, and the Search for the Ideal*, Rodopi, Amsterdam and New York, 2005, pp. 2-4.
[58] Ibid., p. 5.
[59] C. Garcia, 'Art and the Passion of Intellect', 2011, this volume.
[60] Ibid., p. 2.
[61] Ibid., p. 4.
[62] S. Grof, *The Cosmic Game: Explorations of the Frontiers of Human Consciousness*, State University of New York (SUNY) Press, Albany, New York, 1998.

Bibliography

Berger, J., *Ways of Seeing*. British Broadcasting Corporation and Penguin Books, London, 1972.

Berleant, A., *Art and Engagemant*. Tempel University Press, Philadelphia, 1991.

Brentano, F., *Psychologie vom Empirischen Standpunkt* [Psychology from the empirical point of view]. Vol. 1. Meiner, Hamburg, 1955 (original work published 1874).

Breslin, J.E.B., *Mark Rothko: A Biography*. University of Chicago Press, Chicago, 1993.

Casey, E.S., 'Aesthetic Experience'. *Handbook of Phenomenological Aesthetics*. Sepp, H.R. and Embree, L. (eds), Springer, London, New York, 2010.
Collingwood, R.G., *The Principles of Art*. Clarendon, Oxford, 1963.

Crowther, P., *Phenomenology of the Visual Arts (Even the Frame)*. Stanford University Press, Stanford California, 2009.

Dewey, J., *Art as Experience*. Balch, Minton, 1934.

Dufrenne, M., *The Phenomenology of Aesthetic Experience*. Northwestern University Press, Evanston, 1973.

Frijda, N.H., *The Emotions*. Cambridge University Press, Cambridge, 1986.

Frijda, N., 'Emotion Experience and its Varieties'. *Emotion Review*. Vol. 1 (3), 2009, pp. 264-271.

Funch, B.S., 'A Psychological Theory of the Aesthetic Experience'. *Aesthetics and Innovation*. Dorfman, L., Martindale, C. and Petrov, V. (eds), Cambridge Scholars Publishing, UK, 2007.

Gardner, S., 'Aesthetics'. *The Blackwell Companion to Philosophy*. Bunnin, N. and Tsui-James, E.P. (eds), Blackwell, Oxford, 1996, pp. 229-256.

Grof, S., *The Cosmic Game: Explorations of the Frontiers of Human Consciousness*. State University of New York (SUNY) Press, Albany, New York, 1998.

Hagman, G., *Aesthetic Experience: Beauty, Creativity, and the Search for the Ideal*. Rodopi, Amsterdam/New York, 2005.

Heidegger, M., 'The Origin of the Work of Art'. *Martin Heidegger: The Basic Writings*. Harper Collins, New York, 2008.

Higgins, K., 'Refined Emotion in Aesthetic Experience: A Cross-Cultural Comparison'. *Aesthetic Experience*. Shusterman, R. and Tomlin, A. (eds), Routledge, New York, 2008.

Husserl, E., *Cartesian Meditations: An Introduction to Phenomenology*. Springer, New York, 1991.
Husserl, E., 'Phantasie, Bildbewustsein, Erinnerung'. *Husserliana XXIII*. Den Haag, Nijhoff, 1980.

James, W., *Principles of Psychology*. Dover, New York, 1950 (original work published 1890).

Lakoff, G. and Johnson, M., *Metaphors We Live By*. University of Chicago Press, Chicago, 2003.

Lambie, J.A. and Marcel, A., 'Consciousness and the Varieties of Emotion Experience: A Theoretical Framework'. *Psychological Review.* Vol. 109, 2002, pp. 219-259.

Langer, S., 'Feeling and Form'. *Art and Its Significance: An Anthology of Aesthetic Theory.* Ross, S. D. (ed), State University of New York Press, New York, 1984.

Maturana, H.R. and Varela, F.J., *The Tree of Knowledge: The Biological Roots of Human Understanding.* Shambala, Boston, 1987.

Merleau-Ponty, M., 'Eye and Mind'. *Twentieth Century Theories of Art.* Thompson, J.M. (ed), Carleton University Press Inc., Carleton, 1999.

Nagel, T., 'What Is It Like to Be a Bat?' *Philosophical Review.* Vol. 83(4), 1974, pp. 435-450.

Niedenthal, P.M. and Maringer, M., 'Embodied Emotion Considered'. *Emotion Review.* Vol. 1(2), 2009, pp. 122-128.

Oatley, K., 'An Emotion's Emergence, Unfolding, and Potential for Empathy: A Study of Resentment by the Psychologist of Avon'. *Emotion Review.* Vol. 1(1), pp. 24-30.

Oremland, J., *The Origins and Dynamics of Creativity.* International Universities Press, Madison, CT, 1997.

Reisenzein, R. and Doring, S., 'Ten Perspectives on Emotional Experience: Introduction to the Special Issue'. *Emotion Review.* Vol. 1(3), 2009, pp. 195-205.

Rose, G., *The Power of Form (Expanded Edition).* International Universities Press, New York, 1992.

Sartre, J.P., *Esquisse d'une Théorie Phénoménologique des Emotions* [Sketch of a Phenomenological Theory of Emotion]. Hermann, Paris, 1939.

Schutz, A., 'Symbol, Reality, and Society'. *Collected Papers, Vol. 1.* Martinus Nijhoff, The Hague, 1962, pp. 287-356.

Sepp, H.S. and Embree, L., 'Introduction'. *Handbook of Phenomenological Aesthetics*. Sepp, H.R. and Embree, L. (eds), Springer, London, New York, 2010.

Solomon, R.C., 'Emotions in Phenomenology and Existentialism'. *A Companion to Phenomenology and Existentialism*. Dreyfus, H.L. and Wrathall, M.A. (eds), Blackwell Publishing Ltd, Oxford, 2009.

Turner, J., 'The Sociology of Emotions'. *Emotion Review*. Vol. 1(4), 2009, pp. 340-354.

Uzelac, M., 'Art and Phenomenology in Edmund Husserl'. *Axiomathes*. 1-2, 1998.

Выготский, Л., *Психология искусства*. Искусство, Москва, 1986.

Гадамер, Х.-Г., *Истина и метод*. Прогресс, Москва, 1988.

Knowledge Creation in the Intellectual Networks

Nikita Basov

Abstract
The chapter proposes an approach to explain how knowledge is socially created. Such an explanation is essential to understand the emerging knowledge society and the respective changes in the role and place of intellectuals it brings. First, the basic principles of knowledge creation are outlined. Second, we suggest the concept of knowledge creation ritual, which describes co-evolution of knowledge, communication and emotional energy in micro groups as a process of structural coupling between individuals and explains social knowledge generation. Third, the mechanisms of knowledge creation in large-scale network structures - intellectual network ensembles - are analyzed. We introduce the concept of cultural-cognitive domain constituted by three main elements: knowledge fields, communication networks and emotional energy pools as a main unit to analyze knowledge creation in the intellectual network ensembles. Some of the principles of emergence and evolution of the cultural-cognitive domains are outlined. Finally, using the proposed approach we try to address some of the issues discussed by the other authors of this book.

Key Words: Socio-cognitive process, structural coupling, knowledge creation ritual, communication network, emotional energy, intellectual network ensemble, cultural-cognitive domain.

*****

A detailed, multi-dimensional study of knowledge creation mechanisms is urged by the needs of the knowledge society. Whether we study intellectuals in academia, as J. van Andel and J. Moir do in *Part I*; the public sphere, as S. Mahlomaholo and V. Netshandama, T. Adeleke, G. Simet, and O. Procevska in *Part II*; or the arts, like C. García, C. Heaney and O. Nenko in *Part III*, everywhere we see that the ways of how knowledge is socially created are changing dramatically. This also leads to evolving changes to the roles and practices of intellectuals - knowledge creators - as well as changes in their 'natural environment' - academia (scientific knowledge). The other arenas of intellectuals' activity, such as the public sphere (publically promoted knowledge) and the arts (emotionally-driven knowledge) transform as well. The transformations of the intellectual arenas and the changes in knowledge creation practices require new approaches to studying knowledge creation as a collective cognitive process explaining how emerging 'cognizing' society actually operates today.

1. The Principles of Knowledge Creation

Our starting point is the social embeddedness of knowledge. It does not mean that the knowledge creation process is exclusively of a collective nature and doesn't include the elements of individual work. However, even during individual work social factors play a key role. As neurobiologists U. Maturana and F. Varela have prominently shown, consciousness and mind are embedded in social coupling, which is the source of their dynamics.[1] A number of social scientists, e.g., D. Bloor, B. Latour, K. Carley, N. Contractor, S. Grant, J. Law and M. Minski argue a similar position.[2]

The idea that social factors condition knowledge creation is based on the following positions, expressed in extant literature:

(1) Generating of a new idea means systematical combination and recombination of various meanings, which come from the social and cultural environment.[3]
(2) A new idea becomes believed in and institutionalized only through social interaction between individuals.[4]
(3) Knowledge implies a certain grade of social consensus on an idea (or a complex of ideas) offered.[5]
(4) Knowledge is always contextual, and the particular way of how it is created appears to be a key to understanding it. Without being familiar with the context it is often impossible to comprehend an idea or a complex of ideas.[6]

Being socially embedded, knowledge, however, is still rooted in individual structures of the nervous systems; it depends on the mental structures of a specific cognizer, embedded in his/her very organization, his/her biology.[7] As surveys done in Cognition science and Neurophysiology have shown, there exist not only similarities, but also a number of qualitative distinctions between what is represented and what is perceived. This means we cannot consider mental structures simply as some weakened copies of previous sensory influences, especially dealing with products of creative imagination, which are often of hypothetical and even fantastic nature.[8] The plastic richness of the nervous system is realized not in creation of engrams or images of objects in the environment, but in its continuous transformation complementing changes in the environment.[9] Therefore, it appears incorrect to understand mental structures as constructs made of information coming from the outside. Mental structures, apparently, are the states of mental and neural structures, achieved under the influence of external impulses, but not being their direct reflections.[10] Thus, it can be said that there is always a degree of *structural autonomy* any cognizer has.[11]

Nevertheless, any cognizer is still influenced by the environment (including the other actors) and simultaneously influences this environment. Chains of mutual influence lead to structural congruence between individual and environment. This process of recurrent non-linear mutual influence between individual and environment is called *structural coupling*.[12] This mechanism is a key to understanding knowledge creation in society. Combined with the structural autonomy principle it means that knowledge emerges along with sociality as a correlation of individuals' states of nervous systems and mental structures when the latter are structurally coupled. Insights supporting this thesis can be found in the works of H. Garfinkel, R. Collins, B. Latour, S. Fuchs, M. Lynch, E. Livingston, N. Warner, M. Letski, and others.[13] This may be the basis for a specific approach to understanding knowledge creation processes: knowledge is not something that is individually produced, accumulated and then transferred to others (disseminated), but something that is co-created in conjunction with the Other each and every time when a new level of understanding is achieved. According to the proposed approach we suggest to consider the *integral process of knowledge creation* as a socio-cognitive process of joint structural coupling of cognizers. The question is how this structural coupling happens.

We argue that knowledge arises as a result of two basic individual activities, which structurally couple cognizers and build networks of correlations: (1) designing individual mental structures; and (2) modifying the environment (including other actors' mental structures).

The central role in the generation of individual mental structures is played by the mechanism of intrapersonal communication or *auto-communication*, through which structural changes in intrapersonal image of the world (individual mental structures) are stimulated by external factors when performing tasks that require a non-standard, creative approach. The key process in auto-communication is intrapersonal dialogue that is an exchange (not always realized) of messages between 'I' (a set of semantic positions with which an individual identifies him/herself) and the imagined interlocutors representing semantic positions irreducible to each other.[14] Thinking is thus creating 'coalitions in mind,' which reflect social structure.[15]

In order to form and update a heterogeneous set of internally imagined interlocutors individuals interact - *communicate* - with the external environment (including other individuals) and through adaptation to it generate mental structures constituting their images of the world. Here every possible form of communication may be used: face to face and distant, private and group, verbal and non-verbal, etc. The more heterogeneous the communicative environment the higher are the chances for new mental structures to occur. An important role is played by material objects (e.g., books) which feed the cognitive activity of individuals when observed, processed and used. Therefore, material objects are usually involved in collective cognitive processes as mediating elements and appear to be participants of the knowledge creation process (this idea is one of the fundamentals of actor-network theory).[16]

The process of environment modification is crucial for correlating individual mental structures as it is the communicative medium of environment that allows individuals to mutually influence evolution of each other's mental structures. This is done through filling the environment with information, objects, images, verbal expressions and texts, e.g., through discussions, public speaking, writing, painting and drawing schemes. As a result individual mental structures co-evolve internally guided by the auto-communication and are externally influenced by the communicative medium of the environment; hence new combinations of ideas arise.

Knowledge, thus, appears inseparable from its communicative environment and individuals creating it. None of the group members him-/herself can possess knowledge: it is distributed between the individuals, each of which possesses only mental structures on the basis of which the organic integrity of knowledge emerges in the common communicative environment.

However, it is still individual communicative activity that drives knowledge creation and makes mental structures' 'clash' in various communicative interactions, thereby influencing the development of each other via communication mediums and co-evolving as a result.[17] This requires sufficient efforts and energy expenses of individuals.[18] Intellectual work is thus fed by emotional entrainment. Moreover, in the interaction between structurally autonomous individual mental structures, knowledge creation probably relies less on information transferring than on emotional entrainment and intuition, which allows 'feeling the knowledge' of the Other in the process of structural coupling because his/her actual mental structures cannot be directly 'observed.' That is why partiality and enthusiasm can be considered as positive factors of intellectual work; and that is why cognitive processes (with few exceptions) are inseparably linked to affective aspects of mentality, forming an integral stream.[19]

Thus, *emotional energy* - a long-lasting emotion arising at individual level as a cognitive expectation of successful interaction, promising mutual understanding and emotional entrainment - stimulates intellectual activity of an individual.[20] Vise versa, success in intellectual work stimulates inspirational emotional energy charges. Simultaneously, decisions whether to continue communication or not are made on the basis of previous communicative experience with a certain group of people: an individual wishes to repeat interactions only if they promise renewal of the personal emotional energy. So it can be said that communication is determined by emotional energy resonance.

Seen through this perspective knowledge should be considered as an emergent complex of structurally coupled mental structures embedded in a communication network and fed by emotional entrainment in common experience space. To know means to be involved into such communication networks of correlated mental structures and emotional entrainments. To create knowledge means to generate such networks of correlations and emotional entrainments in a common experience space.

Thus, to understand the mechanisms of knowledge creation we are to describe the interplay of the three dimensions: knowledge, communication and emotional energy, which co-create each other in common experience space of a group.

2. Knowledge Creation Ritual

We base the concept of knowledge creation ritual on the concept of *interaction ritual* initially proposed by E. Goffman and elaborated in greater details by R. Collins.[21] Collins describes interaction ritual as an internally structured mechanism through which participants develop a mutual focus of attention and become entrained in each other's bodily micro-rhythms and emotions.[22] The conditions of interaction ritual are: (1) co-presence of two or more people so they affect each other by bodily presence; (2) boundaries to outsiders; (3) focus of attention upon a common object or activity; (4) sharing of a common mood or emotional experience.[23] Bringing collective effervescence these conditions produce the main outcomes of the interaction ritual, which are: (1) group solidarity, a feeling of membership; 2) emotional energy in the individual: a feeling of confidence, elation, strength, enthusiasm, and initiative in taking action; (3) symbols that represent the group; and (4) a feeling of morality.[24] During interaction rituals individuals focus their attention, create a common mood and achieve a state of synchrony. Gestures, voice tones, rhythm of speaking - if everything is synchronized than the closer are the individuals and the longer is the ritual.[25] Through this process individuals produce symbols that carry meanings and emotional energy for those who can decode them. This allows providing a lasting mutual understanding, solidarity and emotional mood. Symbols are then: (1) communicated in social networks where they are reproduced and developed and (2) reflected by individuals in their auto-communication simulating interaction rituals.

Similar mechanisms guide the *knowledge creation ritual* (Fig. 1) where intensive communication mediates interaction of individual mental structures and emotional energy. The major difference of knowledge creation ritual is that it is performed by professional knowledge creators - intellectuals - and focus specifically on generating new correlations of individual mental structures individuals, i.e., knowledge. Numerous rituals of knowledge creation are performed by intellectuals in science, business, education, policy-making and other areas. The few examples may include consulting practices, coaching, trainings, lectures and other public speaking events, seminars, round tables, brainstorming and other forms of group discussions, tutoring, etc.

For the knowledge creation ritual to be productive emotional states and mental structures of its participants should be complementary, it requires participants to be capable of and ready for dialogue. It also requires common experience space, which is a necessary condition for trust and mutual understanding. Under these conditions the knowledge creation ritual provides intensive, focused communication that stimulates coordinated transformation of individual mental structures and levels of emotional energy. The participants achieve emotional resonance, form new correlated mental structures and construct a communication network. As a result, new networks of correlations emerge. If this happens we can say that knowledge is generated.

A successfully performed knowledge creation ritual stimulates subsequent rituals in the same group, and after each new ritual the probability of repeating the rituals grows - a chain is created, in which each previous ritual can stimulate a subsequent ritual. In the chain of rituals mutual understanding and trust between participants strengthen, cognitive integration is empowered and common experience space develops, being structured by more and more complex correlations of meanings based on structurally coupled mental structures. A self-sustaining group is formed connected by a dense communication network, reproducing emotional energy and continuously creating new correlations of mental models.

The knowledge of the group is reflected in sets of symbols embodied in texts, knowledge artifacts, images, sound and video messages, which fill common experience space. Individual mental structures influenced by intra-personal communication develop in this environment and get involved into new knowledge creation rituals. As a result a group's network of correlations structurally drifts. The transformation of this network is more substantial the more diverse individual mental structures the group managed to correlate in the network.

Emotional energy generated through knowledge creation rituals not only feeds further intellectual activity of the group members, but it is also used in the subsequent rituals to enlarge the network of correlations.

As the interacting group evolves, a sustainable *knowledge field* is formed, where key correlations of meanings represent the principal coordination between individuals' mental structures.

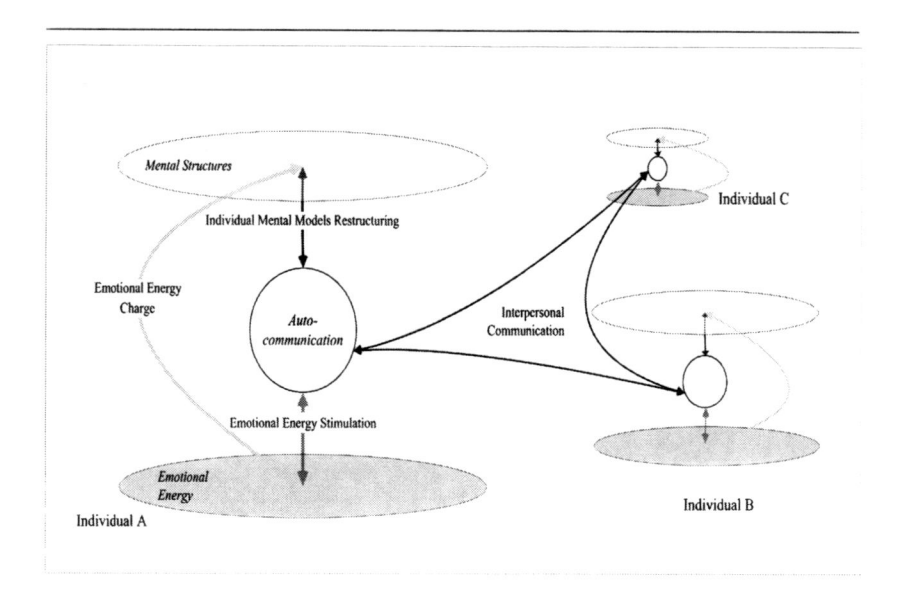

Figure 1: Knowledge Creation Ritual

Similarly to the concept of knowledge field the idea of *emotional energy pool* may be used to define an area in social space where emotional energies of group members get into resonance. As long as group members get involved in a collaboration process the social space is generated in a series of knowledge creation rituals. The *communication network* serves as an interface between the knowledge field and emotional energy pool.

The chains of knowledge creation rituals pull all the three dimensions (knowledge, communication and emotional energy) from an initially separated state (Fig. 1) to a state of synergetic, self-sustaining integrity (Fig. 2), where they co-evolve in a common experience space. Communication conditions information exchange which in turn feeds knowledge creation and charges emotional energy. Emotional energy gives impulses to perform intellectual work and stimulates further communication. Evolution of knowledge transforms network communication structure and evokes splash-outs of emotional energy. Bringing all the dimensions together results in a sustainable socio-cognitive process.[26]

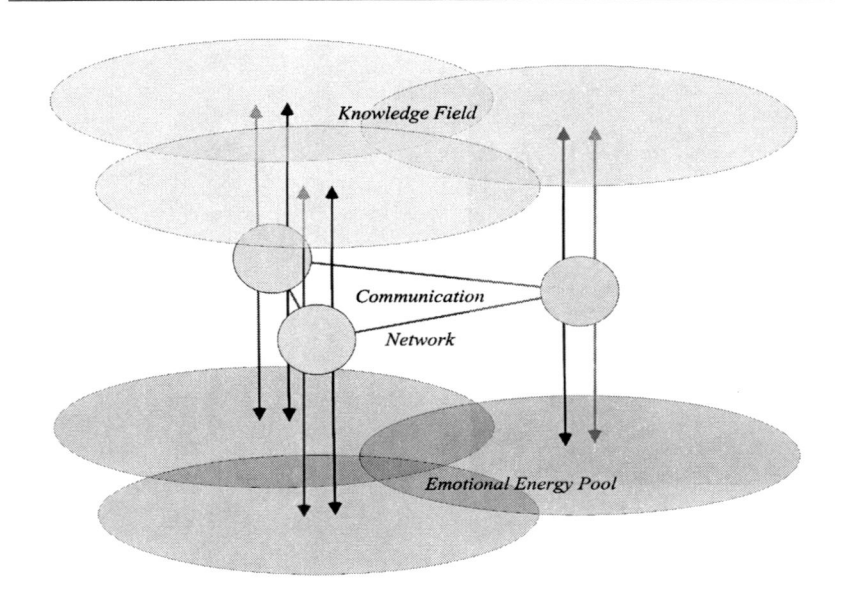

Figure 2 : Co-Evolution Knowledge, Communication and Emotional Energy

3.   Cultural-Cognitive Domains in Intellectual Network Ensemble

Knowledge generated through rituals in micro groups grows to cover a wider social space. Through direct face-to-face and remote interactions, as well as using knowledge artifacts, mass-media and texts, information which reflects the existing knowledge is reproduced in communication and used in new knowledge creation rituals. However, this in itself does not explain emergence of macro-scale knowledge fields covering large communities of intellectuals: as soon as groups are operationally closed systems they usually do not assimilate the information received from outside (i.e., from other groups) easily. Groups tend to build knowledge fields of their own and avoid external influence on these fields, suppressing information that may interfere their own knowledge field or, at least, do not promote such information. For these knowledge fields to be coherent knowledge must be created and re-created in every operationally closed group in a coordinated manner. Thus, there should exist a mechanism of structural coupling that coordinates knowledge correlations between the groups at macro level. Further we will make an attempt to describe this mechanism analyzing network integrity which we name *intellectual network ensemble* - a dynamic, complex, non-linear heterogeneous network structures of intellectual communication consisting of thousands of actors and other network entities and generating knowledge (Fig. 3).

Knowledge, communication and emotional energy within intellectual network ensemble are distributed unevenly. These are also of a heterogeneous nature. This heterogeneity provides the conditions for novelty to emerge. New knowledge and new network structures of intellectual communication, charged by emotional energy in knowledge creation rituals, form *cultural-cognitive domains* - areas of semantic, communicative and emotional couplings in intellectual network ensemble, which consist of actors and network integrities of various stability, linked by communication ties of various density and intensity, exchanging information, resonating emotionally and creating knowledge as a result. The latter are often (but not always) institutionally embodied: in scientific schools, think tanks, universities, research laboratories, editorial offices, political parties' headquarters, etc. Cultural-cognitive domains are filled with strong network ties (solid lines, Fig. 3) providing frequent interactions with high intensity and emotional entrainment (1, 2, 3, 4, 5, Fig. 3). In the domains multiple networks of correlations get structurally coupled through common discourse structures and respective institutions which link knowledge fields and emotional energy pools in communication and create the unique atmosphere of a domain.

Cultural-cognitive domains are characterized by relative cultural stability: behavioral schemes developed in communicative dynamics and knowledge created in a domain becomes an organic part of its structural adaptation. This makes cultural-cognitive domains autonomous self-organizing systems with specific means of structural coupling with their environment. To understand these means it is necessary to analyze every specific domain in each specific environment.

192   Knowledge Creation in the Intellectual Networks

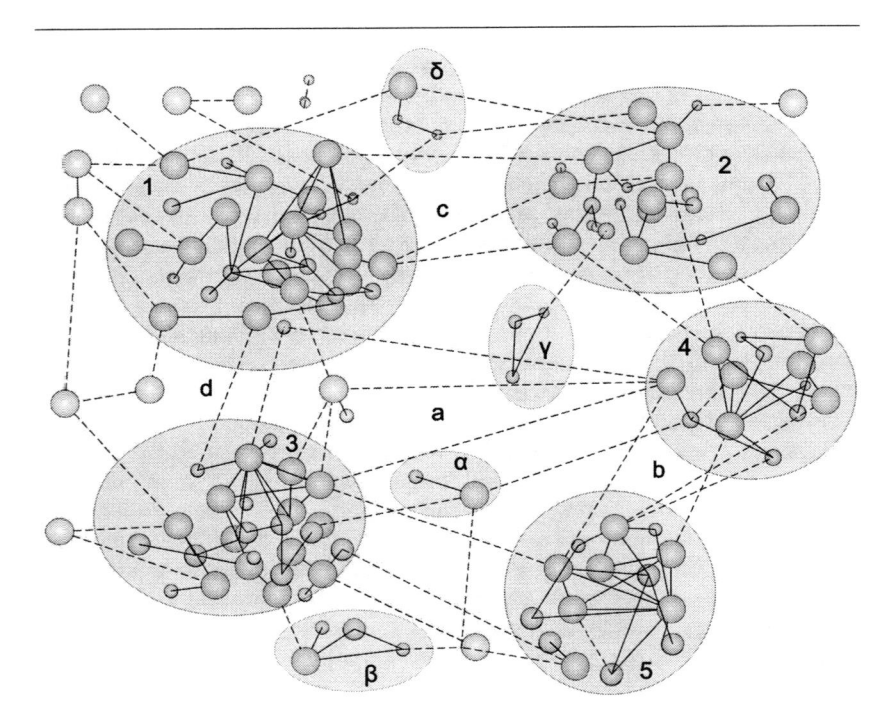

Figure 3: Cultural-Cognitive Domains within Intellectual Network Ensemble

Interactions between the actors belonging to different cultural-cognitive domains are characterized by low intensity of communication and small number of knowledge creation rituals between them. Boundaries of cultural-cognitive domains are marked by *structural holes* (a, b, c, d, Fig. 3).[27] These are spaces with no communication ties at all or with a very small amount of *weak ties* (the dotted lines, Fig. 3).[28] In structural holes the influence of any knowledge norms and conventions is low, independent ideas prevail over correlated ideas. Many small groups claim to know the Truth (that is on legitimacy of knowledge created by them); they form a number of small alternative knowledge fields (α, β, γ, δ, Fig. 3) and respective cultural-cognitive domains. In such rarefied areas the most original practices and unique technologies appear and the most ambitious ideas clash in fight for legitimacy. At the same time, correlation between actors in these areas is sufficiently lower. It leads to dispersion of resources, and knowledge creation rituals are often unsuccessful. As S. Fuchs puts it, in the areas where such kinds of interactions prevail, discussions - not the facts - are produced. The latter are perceived more as social constructs, not as the objective reality. For this reason, knowledge creation in these areas is extremely difficult.[29] For knowledge to be created a cultural-cognitive domain is to form.

The basis for a new cultural-cognitive domain is an intellectual project, emerging from a network of correlations where multiple mental models were structurally coupled with particular success. If participants of the respective intellectual communication network manage to recruit new actors involving them into the chains of knowledge creation rituals and if these actors get successfully structurally coupled with the group's network of meanings - then the knowledge field evolves. The actors possessing various but complementary competencies and resources tied by communication network concentrate in the new knowledge growth point. Communication across micro-groups intensifies and a clot in communication network occurs. Series of knowledge creation rituals are performed within and between groups, and emotional energy pools are generated. The efficiency of communications and quality of discussions gradually grows, mutual understanding and trust increase, the ability to develop concepts, definitions and methods of problem solving develop. Eventually, from the outside it appears that the domain has an integral knowledge field, which generates a steady productive intellectual program. Cultural-cognitive domains act like turbulent funnels among laminar flows, absorbing actors and other domains into their second-order networks of correlations, their specific way to synthesize knowledge, to organize communication and exchange emotional energy.

According to the principles of structural coupling cultural-cognitive domains stimulate internal changes within each other, and knowledge in intellectual network ensemble emerges as a result of co-ontogenesis of knowledge fields of cultural-cognitive domains. Communication networks respective to these knowledge fields provide an infrastructure for their structural coupling and emotional energy feeds and facilitates the process. Knowledge gets spread through structural coupling mechanism, when interactions between cultural-cognitive domains become recurrent. Here to disseminate knowledge means not to transfer it, but to re-create it in a new or an existing cultural-cognitive domain according to its features, usually with the help of those who have already performed similar cognitive operations in the past in other domains and can reproduce respective knowledge-creation rituals. Such collaborative cognitive action requires involvement of all cognizers who are to 'share' knowledge into a common network of correlations. That is why mass production of knowledge with further transfer of it to consumers is impossible: every cultural-cognitive domain generates unique knowledge which can not be copied by other groups of people, only re-created with respective efforts, including knowledge creation rituals. This explains frailty of many existing knowledge and innovation management methods. On the contrary, the methods based on maximum involvement of all network agents into the process of knowledge generation prove to be the most effective. One example represents H. Chesbrough's open innovation methodology.[30] Another example may be E. von Hippel's concept of democratic innovation.[31]

Because knowledge cannot be 'taken' from one domain and 'put' into another, excessive structural autonomy and semantic closure of a domain stops open interaction of meanings which in turn hinders structural coupling between knowledge fields, and new knowledge does not occur. This may lead to disintegration of the cultural-cognitive domain, including its network communication structure and emotional energy pool, because the dynamic metabolic process of structural adaptation stops. To maintain open recurrent interactions between the domains a dialogue of various networks of meanings is required. Only in that case sustainable knowledge creation at macro-level of intellectual network ensemble is possible.

When cultural-cognitive domains in an intellectual network ensemble get structurally coupled, and at the same time the intellectual network ensemble is optimally structurally coupled with the respective social system in which it is embedded, discrete interactions of production and transfer of information are surpassed by a continuous socio-cognitive process of joint knowledge creation. An integral knowledge-creating system operating in real time, 'breathing' and 'pulsing,' emerges. The metabolism of knowledge and emotional energy sufficiently increases and, as P. Lévy names it, a 'creative cycle' starts.[32] It may give life to new knowledge and, moreover, to new levels of structural coupling between intellectual network ensemble and social system, making the latter a collective cognizer which forms its evolutionary path through generating new knowledge and having network collective intelligence. A social system becomes capable to rapidly find new opportunities for knowledge, stimulate intensive communication and emotional energy exchange, develop respective intellectual projects, involve actors with relevant knowledge into a common cultural-cognitive domain, - and then re-configures to solve new problems. This would bring us closer then ever to a true knowledge society built on the intellectual network ensembles organized as knowledge-creating systems.

A knowledge-creating system generates knowledge effectively if it benefits from the co-evolution of knowledge with communication and emotional energy at all levels of intellectual network ensemble: at the level of cultural-cognitive domains, at the level of micro groups, and at the individual level. This mechanism drives both individual and collective cognitive activity of intellectuals. Knowledge fields, communication networks and pools of emotional energy are rooted within individuals and co-evolve in them during intellectual activity. Such activity requires participation in micro group knowledge creation rituals through which mental structures, auto-communication and emotional energy of individuals are structurally coupled. Because each ritual and each individual coupling is unique, an infinite set of variations of individual mental structures is generated. These variations get presented when individuals attempt to influence each other's images of the world. It results in the occurrence of new combinations which feed dynamic evolution of cultural-cognitive domains.

4. Conclusion: Intellectuals in the Networks of Knowledge Creation

The evolution of cultural-cognitive domains in intellectual network ensembles is not an impersonal, mechanistic process. Its key drivers lay in the individual dimensions, where macro-structures reflect in those who generate knowledge, communicate and experience emotions: the intellectuals. The analysis of how intellectuals generate and develop cultural-cognitive domains in multiple network environments of intellectual network ensembles is crucial, as it allows to bring new insights dealing with critical problems of the emerging knowledge society and to provide an integral portrait of intellectuals and their social activity. Further we will try to address some of the key issues discussed in previous chapters of this volume.

The authors of *Part I - Intellectuals in Academia: Institutionalized Knowledge Creation* - deal with a critical issue of a knowledge society: the problem of transformation of academia which is loosing some of its core traditional functions and needs to be re-considered. For Bildung (education) functions of academia to be maintained, Jeroen van Andel advocates in the first chapter, universities should evolve into more democratic forms, as James Moir in his (second) chapter fairly argues.[33] Following the authors' thought and developing it we can conclude that knowledge is to come from below in open dialogic process involving many actors, and it is for academia to secure these conditions, to carefully coordinate knowledge correlations and to involve actors into knowledge creation through education, teaching to ask and answer questions, as well as to participate in open dialogue. We may expect these forms to evolve into a sort of *knowledge-creating network Bildung* when the key function of academia is not searching for Truth with a capital 'T' which is then disseminated through the rest of society, but the coordination of knowledge creation in intellectual networks penetrating the society, where everyone is a potential knowledge creator. The boundaries of academia get thinner and it becomes necessary to look outside its internal scientific knowledge creation processes considering interactions between various types of cultural-cognitive domains which are filled with heterogeneous knowledge and developing new methods to manage knowledge creation within society, other than those traditionally used within academia.

This is, however, not a simple task as academia has to re-think its role and place in society and to re-organize itself, reducing the efforts to retain hegemony in knowledge creation by separating legitimate knowledge from non-legitimate and awarding the diplomas of 'legitimate knowledge creators.'

The ability to create cultural-cognitive domains, involving other social actors into scientific knowledge creation processes (not of much success until now), is now one of the key opportunities to revitalize academia. For academia to survive in the changing world, the boundaries of knowledge fields are to be associated neither with the boundaries of science, nor with the institutional boundaries of academia or any other separate areas, but with the structural holes in cross-disciplinary and cross-institutional communication networks with respective fields of knowledge and pools of emotional energy.

The role of intellectuals under such conditions is to perform knowledge creation rituals and to generate networks of correlations connecting the separated cultural-cognitive domains and building the new ones. This role is explored in greater detail by Olga Procevska in the concluding chapter of *Part II - Intellectuals in the Public Sphere: 'Organic' Knowledge Creation*. Olga analyzes the phenomenon of the post-modern intellectual who is becoming an interpreter connecting different models, traditions and truths and whose function is to facilitate communication between social groups.[34]

The other authors of the second part provide plenty of evidence for the conclusions made by Procevska. Interactive techniques are used by subaltern intellectuals, whom Sechaba Mahlomaholo and Vhonani Netshandama describe as a perfect example of the inclusive methodology of knowledge creation, when researcher and researched social groups co-create knowledge.[35] This methodology allows building sustainable cultural-cognitive domains within intellectual network ensembles, which are capable to resist the pressure of power and social crisis. The role of the intellectual, as Vhonani and Sechaba describe it, is to synthesize seemingly contradictory forces within productive spaces of transformation praxis and facilitate collective knowledge creation thus providing a basis for social consensus and inclusion.

The ability to perform such public practices of building cultural-cognitive domains not only appears to be one of the criteria characterizing the effectiveness of today's intellectuals, but becomes a condition of their very survival as important actors of the social arena. The personal case of Hrant Dink analyzed by Georg Simet in his chapter provides us with a dreadful illustration of this.[36] The life and death of Hrant Dink is an example of a tragedy that was predetermined by his failure to involve a sufficient number of other actors and to create a cultural-cognitive domain within a hostile environment of the closed Turkish society. Dink acted 'non-organically:' not as a group member trying to find correlations of meanings between his ideas and the existing social system of knowledge, but as a lone wolf attempting to break in a forceful blow an operationally closed knowledge field, where the concept of 'turkishness' was embedded. Taking into account the discussed above principles of knowledge creation within intellectual network ensembles it becomes obvious that using such a method he would not succeed even in a much friendlier environment. A friendlier environment, however, would not murder him, while in the closed traditional society Dink's actions were practically suicidal.

Another (class) suicide is exemplified by Tunde Adeleke analyzing the case of Walter Rodney, a true organic intellectual in the Gramscian sense, who sided with the people against the oppressive state.[37] Similarly to Dink, Rodney chose open struggle, but what was different is that he focused on and managed to create knowledge, a network of correlations with the suppressed class, and generate a cultural-cognitive domain. This domain had been successfully used by Rodney as a veritable weapon against vestiges of colonialism and neocolonialism in Africa and was sustainable even when Rodney himself was dead.

Although different methodologies of creating public knowledge may be augmented and adopted, with confidence we can make one general conclusion from the cases analyzed in this part of the book. Whether an intellectual chooses to be subversive through dissemination of alternative ideas that question the current system of knowledge, or through committing a class suicide leading people against the regime, or he/she chooses to communicate groups in a smoother manner, he/she is to create knowledge: involve many actors into collective action and form a cognitive integrity on the basis of a network of correlations. Under such conditions an intellectual operating in an intellectual network of the knowledge society has to be much more responsible, collaborative and 'non-disinterested' than ever: committed to providing heterogeneity of cultures, resolving tensions between social groups and facilitating knowledge creation.

Having left the positivist ideal of a disinterested, non-collaborative, rational and purely academic intellectual overboard, we have to consider a very important yet not sufficiently studied aspect of knowledge creation, which meanwhile appears to be one of its key drivers - emotions. The argumentation of the authors of *Part III - Intellectuals in the Arts: Emotional Knowledge Creation* proves that emotional processes are connected with knowledge creation processes. Carlos Garcia starting the part pictures this bond through a philosophical perspective. He shows that while modernity strived to detach passion from the 'rational thought knowledge,' art sought to return thought to life by understanding and mastering the passions, and there is rational reason for doing so: there is no knowledge that can be created without passion and emotional energy of interactions between the living human beings.[38] Through the perspective suggested by Carlos, disinterestedness in knowledge creation sounds like nonsense: a non-passionate, emotionally uninvolved individual is obviously unable to generate anything except information. Moreover, as convincingly shown by Claire Heaney through the analysis of David Lurie's case in her chapter, personal knowledge transformation (which is a leap to a new level of structural coupling with individual's network of correlations) is emotionally driven and even emotionally determined.[39] Networks of meanings develop as individual emotions clash and evolve at every level, from the individual level to the level of intellectual network ensemble as a whole. Insights and knowledge leaps of different areas of intellectual networks are fed by the evolution of respective emotional energy pools.

Concluding the part Oleksandra Nenko shows how artistic experience of the artist and the spectator may be used to study cognitive changes as influenced by emotional and aesthetic experience through the phenomenological perspective.[40] Results of the analysis allows Oleksandra to state that knowledge arises from multiple sources as a super-subjective substance; art, considered in a broad sense as an effort to make desired changes in the environment that increase our sense of unity with it, can be seen as an important medium, which facilitates structural coupling of a cognizer (whether an individual or a group) with the environment and thus giving grounding to cognizer's knowledge about the world. Thus art may be considered as one of the key drivers of intellectual work and appears an integral and essentially important dimension of intellectual networks. Involvement of intellectuals into artistic and aesthetic practices, as Lurie's case clearly shows, may give additional impulses to the evolution of knowledge creating systems in the knowledge society. For this reason, deep interdisciplinary research of emotions and passions is needed to develop our understanding of how knowledge is generated.

It is now obvious that to understand the intellectual and the processes of knowledge creation driving the emerging knowledge society, as well as to solve the problems faced, we are to reconsider many of the existing beliefs, to go outside into unexplored areas of intellectual activity searching for the new insights and finding new opportunities of widespread yet thoughtful engagement of the society into the totality of knowledge creation.

Notes

[1] У. Матурана и. Ф Варела, *Древо познания. Биологические корни человеческого понимания*, Прогресс-Традиция, Москва, 2001 (See in English: H.R. Maturana and F.J. Varela, *The Tree of Knowledge: The Biological Roots of Human Understanding*, Shambhala, Boston, 1987).

[2] See, e.g.: D. Bloor, *Science and Social Imagery*, University Of Chicago Press, Chicago, 1976; K.M. Carley, 'Knowledge Acquisition as Social Phenomenon'. *Instructional Science*, Vol. 14, 1986, pp. 381-438.

[3] A. Koestler, *The Act of Creation*, Penguin, New York, 1964; D. Rhoten, E. O'Connor and E.J. Hackett, 'The Act of Collaborative Creation and the Art of Integrative Creativity: Originality, Disciplinarity and Interdisciplinarity', *Thesis Eleven*, 96, 2009, pp. 83-108.

[4] M. Gibbons, *The New Production of Knowledge: the Dynamics of Science and Research in Contemporary Societies*, Sage, London, 1994.

[5] Bloor, op. cit.

[6] Матурана и Варела, op. cit., с. 153.

[7] Ibid.

[8] Б.М. Величковский, *Когнитивная наука: основы психологии познания*, т. 2, Смысл, Москва, 2006, с. 56.

[9] Матурана и Варела, op. cit., с. 150.

[10] See Матурана и Варела, op. cit.

[11] See N. Luhmann, *Social Systems*, Stanford University Press, Stanford UP, CA, 1995.

[12] Матурана и Варела, op. cit., с. 160-164.

[13] S. Fuchs, *The Professional Quest for Truth: A Social Theory of Science and Knowledge*, State University of the New York Press, New York, 1992; R. Collins, *The Sociology of Philosophies: A Global Theory of Intellectual Change*, Harvard University Press, Cambridge, MA, 2002, p. 2.

[14] А.М. Пивоваров, 'Внутриличностная коммуникация как предмет социологического анализа'. *Журнал социологии и социальной антропологии*, т. IX (4), 2006, с. 50-65. Messages are understood in a broad sense, including images.

[15] R. Collins, *The Sociology of Philosophies: A Global Theory of Intellectual Change*, op cit., p. 7.

[16] B. Latour, *Science in Action: How to Follow Scientists and Engineers through Society*, Open University Press, Milton Keynes, 1987; J. Law, 'Notes on the Theory of the Actor Network: Ordering, Strategy, and Heterogeneity', *Systemic Practice and Action Research*, Vol. 5, 1992, pp. 379-393.

[17] S.A. McComb, 'Shared Mental Models and Their Convergence', *Macrocognition in Teams: Theories and Methodologies*, M.P. Letsky, et al.

(eds), Ashgate Publishing Limited, Hampshire, 2008, p. 39.

[18] А.В. Россохин и В.Л. Измагурова, *Личность в измененных состояниях сознания в психоанализе и психотерапии*, Смысл, Москва, 2004.

[19] I. Mitroff, *The Subjective Side of Science*, Elsevier, Amsterdam, 1974; M.D. Lewis, 'Bridging Emotion Theory and Neurobiology through Dynamic Systems Modeling', *Behavioral and Brain Sciences*, Vol. 28, 2005, pp. 169-194.

[20] R. Collins, *Interaction Ritual Chains*, Princeton University Press, Princeton, Oxford, 2004, pp. 107-108.

[21] E. Goffman, *Interaction Ritual*, Anchor Books, New York, 1967; Collins *The Sociology of Philosophies: A Global Theory of Intellectual Change*, op. cit.; Collins, *Interaction Ritual Chains*, op. cit.

[22] Ibid., p. 47.

[23] Ibid., p. 48.

[24] Ibid., p. 49.

[25] Ibid., pp. 75-78.

[26] See N. Basov and A. Shirokanova, 'From Distributed Knowledge to Intelligent Knowledge-Creating Systems', *The Intellectual: A Phenomenon in Multidimensional Perspectives*, N. Basov, G. Simet, J. van Andel, S. Mahlomaholo and V. Netshandama (eds), Inter-Disciplinary Press, Oxford, 2010, pp. 57-71.

[27] See R. Burt, *Toward a Structural Theory of Action: Network Models of Social Structure, Perception, and Action*, Academic Press, New York, 1982.

[28] Here under the term 'weak tie' we mean, according to M. Granovetter, communication ties, characterized by seldom, low-intensity interactions with low emotional involvement (M.S. Granovetter, 'The Strength of Weak Ties', *American Journal of Sociology*, Vol. 78, 1973, pp. 1360-1380).

[29] Fuchs, op. cit., p. 90.

[30] See H. Chesbrough, *Open Innovation: The New Imperative for Creating and Profiting from New Technology*, Harvard Business School Press, Boston, 2003; Н.В. Басов, 'Сети межорганизационных взаимодействий как основа реализации открытых инноваций'. *Инновации*, 7 (141), 2010, с. 36-47.

[31] See E. von Hippel, *Democratizing Innovation*, MIT Press, Cambridge, MA, 2005.

[32] P. Lévy, *Collective Intelligence: Mankind's Emerging World in Cyberspace*, Perseus Books, Cambridge, MA, 1997, p. 123.

[33] J. van Andel, 'The Rationalization of Academia: From *Bildung* to Production', 2011, this volume; J. Moir, 'The Democratic Intellect Reconsidered', 2011, this volume.

[34] O. Procevska, 'Not a Sin, but a Side Effect: Collaboration and Knowledge Creation by the Organic Intellectuals', 2011, this volume.

[35] S. Mahlomaholo and V. Netshandama, 'Post-Apartheid Organic Intellectual and Knowledge Creation', 2011, this volume.

[36] G.F. Simet, 'Possibilities and Risks of Influencing Public Knowledge - The Case of Hrant Dink', 2011, this volume.

[37] T. Adeleke, 'Walter A. Rodney and the Instrumentalist Construction and Utilization of Knowledge', 2011, this volume.

[38] C.D.G. Mancilla, 'Art and the Passion of Intellect', 2011, this volume.

[39] C. Heaney, 'Emotional Intelligence: Literature, Ethics and Affective Cognition in J.M. Coetzee's *Disgrace*', 2011, this volume.

[40] O. Nenko, 'Aesthetic Emotional Experience: From Eye Irritation to Knowledge', 2011, this volume.

Bibliography

Basov, N. and Shirokanova, A., 'From Distributed Knowledge to Intelligent Knowledge-Creating Systems'. *The Intellectual: A Phenomenon in Multidimensional Perspectives.* Basov, N., Simet, G., van Andel, J., Mahlomaholo, S. and Netshandama, V. (eds), Inter-Disciplinary Press, Oxford, 2010.

Berger, P. and Luckmann, T., *The Social Construction of Reality: A Treatise in the Sociology of Knowledge.* Anchor, New York, 1967.

Bloor, D., *Science and Social Imagery.* University Of Chicago Press, Chicago, 1976.

Bohm, D., *Science, Order and Creativity.* Routledge, London, 1987.

Böhm, G., 'Cognitive Norms, Knowledge-Interests and the Construction of the Scientific Object'. *The Social Production of Scientific Knowledge.* Mendelsohn, E., Weingart, P. and Whitley, R. (eds), D. Reidel Publishing Company, Dordrecht, 1977, pp. 129-141.

Brandon, D. and Hollingshead, A.B., 'Transactive Memory Systems in Organizations: Matching Tasks, Expertise, and People'. *Organization Science*. Vol. 15, 2004, pp. 633-644.

Burt, R., *Toward a Structural Theory of Action: Network Models of Social Structure, Perception, and Action*. Academic Press, New York, 1983.

——, *Structural Holes: The Social Structure of Competition*. Harvard University Press, Cambridge, 1995.

Carley, K.M., 'Knowledge Acquisition as Social Phenomenon'. *Instructional Science*. Vol. 14, 1986, pp. 381-438.

Chesbrough, H., *Open Innovation: The New Imperative for Creating and Profiting From New Technology*. Harvard Business School Press, Boston, 2003.

Collective Intelligence: Creating a Prosperous World at Peace. EIN Press, Oakton, VA, 2008.

Collins, R., *Interaction Ritual Chains*. Princeton University Press, Princeton, Oxford, 2004.

——, *The Sociology of Philosophies: A Global Theory of Intellectual Change*. Harvard University Press, Cambridge, MA, 2002.

Deleuze, G. and Guattari, F., *What is Philosophy? European Perspectives*. Verso, London and New York, 1994.

Deutsch, K., *Nerves of Government: Models of Political Communication and Control*. Free Press of Glencoe, London, 1963.

Feuer, L., *Einstein and the Generations of Science*. Basic Books, New York, 1974.

Fisher, K. and Fisher, M.D., *Distributed Mind: Achieving High Performance through the Collective Intelligence of Knowledge Work Teams*. AMACOM, New York, 1998.

Florida, R.L., *The Rise of the Creative Class: And How it's Transforming Work, Leisure, Community and Everyday Life.* Basic Books, New York, 2002.

Fuchs, S., *The Professional Quest for Truth: A Social Theory of Science and Knowledge.* State University of the New York Press, New York, 1992.

Gadamer, H.G., *Truth and Method.* Sheed and Ward, London, 1989.

Garfield, E., *Citation Indexing: Its Theory and Application in Science, Technology and Humanities.* John Wiley & Sons, New York, 1979.

Gibbons, M., *The New Production of Knowledge: the Dynamics of Science and Research in Contemporary Societies.* Sage, London, 1994.

Goffman, E., *Interaction Ritual.* Anchor Books, New York, 1967.

Granovetter, M.S., 'The Strength of Weak Ties'. *American Journal of Sociology.* Vol. 78, 1973, pp. 1360-1380.

Habermas, J., *The Theory of Communicative Action, Vol. 1: Reason and the Rationalization of Society.* Beacon Press, Boston, MA, 1984.

Hagstrom, W.O., *The Scientific Community.* Basic Books, New York, 1975.

Hakkarainen, K., Palonen, T., Paavola, S. and Lehtinen, E., *Communities of Networked Expertise: Professional and Educational Perspectives.* Elsevier, Amsterdam, 2004.

Hippel, E. von. *Democratizing Innovation.* MIT Press, Cambridge, MA, 2005.

Hollingshead, A.B., 'Communication Learning, and Retreival in Transactive Memory Systems'. *Journal of Experimental Social Psychology.* Vol. 34, 1998, pp. 423-442.

Johnson-Laird, P.N., 'Mental Models'. *The MIT Encyclopedia of the Cognitive Sciences.* Wilson, R.A. and Keil, F.C. (eds), The MIT Press, Cambridge, MA, 1999.

Kerckhove, (de) D., *Connected Intelligence*. Somerville, Toronto, 1997.

Koestler, A., *The Act of Creation*. Penguin, New York, 1964.

Krohn, R., 'Introduction: Towards the Emperical Study of Scientific Practice'. *The Social Process of Scientific Investigation*. Knorr, K., Krohn, R. and Whitley, R. (eds), D. Reidel Publising Company, Dordrecht, 1980.

Latour, B., *Reassembling the Social: An Introduction to Actor-Network Theory*. Oxford University Press, Oxford, 2005.

——, *Science in Action: How to Follow Scientists and Engineers through Society*. Open University Press, Milton Keynes, 1987.

Law, J., 'Notes on the Theory of the Actor Network: Ordering, Strategy, and Heterogeneity'. *Systemic Practice and Action Research*. Vol. 5, 1992, pp. 379-393.

Lévy, P., *Collective Intelligence: Mankind's Emerging World in Cyberspace*. Perseus Books, Cambridge, MA, 1997.

Lewis, M.D., 'Bridging Emotion Theory and Neurobiology through Dynamic Systems Modeling'. *Behavioral and Brain Sciences*. Vol. 28, 2005, pp. 169-194.

Luhmann, N., *Social Systems*. Stanford University Press, Stanford UP, CA, 1995.

Mannheim, K., *Structures of Thinking*. Routledge & Kegan Paul, London, 1982.

Maturana, H.R. and Varela, F.J., *The Tree of Knowledge: The Biological Roots of Human Understanding*. Shambala, Boston, 1987.

McComb, S.A., 'Shared Mental Models and Their Convergence'. *Macrocognition in Teams: Theories and Methodologies*. Letsky, M.P., et al. (eds), Ashgate Publishing Limited, Hampshire, 2008.

Mitroff, I., *The Subjective Side of Science*. Elsevier Scientific Publishing Company, Amsterdam, 1974.

Monge, P.R. and Contractor, N.S., *Theories of Communication Networks*. Oxford University Press, New York, 2003.

Palazzolo, E.T., Serb, D., She, Y. Su, C. and Contractor, N., 'Co-Evolution of Communication and Knowledge Networks as Transactive Memory Systems: Using Computational Models for Theoretical Integration and Extensions'. *Communication Theory*. Vol. 16, 2006, pp. 223-250.

Raza, A., Kausar, R. and Paul, D., 'The Social Democratization of Knowledge: Some Critical Reflections on E-Learning'. *Multicultural Education & Technology Journal*. Vol. 1(1), 2007, pp. 64-74.

Rhoten, D., O'Connor, E. and Hackett, E.J., 'The Act of Collaborative Creation and the Art of Integrative Creativity: Originality, Disciplinarity and Interdisciplinarity'. *Thesis Eleven*. 2009.

Santerre, L., 'From Democratization of Knowledge to Bridge Building between Science, Technology and Society'. *Communicating Science in Social Contexts*. Donghong, C., et al. (eds), Springer, New York, 2008.

Spiegel-Rösing, I., 'Disziplinäre Strategien der Statussicherung'. *Homo*. 1975, Bd. 25, Heft. 1, s. 11-37.

Stehr, N., *Knowledge Societies*. Sage, London, 1994.

Wegner, D.M., 'Transactive Memory: A Contemporary Analysis of the Group Mind'. *Theories of Group Behaviour*. Mullen, B. and Goethals, G.R. (eds), Springer Verlag, New York, 1986.

Басов, Н.В., 'Инновация как фактор социальной самоорганизации: процессуально-пространственное моделирование'. *Журнал социологии и социальной антропологии*, т. XI(4), 2008, с. 186-204.

Басов, Н.В., 'Сети межорганизационных взаимодействий как основа реализации открытых инноваций'. *Инновации*, 7 (141), 2010, с. 36-47.

Басов, Н.В., 'Становление и развитие инновации в сетевых коммуникативных структурах'. *Общество знания: от идеи к практике. Коллективная монография в 3-х частях. Часть 2. Социальные коммуникации в обществе знания*. В.В. Василькова,

Л.А. Вербицкая (ред.), Скифия-принт, Санкт-Петербург, 2009, с. 149-183.

Величковский, Б.М., *Когнитивная наука: основы психологии познания*, т. 2. Смысл, Москва, 2006.

Кучинский, Г.М., *Диалог и мышление*. Изд-во БГУ, Минск, 1983.

Матурана, У. и Варела, Ф., *Древо познания. Биологические корни человеческого понимания*. Прогресс-Традиция, Москва, 2001.

Пивоваров, А.М., 'Внутриличностная коммуникация как предмет социологического анализа'. *Журнал социологии и социальной антропологии*, т. IX(4), 2006, с. 50-65.

Россохин, А.В. и Измагурова, В.Л., *Личность в измененных состояниях сознания в психоанализе и психотерапии*. Смысл, Москва, 2004.

Notes on Contributors

Tunde Adeleke is Professor of History and Director of African & African American Studies at Iowa State University, USA. He is author of numerous books and articles on African American history and culture, including the critically acclaimed *UnAfrican Americans: Nineteenth Century Black Nationalists and the Civilizing Mission* (Kentucky, 1998).

Nikita Basov is a PhD in Sociology, Postdoctoral Researcher at the Faculty of Sociology, St. Petersburg State University, Russian Federation. He leads and participates in a number of research projects in such research areas as: knowledge creation in inter-personal and inter-organizational networks, creative communities, social integration, innovations, social self-organization, evolutionary and non-linear management.

Carlos David García Mancilla made his MA in Philosophy at National Autonomous University of Mexico (UNAM). He is currently working on his PhD in Philosophy both at his home university and at Free University of Berlin, analyzing Music and Passion from philosophical perspective.

Claire Heaney is currently finishing her PhD at Queen's University Belfast, UK, with her research focused on the relationship between literature and ethics in the writing of J.M. Coetzee.

Sechaba Mahlomaholo is Professor in the School of Education Studies at University of the Free State in Bloemfontein, South Africa. His research interests lie in the creation of sustainable learning environments for social justice based on a spectrum of theoretical positions ranging from critical feminist theory, through critical race theory to postcoloniality.

James Moir is a Senior Lecturer in Sociology at the University of Abertay Dundee, Scotland, U.K. He is currently a Senior Associate of the UK Higher Education Academy's Centre for Sociology, Anthropology and Politics and is also one of the lead facilitators for the Quality Assurance Agency for the Enhancement Themes project, *Graduates for the 21st Century*.

Oleksandra Nenko is a PhD in Sociology, coordinator of the Academic Development Fund in National Research University Higher School of Economics, St. Petersburg, Russia. She manages projects for advances in research and higher education and takes part in projects on culture studies, art networks and social behavior research. Her specific interests lie in such areas as art, emotions and humor research.

Vhonani Netshandama is Professor and Director of Community Engagement at University of Venda in Thoho-ya-Ndou, South Africa. Her research work focuses primarily on understanding processes of *depowering* higher education institutions as they interact with communities, especially those in rural and poor socio-economic environments.

Olga Procevska is a PhD student in communication studies at University of Latvia. She is exploring the identification processes of the post-Soviet intelligentsia, and is also interested in Soviet popular culture and cultural memory studies.

Georg F. Simet is co-founder and Vice President of the Neuss University for International Business, Germany, where he teaches Theory and Propaedeutics of Science. While also interested in Practical Philosophy, he is involved in the Society of Intercultural Philosophy. His main research area in this respect is the development of the EU with a particular focus on Turkey.

Jeroen van Andel is a PhD student in Psychology and Pedagogy at the Centre for Educational Training, Assessment and Research, Netherlands. His major interests and research topics include demand-driven education, higher education, neo-liberalism, rationalization, consumerism and power.